New Inside Out

Sue Kay & Vaughan Jones

with Peter Maggs & Catherine Smith

Pre-intermediate

Student's Book

MACMILLAN

Ⓦ️Ⓑ = **Workbook**. Each unit of the Workbook contains a one-page section which develops practical writing skills.

1 Name

Grammar Tense review. *looks / looks like*. Question forms
Vocabulary Family. Description. Names
Useful phrases Showing interest

Listening

1 🌐 **1.01 Listen to two people talking about their names. Underline the four names you hear for each person.**

> **The man**
> <u>Benjamin</u>   Ben   Benji   Tree   Big Ben
> **The woman**
> Marie   Anne-Marie   Marie Antoinette   Mimi   Baby

2 **Complete these sentences with the words in the box.**

> brother   English friends   French friends
> old friends   parents   sisters

a)   His *parents* call him Benjamin.
b)   His _____ call him Tree.
c)   His _____ call him Big Ben.
d)   Her _____ call her Anne-Marie.
e)   Her _____ call her Marie.
f)   Her _____ calls her Baby.

Listen again and check your answers.

3 **Tell a partner the names that people call you. Which of your names do you like best?**

Vocabulary

1 🌐 **1.02 Listen and repeat the words in the box.**

> aunt   <u>boy</u>friend   <u>bro</u>ther   <u>bro</u>ther-in-law   <u>cou</u>sin   <u>daugh</u>ter   <u>fa</u>ther
> <u>girl</u>friend   <u>grand</u>father   <u>grand</u>mother   <u>half</u>-brother   <u>half</u>-sister   <u>mo</u>ther
> niece   <u>ne</u>phew   <u>sis</u>ter   <u>sis</u>ter-in-law   son   <u>step</u>father   <u>step</u>mother   <u>un</u>cle

2 **Complete the table with words from Exercise 1. Where possible, add the first name of a person from your family as an example.**

♂ Male	♀ Female
boyfriend – No *brother = Paco*	*aunt = Pilar*

Tell your partner about some of the people in your family.

'I don't have a boyfriend. My brother's name is Paco. He's a student. He lives in Vigo ...'

3 **Work with your partner. Look at your names in Exercise 2 and discuss these questions.**

a)   Which names are typical in your country?
b)   Which name is the most unusual?
c)   Which name do you like best?

Reading

1 How did your parents choose your name? Was it for one of the reasons below or for a different reason? Tell a partner.

a) Your parents named you after a relative.
b) They named you after a place.
c) They chose an unusual name.
d) They named you after a famous person.
e) Your name is religious.
f) It has a special meaning.
g) Your parents simply liked the name.

2 Read the article. Which of the reasons (a–g) in Exercise 1 is *not* mentioned?

What's in a name?

Your name is extremely important. It's how you identify yourself. It's how other people identify you. So how do parents make one of the most important decisions of their children's lives – giving them a name?

5   In the past, parents named their children after important family relatives. But people are changing . Nowadays, parents don't want to call their little princess Enid Blodwen after her grandmother.

    It's fashionable to choose names of places for
10 children's names. For example, Madonna named her daughter Lourdes after the town in France. David and Victoria Beckham named their first child Brooklyn after an area in New York. However, it isn't a good idea to follow this trend if your favourite place is your local
15 pizza restaurant or shopping mall!

    Some people name their children after famous people. For example, Leonardo DiCaprio's parents named him after the famous Italian painter. A few years ago the names Beyoncé and Britney were very popular.

20   Some names have a special meaning. Have you ever heard of anyone called Sky, Rain or River? These names come from nature and you can see what they mean. But did you know that actor Keanu Reeves' name

means 'cool breeze over the mountain' in Hawaiian?
25   A recent survey showed that people with unusual or original names feel special. I wonder if this is true for Bruce Willis and Demi Moore's children: Rumer Glenn, Scout LaRue and Tallulah Belle.

    I've chosen the name I want for a daughter. I'm going
30 to call her Lauren. Why? Simply because I like the name. My mother liked the name Lauren too, but unfortunately she named me Enid Blodwen after my grandmother.

▼ Paris   ▼ Gladys   ▼ Dara

3 What name would you choose for a baby girl or a baby boy?

Grammar

Tenses and auxiliary verbs

- Present simple: *do/does*
- Present continuous: *am/are/is*
- Present perfect: *have/has*
- Past simple: *did*
- Future *(be) going to*: *am/are/is*

1 Match each highlighted verb phrase in the article with a tense.

people are changing – present continuous

2 Write the negative form for each sentence and name the tense.

a) I like British pop music.
   I don't like British pop music. (Present simple)
b) I'm reading a good book at the moment.
c) I'm going to have a coffee after the lesson.
d) I went out last night.
e) I've been to Ireland.
f) I can play the piano.

Tick the affirmative or negative sentences which are true for you.

a) I like British pop music. ✓ / I don't like British pop music.

3 Write the question form for each sentence and the short answers *Yes* and *No*. Ask your partner the questions.

a) Do you like British pop music?   Yes, I do. / No, I don't.

Pronunciation

1 🔊 1.03 Listen and repeat the five long vowel sounds: /uː/, /iː/, /ɑː/, /ɜː/, /ɔː/.

2 🔊 1.04 Listen and repeat the names in the table. Then label each group (*1–5*) with the correct vowel sound (/uː/, /iː/, /ɑː/, /ɜː/, /ɔː/).

1 /uː/	2 _____	3 _____	4 _____	5 _____
June	Bert	Charles	Eve	Dawn
Luke	Pearl	Marge	Dean	George
Sue	Kurt	Bart	Pete	Paul

Listening

1 🔊 1.05 How good is your memory for names? Study the photographs of nine people below and listen to their names. Don't write them down.

How many names can you remember? Write them down and compare with a partner.

2 Listen again and check. Who remembered the most names? Do you have any special techniques for remembering names?

'I try to repeat the name in my head.'

Reading

1 Read this advice for improving your memory. Match the headings (*a–d*) with the appropriate paragraphs (*1–4*).

  a) Connect the name and the appearance
  b) Pay attention
  c) Use the name and repeat it
  d) Visualise the name

How to remember names at parties

What's the best way to make a really good impression at a party? By wearing the best clothes? Telling the best jokes? Dancing like a professional? No – you just need to remember people's names. Here are some easy steps.

1 _____
At parties, we sometimes don't hear the other person's name – not because the music is too loud, but because we're too focused on ourselves. So the first step is to pay attention. When you meet someone for the first time, listen carefully to the name and look at the person's face.

2 _____
When you're speaking to the person, use the name. For example, 'Nice to meet you, Danny.' 'What do you do, Danny?' or 'Danny, it was nice talking to you.' Then repeat the new name in your head at least three times.

3 _____
Franklin Roosevelt amazed his staff by remembering the names of nearly everyone he met. His secret? He visualised the name on the person's forehead. It's also a good idea to imagine yourself writing the name in your favourite colour.

4 _____
In your mind, say the name and something memorable about the person's appearance. For example, Charles – looks like a banker; Ann – long blond hair; George – moustache; Sophia – looks friendly.

Finally, if you want to remember other people's names as well as your own name, drink orange juice!

2 Discuss these questions with a partner.

  a) Which of these techniques have you used for remembering names?
  b) Which of these techniques could help you to remember new English words?
  c) What other ways can you think of to help remember and learn new English words?

Grammar

look(s) / look(s) like

look(s) + adjective:
You **look** tired.

look(s) like + noun:
She **looks like** a student.

1 Look at the words and phrases in the box. Write *N* for nouns or noun phrases and *A* for adjectives or adjective phrases.

[A] friendly	[N] a banker	☐ intelligent	☐ shy	☐ a doctor
☐ very young	☐ middle-aged	☐ stressed	☐ about sixty	☐ Greek
☐ a waiter	☐ a student	☐ a retired police officer	☐ rich	

What type of word do you use after *look(s)*? What type of word do you use after *look(s) like*?

2 Write a sentence to describe each person in the nine photographs on page 6. Leave a space for the name.

_____ *looks about fifty and quite friendly. He looks like a banker.*

Ask your partner to complete each sentence with the correct name.

Reading

1 Read the questionnaire and tick the answers that are right for you. What does your score mean? Compare with a partner.

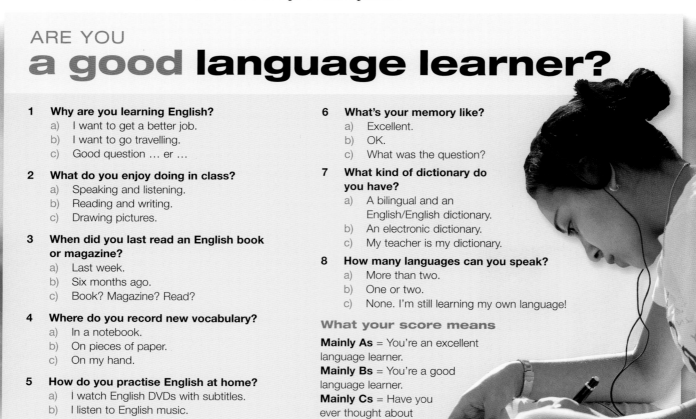

ARE YOU

a good language learner?

1 Why are you learning English?
a) I want to get a better job.
b) I want to go travelling.
c) Good question … er …

2 What do you enjoy doing in class?
a) Speaking and listening.
b) Reading and writing.
c) Drawing pictures.

3 When did you last read an English book or magazine?
a) Last week.
b) Six months ago.
c) Book? Magazine? Read?

4 Where do you record new vocabulary?
a) In a notebook.
b) On pieces of paper.
c) On my hand.

5 How do you practise English at home?
a) I watch English DVDs with subtitles.
b) I listen to English music.
c) I talk to my dog.

6 What's your memory like?
a) Excellent.
b) OK.
c) What was the question?

7 What kind of dictionary do you have?
a) A bilingual and an English/English dictionary.
b) An electronic dictionary.
c) My teacher is my dictionary.

8 How many languages can you speak?
a) More than two.
b) One or two.
c) None. I'm still learning my own language!

What your score means

Mainly As = You're an excellent language learner.
Mainly Bs = You're a good language learner.
Mainly Cs = Have you ever thought about taking salsa lessons?

2 Match these language learning tips with the questions in the questionnaire.
a) Read as much as possible. Graded readers are perfect. *Question 3*
b) Train your memory. Exercise your brain.
c) Participate in class. Speak out. Have a go.
d) Go out and buy a good dictionary.
e) Have a good reason for learning English.
f) Think about how you learned your own or other languages.
g) Record and constantly review new language.
h) Look for more English outside the classroom.

Which tips do you follow? What other tips can you think of?

Speaking

1 Replace the highlighted words and phrases to make five new questions to ask a partner. Use the suggestions or your own ideas.
a) What do you enjoy doing in class ? (watching on TV / reading / doing in your free time)
b) When did you last read an English book ? (go dancing / buy a DVD / drink champagne)
c) Where do you record new vocabulary ? (go on holiday / do your shopping / have lunch)
d) What's your memory like? (house / city or town / family)
e) What kind of dictionary do you have? (computer / car / job)

2 Ask your partner your questions from Exercise 1. What is the most interesting thing you've learned about your partner?

Grammar

Question forms

Is she hungry?
Have they **arrived**?
What **does** 'nephew' **mean**?

1 Look at the table and match the questions (*a–d*) with the correct answers (*1–4*).

a) What are the blue words?
b) What are the red words?
c) What is the word order for statements?
d) What is the word order for questions?

1 (auxiliary) verb + subject
2 subjects
3 auxiliary verbs
4 subject + (auxiliary) verb

Statements				Questions			
You	are	left-handed.			Are	you	left-handed?
Your mother	can	speak English.			Can	your mother	speak English?
You	have	been to Peru.			Have	you	been to Peru?
Your name	means	'first child'.		What	does	your name	mean?

Ask a partner the questions in the table.

2 If necessary, rewrite these sentences with *do, does* or *did* to make correct questions.

a) You play the guitar?
b) You sleep well last night?
c) Can you drive?
d) Where your mother come from?
e) Have you been to the Vatican?
f) What's your favourite colour?

Ask your partner the questions.

3 Rewrite these questions in the correct order. (DON'T ask your partner the questions!)

a) you / are / old / How *How old are you?*
b) in life after death / Do / believe / you ?
c) do / much / earn / you / How ?
d) you / ever / Have / broken the law ?
e) political party / vote / Which / you / do / for ?
f) you / many / boyfriends or girlfriends / How / had / have ?

Work in small groups. Decide which questions it is OK to ask …

- in your English class
- with your best friends
- in your family
- at work
- never!

4 Pairwork **Student A:** page 116 **Student B:** page 121

5 Grammar *Extra* 1 page 126. Read the explanation and do the exercises.

Speaking: anecdote

1 🔊 1.06 Listen to Lee talking about somebody who is important to him. Underline the answers he gives.

a) 'What's this person's name?' '<u>Dan Carter</u> / Carl Daniels.'
b) 'When did you meet him?' '**At university** / When we were five years old.'
c) 'Where does he live?' '**Near London** / In Brussels.'
d) 'What does he do?' 'He's **a teacher** / a doctor.'
e) 'How often do you see him?' '**Every weekend** / In the summer.'
f) 'Why is he important to you?' '**We have the same interests** / He knows me so well.'
g) 'What are his best qualities?' '**He's a really good listener** / He's very funny.'
h) 'Is there anything you don't like about him?' 'He's always **late** / too busy.'
i) 'When did you last see him?' '**On my birthday** / Last weekend.'

▲ Dan Carter

2 You're going to tell your partner about a person who is important to you.

- Ask yourself the questions in Exercise 1.
- Think about *what* to say and *how* to say it.
- Tell your partner about a person who is important to you.

Useful phrases

1 🔊 1.07 **Listen to a conversation between two friends (*Adam* and *Beth*) discussing the weekend. Match the conversation with picture 1 or picture 2.**

2 🔊 1.08 **Listen to another version of the conversation. Does Beth sound more interested this time?**

3 🔊 1.09 **Listen and repeat the useful phrases Beth uses to show that she's interested.**

a) Really?
b) Do they?
c) That sounds interesting.
d) That sounds great.
e) Wow! That's brilliant.
f) I've never heard of it.
g) Oh no! That's terrible.

4 **Complete the conversation with the useful phrases from Exercise 3.**

Adam: Did you have a good weekend?
Beth: Not bad. How about you?
Adam: I had a really good meal on Saturday night.
Beth: (1) *Really?*
Adam: Yes, we went to a new place in town – Edamame.
Beth: (2) _____
Adam: They have a Japanese chef from Tokyo.
Beth: (3) _____
Adam: And the menu is fantastic – they make their own sushi.
Beth: (4) _____
Adam: Yes. It's the best sushi I've ever tasted.
Beth: (5) _____
Adam: And it wasn't expensive. We had starters, main course, dessert and wine, and it only cost £25 each.
Beth: (6) _____
Adam: I know. Unfortunately, when we got back to the car, we had a parking ticket.
Beth: (7) _____

Check your answers and practise the conversation.

5 **Work with a partner. Write a conversation about your last weekend. Include as many of the useful phrases as possible.**

Vocabulary *Extra*

Family and other relationships

1 Complete the table.

	Male	Female	Definition
a)	grandson	*granddaughter*	Your children's children
b)	nephew	niece	Your brother's or _____'s children
c)	_____	grandmother	Your parents' parents
d)	great-grandfather	great-grandmother	Your grandparents' _____
e)	uncle	aunt	Your parents' _____ and sister
f)	cousin	_____	Your aunt's or uncle's children
g)	brother-in-law	sister-in-law	Your wife's or husband's brother and _____
h)	_____	mother-in-law	Your wife's or husband's father and mother
i)	stepfather	_____	Your mother's second husband or your father's second wife
j)	_____	half-sister	The children from your father's or mother's second relationship
k)	_____	ex-wife	The man or woman who you are divorced/separated from
l)	partner	_____	The person you live with but who you are not married to
m)	twin	_____	A brother or sister who was born at the same time as you

2 Work with a partner. Discuss these questions and compare your answers.

a) Who is your oldest relative? Who is your youngest relative?
b) Which side of the family is bigger: your father's side or your mother's side?
c) What are your neighbours like? Do you know all your neighbours' names?
d) How many close friends do you have? Who is your best friend?
e) Who are your favourite colleagues at work? Are there any colleagues you don't like?

Focus on names

1 Underline the correct word.

a) My friends **call** / **name** me 'Chip'.
b) I don't know the **meaning** / **sign** of my name.
c) My parents **identified** / **named** me after my grandmother.
d) I'm married but I use my **maiden** / **feminine** name at work.
e) My **letters** / **initials** are CJP.
f) My **sign** / **signature** is very difficult to read.

Tick the sentences that are true for you.

2 Complete the form in as much detail as you can.

Title: _____ (Mr/Mrs/Ms, etc.)	First name: _____ (Christian name)	Middle name(s): _____ (Second name)	Surname: _____ (Last name / Family name)
Full name: _____	Initials: _____	Maiden name: _____	Nickname: _____	Signature: _____

2 Place

Grammar Countable and uncountable nouns. *so/such*. *very/too*. Quantity expressions
Vocabulary Places in a city. Adjectives. Countries, nationalities. Location. *like*
Useful phrases Saying where you are from

Vocabulary

1 Look at the three photos. Would you like to live in any of these places? Why? Why not? Discuss with a partner.

2 🔘 1.10 Listen and repeat the words in the box. Which of these things can you find in the photos?

> a beach   a bridge   a ca<u>nal</u>   a car park   a <u>cas</u>tle   a ca<u>the</u>dral   a church
> a <u>foun</u>tain   high-rise <u>buil</u>dings   a hill   a <u>lib</u>rary   a mosque   a mu<u>se</u>um
> a park   the sea   a <u>shop</u>ping <u>cen</u>tre   a square   a <u>sta</u>tue

3 How many of the things in Exercise 2 can you find near your school? Put them in the right order on this line.

Nearest ⟵————————————————————⟶ Furthest away

▲ Venice, Italy

▲ La Bastide, France

▼ Rio de Janeiro, Brazil

▲ Paulo

▲ Armelle

▲ Luigi

Listening

1 🌐 **1.11 Listen to Paulo, Armelle and Luigi talking about the three places in the photos on page 12. Match each speaker with a photo. Who likes living where they live? Who doesn't?**

2 Use the adjectives in the box to complete Paulo, Armelle and Luigi's descriptions.

| boring   clean   crowded   ~~exciting~~   humid   polluted   romantic   small |

a) … a city that's so big and *exciting*

b) … it's too hot and _____

c) … the air is lovely and _____

d) … I find it so dull and _____

e) … it's such a _____ city.

f) … it gets very noisy and _____

g) … the canals are so dirty and _____

h) … my city is too _____ for all these people

Listen again and check your answers.

Grammar & Vocabulary

so/such

so + adjective
It's **so** romantic.

such + noun phrase
It's **such** a romantic city.

1 Look at the sentences with *so* and *such a/an* in Exercise 2 in the Listening section. Complete the rules.

a) You use _____ + a negative or positive **adjective** for emphasis.

b) You use _____ + a negative or positive **noun phrase** for emphasis.

2 Use *so* and *such a/an* to complete the email. Is the person happy or unhappy?

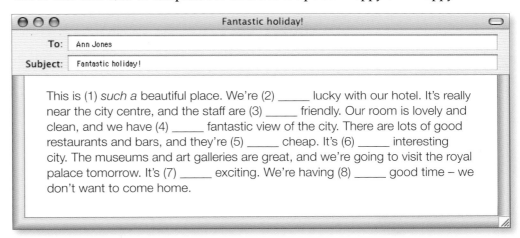

○ ○ ○   Fantastic holiday!   ⊂⊃

To: Ann Jones

Subject: Fantastic holiday!

This is (1) *such a* beautiful place. We're (2) _____ lucky with our hotel. It's really near the city centre, and the staff are (3) _____ friendly. Our room is lovely and clean, and we have (4) _____ fantastic view of the city. There are lots of good restaurants and bars, and they're (5) _____ cheap. It's (6) _____ interesting city. The museums and art galleries are great, and we're going to visit the royal palace tomorrow. It's (7) _____ exciting. We're having (8) _____ good time – we don't want to come home.

3 Change the email in Exercise 2 to make it sound negative.

This is such an ugly place. We're …

very/too

very + adjective/adverb
We were **very** late (but we caught our train).

too + adjective/adverb
We were **too** late (so we missed our train).

4 Look at the sentences with *very* and *too* in Exercise 2 in the Listening section. Complete the rules.

a) You use _____ + an **adjective** or an **adverb** to emphasise something.

b) You use _____ + an **adjective** or an **adverb** to show that there is a problem: something is excessive or more than necessary.

5 Complete the sentences with *very* or *too*.

a) My neighbours are _____ quiet. I never hear them.

b) I can't walk to work. My office is _____ far from my house.

c) I take the bus to work. It's _____ crowded, but I usually get a seat.

d) It's _____ hot in the summer, but fortunately my office has air-conditioning.

e) Time goes _____ quickly, and I never finish my work.

f) I want to move into the city, but I can't because apartments are _____ expensive.

Tick any sentences that are true for you.

Place

Grammar

Nouns

Countable
a shop / shops
a city / cities
a person / people

Uncountable
architecture
weather
traffic

1 Match each question with the most appropriate response.

a) What's the weather like?
b) What are the shops like?
c) What are the people like?
d) What's the architecture like?

1 It's a mixture of old and new.
2 They're really friendly.
3 They're too expensive.
4 It's hot and humid.

2 Complete the table with the nouns in the box.

cinema   nightlife   park   person   public transport   restaurant   traffic

Singular form	Plural form	Countable or uncountable?
cinema	cinemas	countable
nightlife	—	uncountable

Work with a partner. Discuss these questions.

a) How do you make plural forms of these nouns: *shop, bus, church, city, country, leaf*?
b) Which countable noun in the table has an irregular plural form?
c) How do you make plural forms of these nouns: *man, woman, child, foot, tooth*?

3 Work with your partner. Note down the names of two cities or villages you know well. Ask each other questions about the places you have noted down.

'What's the nightlife like?' 'It's great! There are lots of bars and clubs.'

Vocabulary & Pronunciation

1 Complete the following sets (*A*, *B* and *C*). Underline the stressed syllable in each word.

A Country	Nationality	B Country	Nationality	C Country	Nationality
Cuba	C_____	E_____	Egyptian	China	C_____
T_____	Turkish	Italy	I_____	V_____	Vietnamese
B_____	Brazilian	Hungary	H_____	P_____	Portuguese
Morocco	M_____	C_____	Canadian	Japan	J_____

🔘 1.12 Listen, check and repeat. What do you notice about the word stress in each set?

2 Write down six other countries you know and their nationalities. Mark the stress.

Which countries would you most like to visit? Tell your partner.

Speaking

1 Work in small groups. Do you agree with these statements?

French wine is the best in the world.   Japanese cars are the best in the world.

2 Write similar statements which you all agree on. Combine a nationality with a noun from the box (or your own ideas).

beer   chocolate   coffee   fashion   films   food   football players   men
nightlife   perfume   pop music   universities   watches   women

German beer is the best in the world.

Compare your statements with other groups.

Reading

1 Read the four fifty-word descriptions of holiday destinations in this competition. List them in order (*1* = the place you would *most* like to go to; *4* = the place you would *least* like to go to). Explain your choices to a partner.

2 Read the *How to enter* section and do Part *A* and Part *B*.

3 Check your answers to Part *A* at the bottom of the page and compare your descriptions with other people in the class. Choose a class winner!

WIN A
Dream holiday
FOR TWO!

The winner of our exciting competition can choose a dream holiday for two in one of these fabulous destinations.

Shanghai

This is the best place on earth for shopping. No, it isn't New York – New York is too crowded. Not Dubai – Dubai is too hot. Not even Paris – Paris is too expensive! Our shopping heaven is Shanghai. We shopped till we dropped and then ate delicious noodles in the street. **(50 words)**

Kenya

Now I understand why people fall in love with Africa. The people are friendly and welcoming. The scenery is spectacular. And the best thing is the lions. No, wait, the flamingos, or maybe the hippos. OK, everything is great, and I want to go back there as soon as possible. **(50 words)**

Gulf of Aqaba

Are you looking for excitement and adventure? Well, don't come to Dahab on the Gulf of Aqaba. Here you'll find peace and quiet, beautiful beaches, perfect weather and the best welcome in Egypt. Oh, and you can go diving if you like! Personally, I prefer to relax on the beach. **(50 words)**

Iceland

Iceland, the land of ice and fire, is full of contrasts. The air is freezing, but the hot springs are … well, hot. Reykjavik, the capital, is small, but the nightlife is buzzing. It's a very long way from the rest of Europe, but Iceland is completely up-to-date in every way. **(50 words)**

HOW TO ENTER

Part A
To enter this fabulous competition and win a dream holiday for two, complete the following sentences with option *a*, *b* or *c*.

1 The official language of Brazil is …
   a Portuguese b French
   c Italian

2 Ankara is the capital of …
   a Morocco b Turkey
   c Malta

3 The third largest country in the world is …
   a China b Argentina
   c Australia

4 The dong is the currency of …
   a Morocco b Thailand
   c Vietnam

5 The Alhambra Palace is in …
   a Egypt b Spain c Mexico

6 Kyushu is an island in the south of …
   a Thailand b Greece
   c Japan

Part B
Now write a review of the best holiday destination you've been to. Use exactly 50 words!
Send your answers before 1st April to *Dream Holiday*, PO Box 437, London NW1 48B.

(Part A answers: 1a, 2b, 3a, 4c, 5b, 6c)

Reading

1 Complete the following description of a country. Use the nouns in the box.

| cars | cigarettes | coffee | hours | ~~meat~~ | noise | people | sleep | wine |

Everything's wrong here!

They do everything wrong here! They eat far too much (1) *meat* and they eat it at 11.00 p.m. Yesterday we went out to dinner at 11.30 p.m. and we had trouble getting a table! At 1.00 a.m. we were still eating, and the restaurant was still half-full!

They smoke too many (2) _____ . They drink lots of strong (3) _____ and a lot of (4) _____ .

They spend too many (5) _____ in the sun and they certainly don't get enough (6) _____ . One Saturday night we went to a disco at 2.00 a.m. and were surprised to see that there were only a few (7) _____ on the dance floor. Then the DJ arrived at 3.00 a.m. and the party began!

There are far too many (8) _____ in the cities, and there's too much (9) _____ everywhere!

They do everything wrong here, but the quality of life is great, and people really know how to enjoy themselves. I don't want to go home!

2 Which country do you think it is? Could it be your country? Why? Why not?

Grammar

Quantity expressions

With **countable** nouns

How **many** people?
too many, lots, a lot,
not many, a few,
not enough

With **uncountable** nouns

How **much** traffic?
too much, a lot, lots,
not much, a little,
not enough

1 Complete the headings for each category (*A*, *B*, *C*) with *countable* or *uncountable*.

A: With _____ nouns	B: With _____ nouns	C: With _____ and _____ nouns
How many? *(far) too many* *not many* *(only) a few*	*How much?* *(far) too much* *not much* *(only) a little*	*not enough* *a lot (of)* *lots (of)*

2 Underline the correct quantity expression in each of these sentences.

a) I don't eat **much** / **many** bread.
b) I eat **a few** / **lots of** fruit.
c) I drink **far too much** / **far too many** tea.
d) I don't eat **much** / **enough** vegetables.
e) I eat **a lot of** / **a little** cakes.
f) I don't drink **enough** / **many** water.

How many of the sentences are true for you? Rewrite the sentences so that they are all true for you. Compare your sentences with a partner.

3 Use the table to ask your partner questions about daily habits. Add your own nouns and verbs to make different questions.

	Nouns		**Verbs**	
How much How many	chocolate coffee emails exercise friends meat money people sleep text messages wine	do you	do drink eat get have make phone see send spend	every day?

'How much chocolate do you eat?' 'Not much.
'How many emails do you get?' 'Lots. Far too many!'

4 Grammar *Extra* 2 page 128. Read the explanation and do the exercises.

Vocabulary

1 Complete the labelling of the compass.

a) *North*

f) _____-west

North-east

e) _____

b) _____

d) _____-west

South-east

c) _____

2 Match the descriptions (*a–d*) with the cities on the maps (*1–4*).

a) It's in the centre.
b) It's in the east.
c) It's on the west coast.
d) It's in the south-east.

▲ The USA

▲ Turkey

▲ Britain

▲ Germany

3 Pairwork **Student A:** page 116 **Student B:** page 121

Speaking: anecdote

1 ● 1.13 Listen to Emma talking about the best place she has ever visited. Read the questions and tick the ones she gives information about.

a) Where is the place? ✓
b) When did you first go there?
c) Were you on holiday?
d) Where did you stay?
e) What did you do there?
f) How many times have you visited the place?
g) When was the last time?
h) What do you most like about this place?
i) Are there any things you don't like about this place?
j) Would you like to live there? Why? Why not?

2 You're going to tell your partner about the best place you have ever visited.

- Ask yourself the questions in Exercise 1.
- Think about *what* to say and *how* to say it.
- Tell your partner about the best place you have ever visited.

Useful phrases

1 🌐 1.14 **Listen and read the conversation. What nationalities are Josh, Matt and Erica?**

Josh:	Matt, this is Erica.
Matt:	Nice to meet you, Erica.
Erica:	Nice to meet you, too.
Matt:	You're not American are you? Where are you from?
Erica:	I live in New York, but I'm originally from England.
Matt:	Oh, where exactly?
Erica:	A small town just outside Manchester.
Matt:	Manchester? Is that near London?
Erica:	No, Manchester's in the north. And where are you from?
Matt:	Well, I live in New York, too, but I'm actually from Los Angeles.
Josh:	Hey, I'm from LA, too. Which part of the city are you from?
Matt:	Santa Monica, not far from the airport.
Josh:	Oh great. My family live in Hollywood.
Erica:	Wow, really?
Josh:	No, I'm kidding. They live in the south. Near South Beach.

2 **Match each person with one of the maps below. Put a cross on each map to show exactly where each person comes from.**

3 **Complete the useful phrases with the words in brackets.**

a) Where you from? (are) *Where are you from?*
b) I'm originally England. (from)
c) Where? (exactly)
d) A small town outside Manchester. (just)
e) Manchester's the north. (in)
f) I live in New York but I'm from Los Angeles. (actually)
g) Which part of the city are from? (you)
h) Not far the airport. (from)
i) They live in south. (the)

🌐 1.15 **Listen, check and repeat the useful phrases.**

4 **Write a conversation between you and a partner about where you come from and where you live now.**

Vocabulary *Extra*

Places

1 Match the places in the picture with the words.

- [6] art gallery
- [ ] car park
- [ ] castle
- [ ] church
- [ ] library
- [ ] mosque
- [ ] museum
- [ ] shopping centre
- [ ] square
- [ ] theatre

2 Think about the last time you were in some of the different places in Exercise 1. Ask a partner.

'When was the last time you were in an art gallery?'
'I'm not sure. Maybe when I went to Paris a few years ago.'

Adjectives

1 Look at the adjectives to describe cities. Decide which are positive and which are negative.

> beautiful   big   boring   crowded   dirty   dull   exciting   expensive   fabulous
> interesting   modern   noisy   polluted   romantic   spectacular

Positive: beautiful, …   Negative: boring, …

2 What are the best five adjectives to describe *your* city. Compare your answers with your partner.

Focus on *like*

1 Match the uses of *like* (a–f) with the example sentences (1–6).

Uses of like		Examples	
a)	*What + be +* somebody / something *+ like* = asking for a description	1	We like going out every Saturday night. I like cooking but I don't like washing up.
b)	verb *+ like* = similar to somebody / something	2	I really like *Harry Potter*. I've seen all the films. I don't like her very much and she doesn't like me.
c)	*like (+ this/that)* = in this or that way	3	She looks like her mother. They have the same eyes. It's plastic, but it feels like leather.
d)	*like +* noun / pronoun = somebody / something pleases you	4	'What's your new teacher like?' 'He's really nice.' 'What was the weather like?' 'Terrible. It rained every day.'
e)	*like + ing* = enjoy an activity	5	'Would you like a drink?' 'Yes. I'd like a glass of cold water, please.'
f)	*would like +* noun = want something	6	Click on the 'send' icon, like this. Cut the paper into squares. No, not like that, like this!

2 Write your own example sentence for each use of *like*.

3 Love

Grammar Past simple and continuous. Adverbs of manner
Vocabulary Relationship expressions. Narrative linkers. *ed/ing* adjectives. *get*
Useful phrases Things in common

Listening

1 🌐 **1.16 Listen to Fred and Edna talking about their relationship and answer the questions.**

a) When did they first meet?
b) When did they get married to each other?

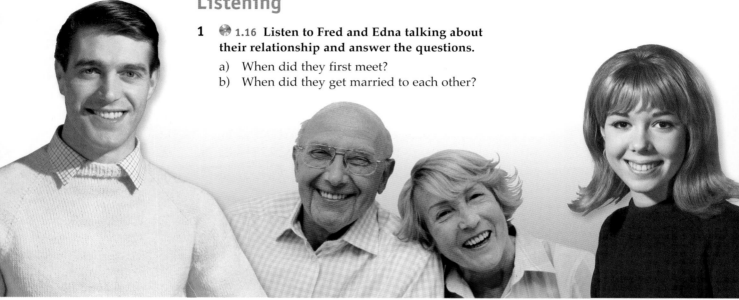

▲ Fred fifty years ago   ▲ Fred and Edna now   ▲ Edna fifty years ago

2 **Write *He*, *She*, or *They* in these sentences about Fred and Edna's story.**

a) *They* first met in Blackpool and went out together for three months.
b) _____ moved to different places and lost touch with each other.
c) _____ was married to another person for forty-eight years.
d) _____ got divorced after thirty years of marriage.
e) _____ went to Blackpool with her grandson and visited all the old places.
f) _____ thought about Fred and wanted to find him.
g) _____ wrote a letter to the local newspaper.
h) _____ had a cousin in Blackpool who told him about the letter.
i) _____ met soon after that and moved in together.
j) _____ got married – fifty years after they first met!

Listen again and check your answers.

Vocabulary & Speaking

1 **Complete the expressions in the sentences below with the words in the box.**

| ~~get~~ have live lose love |

a) The best age to *get* married is twenty-five for women and twenty-seven for men.
b) The main reason for getting married is to _____ children.
c) A big difference in age isn't a problem for a couple if they are in _____ .
d) It's a good idea for a couple to _____ together for a few years before getting married.
e) It doesn't matter if children _____ touch with one of their parents.

2 **Work in small groups. Discuss the statements in Exercise 1. Do you agree or disagree?**

Vocabulary

1 Match each of the verb phrases in the box with an appropriate picture (*a–d*).

> chat somebody up   fancy somebody   have a row   move in together

2 Put the stages of a relationship in a logical order (*1–12*). Add or take away stages if you think it's necessary.

a) You get married.
b) You chat somebody up.
c) You ring somebody up.
d) You fancy somebody.

e) You move in together.
f) You have children.
g) You meet the parents.
h) You go out together.

i) You have a row.
j) You kiss.
k) You split up.
l) You fall in love.

Compare your ideas with a partner.

Grammar

Past simple

He **went** to Blackpool.
He **didn't go** to Liverpool.

Did he **go** to London?
Yes, he **did**.
No, he **didn't**.

1 Write the affirmative and negative past simple forms of the verbs in the box.

> be   can   chat   fancy   get   go   have   kiss   meet   move   study   want

be – was/were, wasn't/weren't

2 Write true sentences – affirmative or negative – with the verbs in brackets.

a) My mother and father (meet) at university.
b) My grandparents (get) married in a church.
c) I (have) a big breakfast this morning.

d) I (go) skiing last winter.
e) I (study) German at school.
f) I (be) very busy yesterday.

Make questions and ask your partner.
'Did your mother and father meet at university?' 'No, they didn't.'

3 Grammar *Extra 3, Part 1* page 130. Read the explanation and do the exercises.

Pronunciation

1 Complete these irregular verb sets. Label the past forms in each group (*1–3*) with these sounds: /æ/, /e/, /ɔː/.

1 Infinitive	Past: /e/	2 Infinitive	Past: _____	3 Infinitive	Past: _____
keep	kept	begin	c) _____	bring	brought
mean	a) *meant*	drink	d) _____	e) _____	bought
b) _____	met	ring	rang	catch	f) _____

🔊 1.17 **Listen, check and repeat.**

2 Add the verbs in the box to the correct groups in the table in Exercise 1.

> fight   read   sing   sleep   swim   teach

🔊 1.18 **Listen, check and repeat.**

Listening

1 Read about a television game show called *Get Personal* and answer these questions.

a) Who are the two people playing *Get Personal* tonight?
b) How much is the prize money?
c) How can they win?

Get Personal

Game show *Get Personal* is hosted by Bobby Brown. In tonight's show, contestants Rosie and Dave try to win the £10,000 prize. The game is very simple. Bobby interviews Rosie and Dave in separate studios. He asks them the same questions about how they first met, and they have to give the same answers. Can they do it? Watch OTV at 8.30 tonight and find out.

2 1.19 Read the questions and answers in the table below. Listen and choose the answers (*a*, *b*, or *c*) that Rosie gives.

Questions	Rosie's answers	Dave's answers
1 How did you first meet?	a) She was a nurse. He was a patient. b) She was a patient. He was a nurse. c) She was a doctor. He was a nurse.	✓ / ✗
2 What time of day was it?	a) Early morning. b) Early afternoon. c) Early evening.	✓ / ✗
3 What was the weather like?	a) The sun was shining. b) It was raining. c) It was snowing.	✓ / ✗
4 What were you both wearing?	She was wearing … He was wearing … a) a white coat. a) blue pyjamas. b) a nurse's uniform. b) green pyjamas. c) a nightdress c) pink pyjamas.	✓ / ✗
5 Who spoke first and what did they say?	a) She said: 'How are you feeling?' b) He said: 'I'm going to be sick.' c) He said: 'I feel terrible.'	✓ / ✗

3 1.20 Listen to Dave answering the same questions. Circle the ✓ if he gives the same answer as Rosie. Circle the ✗ if he gives a different answer.

How many points did Rosie and Dave score out of five?

4 Think about your closest friend. How many of the questions from *Get Personal* could you answer? Discuss with a partner.

Grammar

Past continuous

I **was**
You **were**
He **was**
She **was** working.
It **was**
We **were**
They **were**

Were you **working**?
Yes, I **was**.
No, I **wasn't**.

1 Look at these extracts from Bobby Brown's interview with Rosie. Answer questions (*a–d*) with *Past simple* or *Past continuous*.

'I <u>was working</u> as a nurse, and Dave <u>came</u> into the hospital for an operation.'
'Yes, it <u>was raining</u> when I <u>arrived</u> at work.'
'What <u>were</u> you <u>wearing</u> when you <u>saw</u> each other for the first time?'

a) What tense is used for the verbs *come*, *arrive* and *see*? *Past simple.*
b) What tense is used for the verbs *work*, *rain* and *wear*?
c) Which tense describes something that was in progress when another event happened?
d) Which tense describes an event that happened at a particular moment in the past?

2 Pairwork **Student A:** page 116 **Student B:** page 121

3 🌐 **1.21** Look at the pictures (*1–5*) and listen to the recordings. Work with a partner. Write sentences about Jake and Fiona to describe the five situations.

1 Jake was having a shower when his mobile phone rang.

4 Grammar *Extra* 3, Part 2 page 130. Read the explanations and do the exercises.

Reading

1 Complete the funny story with past continuous or past simple verb forms. Predict the ending of the story.

A Hollywood director (1 film) *was filming* an important film in the desert when an old Native American man (2 come) _____ up to him and said, 'Tomorrow rain.' The next day it rained.

A few days later, the director (3 talk) _____ to the cameraman about the next day's filming. The Native American went up to him and said, 'Tomorrow storm.'

He was right again, and he saved the director thousands of dollars.

The director was very impressed and (4 give) _____ the old man a job.

The old man (5 continue) _____ to predict the weather correctly, but then he (6 not come) _____ for three weeks.

The director (7 plan) _____ to film an important scene and he needed good weather. So he (8 go) _____ to look for the Native American.

When he (9 find) _____ the old man, he said, 'Listen, I have to film an important scene tomorrow. What will the weather be like?'

The old man (10 shake) _____ his head and said, '……'

2 🌐 **1.22** Listen and check your answers.

Reading

1 Look at the pictures and complete the noun phrases with the words in the box.

bag   club   ~~paint~~   party   scissors   wine

a) a pot of *paint*

b) a dinner _____

c) a pair of _____

d) a night _____

e) a plastic _____

f) a bottle of _____

2 🔘 1.23 Read the stories and match the things (*a–f*) in Exercise 1 to the appropriate story. What is the importance of each thing in the stories?

REVENGE *is sweet*

When Lady Sally Moon found out that her husband was having an affair, she didn't leave him. She thought it was better to be unhappily married than not married at all. But her husband
5 didn't hide his affair, and this made her feel really bad.
   One day she was driving home when she saw his car parked outside his lover's house. She was angry and she decided to get her revenge.
10 She quickly drove home, put a pot of paint into her car and drove to the lover's house.
   Then she poured thick white paint all over her husband's beautiful, new, black car.
   Next, she carefully took his collection of
15 fine wines from the cellar. That night, she went round the village where she lived, and quietly placed a bottle of wine on each doorstep. She left the other bottles on the war memorial in the centre of the village.
20 Finally, she took a pair of scissors and cut off the arms and legs of all his suits – thirty-eight of them in all.

DINNER BY POST

Last year, I went out with Hermione for four months. We were very different. I always arrived early; she always arrived late. I was very tidy; she was terribly untidy. But to be honest, I
5 found the differences rather attractive.
   At first, she was only fifteen or twenty minutes late. But she got later and later.
   At the end of August, it was my birthday. I'm a good cook, so I decided to have a dinner
10 party and I invited four friends.
   That evening, my four friends arrived on time, but unsurprisingly Hermione wasn't there at eight o'clock. But then she wasn't there at nine o'clock, half past nine or ten o'clock.
15 This was extremely late, even for Hermione. So I phoned her mobile. When she answered, music was playing loudly in the background. 'Where are you?' I shouted angrily. 'I'm at a
20 night club,' she shouted back. I was furious. I went into the kitchen and put her meal into a plastic bag.
   The next morning I posted it to her with a note saying, 'Here's your dinner.' A week later,
25 I got a postcard from Hermione. It said, 'Too much salt.'

3 Which story do you prefer? Tell your partner why.

Vocabulary & Speaking

1   Find and underline the time adverbials from the box in the stories on page 24.

> One day   Last year   At first   Then   At the end of August   Next
> That night   That evening   The next morning   Finally   A week later

List the time adverbials in the order in which they appear in the stories.

Revenge is sweet

a) *One day*	d) _____
b) _____	e) _____
c) _____	

Dinner by post

1 *Last year*	4 _____
2 _____	5 _____
3 _____	6 _____

2   Choose a story and use the time adverbials in Exercise 1 to retell the story to a partner. Don't look at the text on page 24.

Grammar

Adverbs of manner

Add *ly* to most adjectives.
bad**ly**, careful**ly**, ang**ri**ly

Exceptions:
well, early, late, fast

1   Work with a partner. Complete the tables with adverbs or adjectives from the stories on page 24.

Revenge is sweet			Dinner by post		
	Adjective	**Adverb**		**Adjective**	**Adverb**
a)	unhappy	*unhappily*	1	*different*	differently
b)	_____	badly	2	early	_____
c)	_____	angrily	3	late	_____
d)	quick	_____	4	_____	tidily
e)	_____	beautifully	5	_____	attractively
f)	careful	_____	6	_____	well
g)	quiet	_____	7	loud	_____

Answer these questions.

a)   How do you make adverbs from most adjectives?
b)   How do you make adverbs from adjectives ending in *y*?
c)   What are the adverbs for the adjectives *good, early, late*?

2   Rewrite these sentences in the usual order.

subject + verb   +   object   +   adverb
a)   I / very quickly / eat / my lunch   *I   eat   my lunch   very quickly.*
b)   drive / my car / I / very slowly
c)   plan / my days / very carefully / I
d)   I / my money / spend / very intelligently
e)   play / I / tennis / very badly
f)   very regularly / clean / I / my house
g)   I / speak / very well / English

How many sentences are true for you? Rewrite the sentences so that they are all true for you.

Compare your sentences with your partner.

Useful phrases

1 ⊕ **1.24 Listen to a conversation between a man (*Tim*) and a woman (*Anna*) on a train. Do they know each other?**

2 **Are these sentences true or false?**

a) The man and woman are going to London.
b) She's reading *Pride and Prejudice*.
c) They both like Keira Knightley.
d) They're both going to see Johnny Depp's new film tomorrow night.
e) They're both single.

Listen again and check your answers.

3 **Complete the useful phrases in the table using the phrases in the box.**

> So do I   So am I   Me too   Neither do I   Oh, I did

Comment	Agree	Disagree
a) I didn't like the film much.	Neither did I. / Me neither.	(1) _____ .
b) I really like Keira Knightley.	(2) _____ . / Me too.	Oh, I don't.
c) I think she's really good.	So do I. / (3) _____ .	Oh, I don't.
d) I'm going to see Johnny Depp's new film.	(4) _____ . / Me too.	Oh, I'm not.
e) I don't know what time it starts.	(5) _____ . / Me neither.	Oh, I do.

⊕ **1.25 Listen, check and repeat the useful phrases.**

4 **Write true comments using these sentence beginnings.**

I think …
I really like …
I don't like …
I'm going …
I'm not going …
Yesterday evening I …
Last weekend I didn't …

5 **Work with a partner. Take it in turns to read out your sentences. Agree or disagree with your partner's comments.**

Vocabulary *Extra*

Adjectives ending in *ed* or *ing*

1 Match the pictures with the pairs of adjectives.

- [5] ann<u>oy</u>ed / ann<u>oy</u>ing
- [ ] bored / <u>bor</u>ing
- [ ] con<u>fu</u>sed / con<u>fu</u>sing
- [ ] de<u>pre</u>ssed / de<u>pre</u>ssing
- [ ] em<u>bar</u>rassed / em<u>bar</u>rassing
- [ ] ex<u>ci</u>ted / ex<u>ci</u>ting
- [ ] <u>frigh</u>tened / <u>frigh</u>tening
- [ ] <u>in</u>terested / <u>in</u>teresting
- [ ] sur<u>pri</u>sed / sur<u>pri</u>sing
- [ ] <u>ti</u>red / <u>ti</u>ring

2 Underline the correct adjective.

1 The students are **boring** / <u>**bored**</u>.
2 The teacher is **interesting** / **interested**.
3 The score is **depressing** / **depressed**.
4 The daughter is **embarrassing** / **embarrassed**.
5 The dog is **annoying** / **annoyed**.
6 The people are **frightening** / **frightened**.
7 The boy is **surprising** / **surprised**.
8 The race is **exciting** / **excited**.
9 The man is **tiring** / **tired**.
10 The map is **confusing** / **confused**.

Focus on *get*

1 Match the uses of *get* (*a–e*) with the examples (*1–5*).

Some uses of *get*	Examples
a) *get* + adjective = become	1 Did you get my text message? I got my new shoes in the sale. She's trying to get a new job.
b) phrasal verbs with *get*	2 It doesn't get dark till 10.00 p.m. in the summer. He's getting better at English. This room never gets warm enough.
c) *get* + noun = buy, obtain or receive	3 What time do you get to work? I got home very late last night. We'll never get there in time.
d) *get* = arrive	4 Where can I get changed? They got married in a hotel. I always have breakfast before I get dressed.
e) Expressions with *get* + past participle	5 He never gets up before 10.00 a.m. We don't get on with our neighbours. The whole family gets together at Christmas.

2 Use a dictionary. Find and write your own example sentence for each use of *get*.

Review A

► Grammar *Extra* pages 126–131

Grammar

1 Complete the questions with the correct auxiliaries and name the tenses.

> am / is / are   do / does   did   have / has

a) *Have* you been to Oslo? *Present perfect*
b) _____ you like jazz?
c) Where _____ you go on holiday last year?
d) Where _____ you going to go on holiday this year?
e) Where _____ you living at the moment?
f) _____ you seen the Pyramids?
g) What _____ you do for a living?

Ask and answer the questions with a partner.

2 Complete the sentences with *look(s)* or *look(s) like*.

a) I *look like* my aunt.
b) My dad _____ young for his age.
c) I _____ English.
d) I _____ a famous person.
e) I _____ a student.
f) My mum _____ friendly.

Which sentences are true for you? Compare with a partner.

3 Underline the correct words.

Di: Rome is (1) **such a** / **so** lovely city, isn't it?
Jo: I don't like it. It's (2) **too** / **very** hot for me.
Di: The weather's perfect. It's really (3) **too** / **very** nice.
Jo: But the streets are (4) **such a** / **so** crowded.
Di: Yes, but it's (5) **such a** / **so** wonderful experience.
Jo: Well, I'm not enjoying it. It's (6) **too** / **very** noisy!
Di: Jo, don't be (7) **such a** / **so** boring. We're in a (8) **too** / **very** beautiful place. Come on, smile. …

4 Complete the conversation with *lot*, *many* or *much*.

Chris: How (1) *many* people live in your town?
Rob: Not (2) _____ . Around 20,000, maybe.
Chris: And is there (3) _____ traffic?
Rob: Yeah! Too (4) _____ ! The streets are always full of cars. What about your city?
Chris: There are a (5) _____ of people – around a million – but there isn't (6) _____ traffic. We've got good public transport.
Rob: How (7) _____ cinemas do you have?
Chris: We have a (8) _____ . Maybe forty or fifty. You?
Rob: Wow! We don't have (9) _____ . Only three, in fact.
Chris: So what else can you do in the evenings?
Rob: We go to the pub. It's a small town, but there are a (10) _____ of pubs.

5 Write one verb in the past simple and the other in the past continuous for each sentence.

a) I (work) *was working* in Oxford when I (meet) *met* Tony for the first time.
b) It (rain) _____ when Sara (arrive) _____ home.
c) We (have) _____ lunch when you (ring) _____ .
d) You (chat) _____ when I (come) _____ in.
e) Joe (cook) _____ when he (cut) _____ his finger.
f) Dave and Becky (watch) _____ TV when the baby (wake) _____ up.

6 Change the adjectives in the box into adverbs and use them to complete the sentences.

> careful   early   good   quiet   ~~regular~~

a) I wash my car *regularly* – every Saturday.
b) I don't cook very _____ – everyone hates my food!
c) I usually speak very _____ – no-one can hear me!
d) I always get up _____ – at 6.00 a.m.
e) I do my work _____ – I never make mistakes!

Tick the sentences that are true for you. Compare with your partner.

7 Spot the mistake! Cross out the incorrect sentence.

1   a) ~~What means your name?~~
    b) What does your name mean?

2   a) Did they been to Venice?
    b) Have they been to Venice?

3   a) What was the weather like in Greece?
    b) How was the weather like in Greece?

4   a) We eat far too much chocolate.
    b) We eat far too many chocolate.

5   a) You eat your food very slowly.
    b) You eat very slowly your food.

6   a) They speak French very good.
    b) They speak French very well.

Vocabulary

1 Complete the text about Simon and his family with the words in the box.

> brother-in-law   daughter   half-brother
> half-sister   nephew   niece   ~~stepfather~~
> stepmother   uncle

'Hi, I'm Simon, and this is my family. My dad, Pete, and my mum, Lisa, are divorced. Dad is single, but Mum remarried. Her husband – my (1) *stepfather* – is called Sam. Mum and Sam have two children, Jack and Cathy – my (2) _____ and my (3) _____ . Sam and his ex-wife, Eva, have a (4) _____ , Debra. My mum is Debra's (5) _____ . My sister's name is Ann. She's married to Ted – (6) my _____ . They have two children. Bea is my (7) _____ and Harry is my (8) _____ , and, of course, I'm their favourite (9) _____ . They're lovely children.'

2 Match the two halves of the questions about names.

a) What are your   1 maiden name?
b) What do your friends   2 initials?
c) What name do you   3 name you after?
d) Who did your parents   4 like best?
e) What's your mother's   5 call you?

Answer the questions. Work with a partner and compare your answers.

3 Complete the names of places you might find in a city.

a) *art g*allery
b) br__dg__
c) c__n__l
d) c__r p__rk
e) c__stl__
f) f____nt____n
g) l__br__ry
h) m__s____m
i) p__rk
j) sh__pp__ng c__ntr__

4 Write an adjective from the box next to each definition.

> beautiful   ~~crowded~~   dull   expensive
> polluted   romantic   spectacular

a) full of people *crowded*   e) costs a lot of money
b) too much smoke / traffic   f) very good-looking
c) not interesting   g) dramatic and exciting
d) ideal for lovers

5 Write the nationality in the correct column.

> ~~Brazil~~   Canada   ~~China~~   Egypt   Hungary
> Italy   Japan   Morocco   Portugal   Vietnam

-an	-ese
Brazilian	*Chinese*

6 Look at the map of Australia and write sentences about the places using the words in the box.

> centre   east   ~~north~~   north-east   south
> south-east   south-west

Darwin is in the north.   Cairns is in …

7 Match the two halves of the phrases that describe stages of a relationship.

a) chat   1 in love
b) go   2 somebody up
c) fall   3 children
d) move   4 in together
e) get   5 up
f) have   6 out together
g) split   7 married

Pronunciation

1 Look at some words from Units 1–3. Say the words and add them to the table.

> ~~annoyed~~   ~~beautiful~~   ~~cathedral~~   Chinese
> ~~chocolate~~   cousin   dessert   Egyptian
> extremely   granddaughter   perfume
> surprised   together   Turkish   uniform
> vegetables

A: □▢	B: ▢□	C: □□□	D: □▢□
annoyed	*chocolate*	*beautiful*	*cathedral*

2 Underline the stressed syllable in each word.

🔊 **1.26** Listen, check and repeat.

Reading & Listening

1 🔘 **1.27 Read the descriptions of two friendships and answer the questions.**

a) How did these best friends meet?

b) How often do they see each other?

My best friend

Liz Krebbs

'My best friend is Deb Evans. We met on an internet chat site in 2003. We both liked chatting about music and fashion, and then we discovered that we live only ten miles from each other.

5 We talked online all the time, and one day we arranged to meet in a café. I felt really nervous, because I'm shy with new people, but we liked each other immediately. We are very similar. We both lived abroad when we were children, and we

10 both had parents who got divorced when we were young. We both have busy lives, but we still talk every day on the phone and we see each other once a week. I think Deb's a fantastic person. She's very generous and a lot of fun. I'm so happy I met her!'

Paul MacIntyre

15 'James Wood is my best friend. We met at primary school. His real name is James, but everybody calls him 'Woody'. He sat behind me in class. We were both very naughty at school and we got into trouble a lot! When we were teenagers we didn't

20 spend much time with each other. Woody was a punk, and I liked rock music. Then, after school I went to university, and we didn't see each other for four years. But after that, I moved back to our home town and met Woody again. Now we see

25 each other every month at the pub. He's just the same as twenty years ago.
He made me laugh then,
and he makes me
laugh now.'

2 **Read the descriptions again. Are these statements true or false? Correct the false sentences.**

a) Liz and Deb live ten miles from each other. *True.*

b) Liz and Deb didn't like each other at first.

c) Liz is very different from Deb.

d) Liz likes Deb because she's generous and fun.

e) Woody and Paul were always very good students at school.

f) Woody and Paul were both punks when they were teenagers.

g) Paul thinks Woody is the same now as twenty years ago.

3 🔘 **1.28 Listen to the conversation between Carol and Jessica. What nationality is Mark?**

Listen again and underline the correct information.

Jessica's boyfriend: Mark

• Where Jessica and Mark met:
  (1) **At school / At university**.

• When they met:
  (2) **Five years ago / Ten years ago**.

• First impression:
  (3) **She didn't like him. / She thought he was very interesting**.

• Things they really like doing together:
  (4) **Windsurfing / Scuba diving**.

---

4 **Listen again and answer the questions.**

a) What did Jessica and Mark do at the beach?

b) Where did Mark go after university?

c) Why did they go to Egypt?

d) Has Jessica been to the USA?

e) When did Mark come back to England?

f) Where are Jessica and Mark going to travel to next?

Writing & Speaking

1 Work with a partner. Match the questions (*a–e*) with the answers in note form (*1–5*).

   a) What's your best friend's name? 3
   b) Where and when did you meet him/her?
   c) What was your first impression of him/her?
   d) What do you like about him/her?
   e) What do you like doing together?

2 Match the parts of the text below to the questions (*a–e*) in Exercise 1.

1 relaxed, good listener, funny
2 secondary school – 1st day
3 Adriana Costa
4 theatre, museums, shopping
5 she knew everybody

How I met
my best friend

☐ We met on the first day of secondary school. I was very shy, and I felt nervous on my first day.

☐ We are very different. I'm quite serious. But Adriana is a very relaxed person, and she's a really good listener. And she's the funniest person I've ever met. We laugh all the time.

a My best friend is Adriana Costa.

☐ We do everything together! We both like the theatre and art. We visit museums and we love shopping!

☐ Adriana knew everybody, and everybody liked her. I liked her too, but I thought she was too cool, and I was too shy. But she still liked me! I was sitting alone in the classroom when she sat down next to me. She was very kind to me, and we became good friends.

3 How did you meet your best friend? Write answers in note form to the questions in Exercise 1.

4 Tell your partner about how you met your best friend.

5 Write about how you met your best friend. Give longer answers to the questions in Exercise 1.

▶ 🎵 1.29 **Song:** *Stand By Me*

4 Shopping

Grammar Adverbs of frequency. Verb patterns. Present simple and continuous
Vocabulary Collocations: *a bunch of ...*, *a box of ...*, etc. Clothes and accessories
Useful phrases In a clothes shop

Speaking

Work in small groups. Discuss the questions.

a) When do you give presents?
b) What's the best present you've ever given or received?
c) Which is easier: buying presents for men or buying presents for women?

Reading

1 Read this article and answer the questions.

a) Did a man or woman write the article?
b) Does he or she think men are good at choosing presents?
c) Does he or she think women are good at choosing presents?
d) What do women and men really want for their birthday? Do you agree?

What people really want for their birthday

It was my birthday recently and as usual I didn't get what I really wanted. I usually get a bunch of flowers, a cookery book, a box of chocolates and electronic gadgets. My family always ask me what I want, and I always tell them
5 the same thing – I want a surprise. So this year I got flowers, a cookery book, chocolates and gadgets.

Flowers are lovely but they hardly ever last for more than a week, and a real present is something you can keep. I always look for the diamond ring hidden in the flowers,
10 but it's never there.

Cookery books are boring, and I hate getting chocolates because I'm usually on a diet.

But gadgets are the worst. Most women are not interested in gadgets. Men buy gadgets for women because
15 men love gadgets.

But women are sensitive and intuitive so they always know the right thing to buy. Right? Wrong.

The big mistake that women make is that they
20 usually buy clothes. They buy clothes because they like them and they want other people to wear the clothes they like. 'You always wear dark colours, and I want to change you, so I'm going to buy you a brightly coloured tie or a pair of Mickey Mouse socks.'

25 This is a big mistake. Men don't usually want brightly coloured ties or silly socks. The word to remember when you're buying a present for a male is *gadgets*. Men like anything digital, electronic and fun.

For his last birthday, I gave my husband a small torch
30 and a Swiss army knife. He was overjoyed.

It's very simple. You can't go wrong if you always remember the 'J' word for women (that's 'J' for jewellery) and the 'G' word for men.

2 Rearrange the words below to make six statements from the article.

a) A / can / real / you / something / is / present / keep
    A real present is something you can keep.
b) Cookery / boring / books / are
c) Most / in / are / interested / women / gadgets / not
d) Women / and / intuitive / are / sensitive
e) Men / usually / brightly / coloured / want / don't / ties
f) Men / fun / anything / like / electronic / digital / and

Do you agree with these statements? Discuss with a partner.

Vocabulary

1 *A bunch of flowers* is a collocation from the article on page 32. Match words from column *A* with words from column *B* to make similar collocations.

A		B	
a)	a bunch of	1	socks / scissors / jeans
b)	a box of	2	cake / furniture / wood
c)	a pair of	3	cigarettes / crisps / biscuits
d)	a packet of	4	flowers / grapes / keys
e)	a piece of	5	wine / perfume / whisky
f)	a bottle of	6	beans / petrol / tomatoes
g)	a jar of	7	chocolates / matches / tissues
h)	a can of	8	jam / instant coffee / mayonnaise

2 Work with a partner. Discuss the questions about the things in Exercise 1.

- Have you ever given or received any of these things as a present?
- Which things are common presents in your country?
- Which things would be very strange or unusual presents?

Pronunciation

1 🔊 1.30 Listen and repeat the plural forms in the table.

/s/, /z/ or /ɪz/ ?	Examples
A: /s/ after /p/, /k/, /f/, /t/, /θ/	*cakes, crisps, suits*
B: /z/ after /b/, /g/, /v/, /d/, /ð/, /l/, /m/, /n/, /ŋ/ and all vowel sounds	*clothes, rings, views*
C: /ɪz/ after /s/, /z/, /ʃ/, /tʃ/, /dʒ/	*beaches, places, stages*

2 Add the plural forms of these nouns to the appropriate line in the table in Exercise 1.

bar /bɑː/ bridge /brɪdʒ/ bunch /bʌntʃ/ grape /greɪp/ key /kiː/
piece /piːs/ pot /pɒt/ sock /sɒk/ tie /taɪ/

🔊 1.31 Listen, check and repeat.

Grammar

Adverbs of frequency

100% ↑ always
usually
normally
often
sometimes
occasionally
rarely
hardly ever
0% ↓ never

adverb before <u>main verb</u>
We don't **usually** <u>drive</u>.

be before **adverb**
<u>I'm</u> **always** tired.

1 Look at the highlighted examples of adverbs of frequency used in the article on page 32. Are these sentences true or false?

a) Adverbs of frequency come <u>before</u> the main part of the verb, but <u>after</u> auxiliary verbs.
b) Adverbs of frequency come <u>after</u> the verb *be*.

2 How well do you know the person sitting next to you? Add an adverb of frequency to these sentences to make them true. Write affirmative or negative sentences.

a) He/She spends more than €25 on a present.
She rarely spends more than €25 on a present.
He doesn't usually spend more than €25 on a present.
b) He/She is positive about life.
c) He/She goes out at the weekend.
d) He/She is late for appointments.
e) He/She has lunch at home during the week.
f) He/She walks to school/work.

Check your sentences with your partner. How many are true? How similar or different are you?

Speaking: anecdote

1　🔘 1.32 **Listen to Eddie talking about the last time he bought somebody a present. Underline the answers he gives.**

a) 'Who was the present for?' 'My **friend** / <u>sister</u>.'
b) 'What was the occasion?' 'Her **birthday** / **wedding anniversary**.'
c) 'Where did you go shopping for the present?' '**To the city centre** / **On the internet**.'
d) 'Did you know what you were going to buy?' '**Yes, I did** / **No, I didn't**.'
e) 'What did you buy in the end?' '**Jewellery** / **A foot spa**.'
f) 'How much did you spend?' 'About **£50** / **£15**.'
g) 'Did you buy a card too?' '**Yes, I did** / **No, I didn't**.'
h) 'Did the person like the present?' '**Yes, she did** / **No, she didn't**.'
i) 'Was it the sort of present you would like to receive?' '**Yes, it was** / **No, it wasn't**.'

2　**You're going to tell your partner about the last time you bought somebody a present.**

- Ask yourself the questions in Exercise 1.
- Think about *what* to say and *how* to say it.
- Tell your partner about the last time you bought someone a present.

Grammar & Vocabulary

Verbs patterns 1

Verbs with two objects

buy somebody something
send somebody something
give somebody something

somebody = indirect object
something = direct object

1　**Look at these two sentences and answer the questions.**

*Eddie bought **a foot spa** for his sister.*
*Eddie bought his sister **a foot spa**.*

a) Do the sentences mean the same thing?
b) What colour is the direct object in each sentence?
c) What colour is the indirect object in each sentence?

2　**Complete the table to show two ways of saying the same thing.**

subject + verb + thing + *to/for* + person	subject + verb + person + thing
a)　I never lend **my car** to anybody.	I never lend anybody **my car**.
b)　My friends send **lots of texts** to me.	_____
c)　I sometimes buy **flowers** for my mum.	_____

Tick the sentences that are true for you.

3　**Insert the indirect object in brackets to complete the questions.**

When was the last time …
a) you bought presents? (your family)
　　you bought your family presents?
b) you made a cup of coffee? (somebody)
c) your bank sent a letter? (you)
d) you gave a lift? (somebody)
e) you lent some money? (your best friend)
f) a friend told a joke? (you)

Ask your partner the questions.

4　**Grammar** *Extra* 4, Part 1 page 132. Read the explanation and do the exercises.

Speaking

1 Complete these statements with *Men* or *Women* as you think appropriate.

a) _____ can't stand shopping for clothes.

b) _____ don't mind spending hours and hours shopping for clothes.

c) _____ spend a lot of time going from shop to shop, comparing prices and quality.

d) _____ never forget to look at the price tag before they buy.

e) _____ only agree to go shopping when they really need to buy something.

f) _____ like going to the dentist's more than going shopping.

2 Discuss your ideas with a partner. Which statements in Exercise 1 are true for you?

Grammar & Vocabulary

Verb patterns 2

Verbs + *ing*-form
avoid   can't stand
don't mind   enjoy   hate
like   love   spend time

I can't stand **shopping**.

Verbs + *to*-infinitive
agree   can't afford
choose   decide   forget
manage   need   refuse
want   would like

I can't afford **to buy** it.

1 Complete these interviews with two men about shopping. Use the *ing*-form or the *to*-infinitive.

Questions	Conor, 26, writer	Jim, 32, designer
Question 1 'Do you mind (1 go) *going* round the shops?'	'Not really. But after about an hour I want (2 go) _____ home.'	'Actually, I can't stand (3 go) _____ round the shops. My girlfriend knows this, so she usually chooses (4 go) _____ without me.'
Question 2 'What kind of shops do you enjoy (5 go) _____ into?'	'Book shops. I spend a lot of time (6 read) _____ book reviews so I always have a list of books I'd like (7 buy) _____ .'	'I enjoy (8 look) _____ at electronic equipment but I can't afford (9 buy) _____ it. It's usually far too expensive.'
Question 3 'Are there any kinds of shops you hate (10 go) _____ into?'	'I hate supermarkets. I usually forget (11 buy) _____ the things I went there for, so I avoid (12 go) _____ into them. Fortunately, I can do most of my food shopping online.'	'I refuse (13 go) _____ into shoe shops with my girlfriend. She tries on ten pairs and then decides (14 buy) _____ the first pair.'
Question 4 'Do you enjoy (15 buy) _____ clothes for yourself?'	'Not really. I only go into a clothes shop when I need (16 buy) _____ a new shirt or something. For me, shopping is a necessity, not a pleasure.'	'I love (17 have) _____ new clothes, but I never manage (18 find) _____ time to go shopping.'

🌐 **1.33** Listen and check your answers. Do you know any men with similar attitudes?

Ask your partner the questions (*1–4*) from the interview.

2 Complete the following sentences with your own ideas.

a) I enjoy …

b) I don't mind …

c) I can't stand …

d) I avoid …

e) I'd like …

f) I need …

g) I can't afford …

h) I've decided …

Compare your sentences with your partner.

Reading & Vocabulary

1 Look at the photos from a fashion magazine and complete the descriptions with the words below.

boots	earrings	necklace	sandals	scarf	shirt
skirt	top	trousers	~~waistcoat~~		

MEN'S OR WOMEN'S FASHION?

KEIKO is wearing a black silk (1) *waistcoat*, a white cotton (2) _____ , black woollen (3) _____ and black leather (4) _____ .

ROBERT is wearing a plain green linen (5) _____ , a red cotton (6) _____ , a light green silk (7) _____ around his head, gold (8) _____ , a gold (9) _____ , and yellow leather (10) _____ .

🌐 1.34 **Listen and check.**

2 What do you think of the clothes in the photos? Tell a partner.

3 Complete the table with words from the descriptions in Exercise 1 above.

Design/Colour	Material	Clothes and accessories
black	silk	waistcoat

4 🌐 1.35 **Listen and repeat the items of clothing (*a–d*).**

Add the words to the table in Exercise 3.

5 Complete the sentences below in as much detail as possible so that they are true for you. Compare your sentences with a partner.

a) I never wear …   b) I often wear …   c) Today, I'm wearing …

I never wear checked shirts. Today I'm wearing a blue cotton top.

Reading

1 Read the article. According to environmental groups, are cheap clothes good or bad?

The **real price** of fashion

In 2005, a military jacket appeared on the fashion pages of *Vogue*. There's nothing unusual about that, except that the price tag was not £1,200, nor
5 even £120. The jacket was made by Primark, and it was on sale for just £12! Women went mad for it, and Primark was renamed 'the new Prada'.
At Primark T-shirts cost £2, pyjamas
10 cost £5, suits cost £15 and women's tops cost less than £5. So it's no surprise that Primark's profits are increasing and new stores are opening across the UK, Spain and Ireland.
15 So everybody's happy then. Well, no. According to environmental groups such as Friends of the Earth,

cheap clothes are damaging the environment. Consumers are paying
20 low prices for their clothes, but the planet is paying a high cost.
The result of low prices is that people are buying more. On average, people now buy fifty items of clothing
25 a year – an increase of 33%. But these clothes are poor quality and they don't last. You can't sell them second-hand or recycle them for charity. They are disposable.
30 A spokesperson from the Green Party said, 'We are not against fashion, but cheap clothes, not designed to last, are bad for the consumer and the planet.'

2 Complete the diagram with *stores* or *consumers*.

3 Is this trend happening in your country? Discuss these questions with your partner.

a) Where can you buy cheap clothes in your city?
b) How much do you pay for casual clothes such as jeans, trainers, tops, etc.?
c) Do you recycle your clothes? How?

More (1) _____ are selling poor quality clothes.

(2) _____ are paying lower prices.

(3) _____ are buying more clothes.

(4) _____ are making more profits.

(5) More _____ are opening.

Grammar

Present tenses

Present simple
I **work** in an office.
We **start** work at nine.

Present continuous
I'm **not working** now.
I'm **having** lunch.

My job **is getting** more difficult to do.

1 Match the underlined verb forms (1–3) in these sentences with their uses (a–c).

Today (1) I'm wearing a top from Primark. (2) I usually wear designer clothes but these days (3) I'm buying more high street clothes because they look great.

a) Actions that happen **all the time, often, sometimes, never, etc.** (Present simple)
b) Actions that are **in progress** *at* **the moment of speaking.** (Present continuous)
c) Actions that are **in progress** *around* **the moment of speaking.** (Present continuous)

2 Write these sentences in the negative and match them with the uses (a–c) in Exercise 1.

a) I'm sitting near the door.
   I'm not sitting near the door. = Use 'b'
b) My parents go to church.
c) I'm saving money for my next holiday.
d) My mother works in a shop.

e) I'm studying for an exam.
f) It's raining.
g) I'm learning to play the piano.
h) The cost of living is going up fast.

Tick the sentences – affirmative or negative – that are true. Compare with a partner.

3 Pairwork **Student A:** page 117 **Student B:** page 122

4 Grammar *Extra* 4, Part 2 page 132. Read the explanation and do the exercises.

Useful phrases

1 Russell wants to buy a present for his girlfriend. Read the useful phrases. Put *R* if you think Russell says them. Put *SA* if you think the shop assistant says them.

a) I'm just looking, thanks. *R*
b) I'll take it.
c) Can I help you?
d) What colours do you have?
e) How would you like to pay?

f) Can she exchange it if it doesn't fit?
g) What size is she?
h) Here's your receipt.
i) What sort of thing are you looking for?
j) By credit card.

🌐 **1.36** Listen, check and repeat the useful phrases.

2 Put the useful phrases in the correct place in the conversation.

SA: (1) *Can I help you?*
R: (2) _____ Well, actually, I'm looking for something for my girlfriend.
SA: (3) _____
R: I don't really know. A top?
SA: OK, and what colour would you like?
R: (4) _____
SA: We have any colour you want, sir. Purple is very fashionable at the moment.
R: Purple's fine.
SA: Right. (5) _____
R: Ah, well, she isn't very big, but she's not particularly small.
SA: So she's medium.
R: Yes, medium.
SA: Well, we have this rather nice purple top here ...
R: Good. (6) _____
SA: Are you sure you don't want to see any more ...?
R: No, that's great. I'll take it. Thank you. How much is it?
SA: That's £70, sir. (7) _____
R: Seventy?! (8) _____ , please.
SA: Fine. If you could just sign ...
R: Here you are. Goodbye.
SA: Just a minute, sir. (9) _____
R: Oh yes, er ... (10) _____
SA: Yes, but she needs to keep the receipt.

🌐 **1.37** Listen and check your answers.

Practise the conversation with a partner.

3 Work with your partner. Write your own shopping conversation.
a) Decide on the shop and what the customer is buying.
b) Decide on the character/personality of the shop assistant and the customer.
c) Include at least six of these eight words.

by	fit	help	just	pay	receipt	size	sort

d) Practise your conversation and perform it for the rest of the class.

Clothes and accessories

1 Match the pictures with the descriptions. Then complete the descriptions.

7	a checked *scarf*
	brown leather _____
	a plain white cotton _____
	a blue denim _____
	a pinstriped _____
	a silver _____
	a patterned woollen _____
	a floral _____
	gold _____
	striped _____
	plastic _____
	a light blue silk _____

2 Work with a partner. Cover the words. Look at the pictures. Ask and answer questions.

'What's this?'
'It's a checked scarf.'

'What are these?'
'They're brown leather gloves.'

Focus on verbs used with clothes

1 Match the verb phrases with their meanings

a) get dressed
b) get undressed
c) get changed
d) clothes fit you
e) clothes suit you
f) try something on

1 take your clothes off
2 put something on to see if it fits / suits you
3 clothes are the right size for you
4 put your clothes on
5 clothes are the right colour, shape and style for you
6 take your clothes off and put different clothes on

2 Underline the most appropriate verb phrase.

a) I always **get dressed** / **get undressed** before breakfast.
b) I usually **try on** / **wear** formal clothes at work.
c) When it's cold I **put on** / **take off** my leather coat.
d) I like **trying on** / **taking off** new clothes.
e) Yellow and orange don't **suit** / **fit** me.
f) I **get dressed** / **get changed** when I get home from work.

Tick the sentences that are true for you. Compare with your partner.

5 Fit

Grammar Comparatives and superlatives. Phrasal verbs
Vocabulary *How* + adjective/adverb. Sport. Numbers
Useful phrases Giving instructions

Reading

1 Read and answer the questionnaire.

ARE YOU
dangerously unfit?

1 In an average day, do you …
a) climb more than a hundred stairs?
YES / NO
b) do at least one hour of housework?
YES / NO
c) walk or cycle to school or work?
YES / NO

2 How often do you walk five kilometres or more?
a) Once a month.
b) Once a week.
c) Never.

3 How much sport do you do every month?
a) More than nine hours.
b) Between two and nine hours.
c) Less than two hours.

4 How often do you spend twenty minutes or more doing an activity that makes you hot or sweaty?
a) Three or more times a week.
b) Once or twice a week.
c) Not at all.

5 How long does it take you to walk a kilometre?
a) Less than ten minutes.
b) Between ten and twenty minutes.
c) I can't walk that far.

6 How many of the following activities do you do at least once a week?
a) Go jogging. YES / NO
b) Play a ball game. YES / NO
c) Do some aerobic exercise (cycling, rowing, etc.). YES / NO

7 Tick the activities you often do when you're on holiday.
a) Go hiking.
b) Go swimming.
c) Go sightseeing.
d) Go dancing.
e) Lie on the beach.
f) Eat and drink a lot.

8 Do you smoke? YES / NO

How to score

1 a) YES: 5   NO: 0
   b) YES: 5   NO: 0
   c) YES: 5   NO: 0

2 a) 3 b) 5 c) 0

3 a) 5 b) 3 c) 0

4 a) 5 b) 3 c) 0

5 a) 5 b) 3 c) 0

6 a) YES: 5   NO: 0
   b) YES: 5   NO: 0
   c) YES: 5   NO: 0

7 a) 5 b) 5 c) 3 d) 3 e) 0 f) 0

8 YES: 0   NO: 10

What your score means

20 or less: Your health and your life are in danger! You must do more exercise.

21–30: Could be worse, but not much worse.

31–40: Not bad, but could be better.

41–50: You are healthier than the average person and you probably find your life more enjoyable as a result.

51 or more: You are super-fit. Are you a professional athlete? (Are you telling the truth?!)

2 Calculate your score and compare your answers with a partner.

Vocabulary

1 Look at the table. How long does it take you to do each activity?

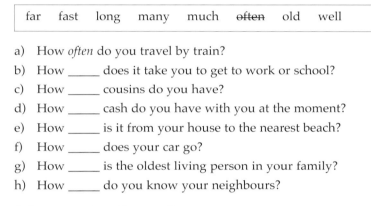

	Activity
How long does it take you to …	(1) get up in the morning? (2) buy presents for people you love? (3) choose from a menu in a restaurant? (4) decide whether you like someone? (5) read a novel? (6) get ready to go out for the evening? (7) get to sleep at night?

Guess the time it takes your partner to do the same things.

Ask a partner questions to check your ideas.

'How long does it take you to get up in the morning?'
'About twenty minutes.'

2 Complete more questions with *How* + adjective/adverb. Use the words in the box.

far   fast   long   many   much   ~~often~~   old   well

a) How *often* do you travel by train?

b) How _____ does it take you to get to work or school?

c) How _____ cousins do you have?

d) How _____ cash do you have with you at the moment?

e) How _____ is it from your house to the nearest beach?

f) How _____ does your car go?

g) How _____ is the oldest living person in your family?

h) How _____ do you know your neighbours?

Ask your partner the questions.

Speaking: anecdote

1 🌐 2.01 Listen to Tina, talking about her experiences of doing sport at school. Are the answers here right (✓) or wrong (✗)?

a) 'How many hours of sport did you do each week at school?'
'Three hours a week.' ✗

b) 'What different sports did you do during the school year?'
'Swimming, tennis and hockey.'

c) 'Which sports did you like/hate the most?'
'I hated hockey.'

d) 'What kind of sports facilities did your school have?'
'A gym and a football pitch.'

e) 'What did your sports teacher look like?'
'She looked like a boxer.'

f) 'Did you ever play for a school team?'
'Yes, I played for the school hockey team.'

g) 'What was your best/worst sporting moment?'
'My best moment was winning a disco dancing competition.'

2 You're going to tell your partner about your experiences of doing sport at school.

- Ask yourself the questions in Exercise 1.
- Think about *what* to say and *how* to say it.
- Tell your partner about your experiences of doing sport at school.

Listening

1 Work with a partner. Try to match each of these famous sports stars with their date of birth.

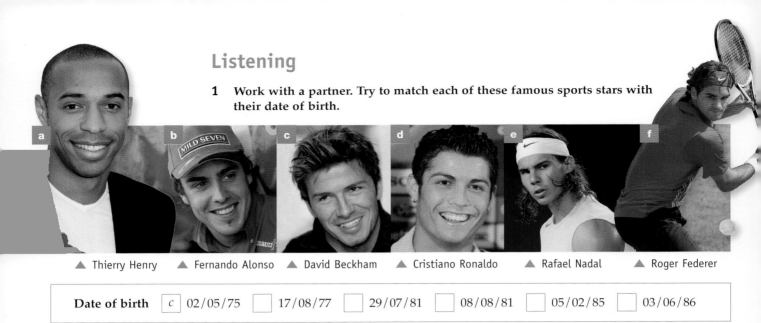

▲ Thierry Henry ▲ Fernando Alonso ▲ David Beckham ▲ Cristiano Ronaldo ▲ Rafael Nadal ▲ Roger Federer

Date of birth	c 02/05/75	17/08/77	29/07/81	08/08/81	05/02/85	03/06/86

🕐 2.02 **Listen and check your answers**

2 🕐 2.03 **Listen to a discussion between a marketing director and an advertising executive. Which sports star do they choose to advertise a new energy drink?**

Listen again and complete these sentences. You need to use some names more than once.

a) *Beckham* is more famous than *Henry*.

b) _____ isn't as interesting as _____ .

c) _____ is a bit older than _____ .

d) _____ isn't as successful as _____ .

e) _____ is much younger than _____ .

f) _____ is the best-looking, most ...

3 Work with a partner. List the most famous sports stars in your country.
* Complete the sentences in Exercise 2 with names from your list.
* Choose one sports star from your list to advertise a new sports car.
* Compare your ideas with other students in the class.

Grammar

Comparatives

He's **a bit older**

He's **older**   **than** her.

He's **much older**

She's **not as old as** him.

1 Test your general knowledge! Use the adjective in brackets with *a bit / much / not as ... as* to make true comparisons.

a) Mount Kilimanjaro (high) _____ Mount Fuji.
Mount Kilimanjaro is much higher than Mount Fuji.

b) London (wet) _____ Rome.

c) The US Army (small) _____ the North Korean Army.

d) Heathrow Airport (busy) _____ Los Angeles International Airport.

e) Ireland (big) _____ Cuba.

f) Big Ben (tall) _____ the Statue of Liberty.

🕐 2.04 **Listen and check your answers.**

2 Combine the noun phrases with the adjectives – or your own ideas – to make comparative statements that you agree with.

English food   Flying
French wine   German cars
Living in a city   Men
Shopping online   Women

cheap   complex   convenient
exciting   expensive   funny
interesting   noisy   reliable
safe   sensitive   sophisticated

Compare your statements with a partner. Do you agree or disagree?

'I think women are much more complex than men.'

3 Grammar *Extra* 5, Part 1 page 134. Read the explanation and do the exercises.

Pronunciation

1 Complete the following expressions with the appropriate word.

a) It's as light as a *feather*.   c) They're as good as _____.   e) It's as solid as a _____.

b) He's as free as a _____.   d) She's as pretty as a _____.   f) It's as old as the _____.

2 🌐 **2.05 Listen, check and repeat. Practise the red schwa (/ə/) sounds.**

Can you think of people or things you could describe in this way? Do you have similar expressions in your language?

Grammar

Superlatives

Short adjectives
the rich**est**, the big**gest**, the funn**iest**

Irregular forms
the best, the worst, the furthest

Long adjectives
the **most** interesting, the **most** modern

1 Write out the superlative forms for the following groups of adjectives.

Adjectives	Superlative forms
a) old / rich / exciting / great b) valuable / big / hot / thin c) funny / interesting / sexy / happy d) bad / far / good / talented	*the oldest / the richest / the ...*

In each group, underline the superlative adjective which is formed in a different way from the other three.

2 Complete the questions with different superlative adjectives. Use the adjectives in Exercise 1 or your own ideas.

a) Who is _____ sports person in the world?

b) What is _____ music group of all time?

c) What is _____ place you've ever visited?

d) Who is _____ person you know?

e) What is _____ possession you have?

f) Who is _____ actor/actress in your country?

g) Where is _____ nightlife in town?

h) Who is _____ person in the class?

Ask a partner your questions.

Vocabulary

1 🌐 **2.06 Listen and repeat the numbers in the box.**

> ³/₄   0.25   0.33   1¹/₂   ¹/₈   ¹/₄   1.5   0.125   ¹/₃   0.75

Make pairs of numbers with the same value. Practise saying the numbers.
³/₄ is the same as 0.75.

2 🌐 **2.07 Listen and repeat the numbers in column *A*. Write each number in full.**

A		B	
a)	249 km/hr *two hundred and forty-nine kilometres an hour*	1	Cristiano Ronaldo's earnings in 2007
b)	42.195 km	2	The percentage of the UK population who trust the government
c)	8.2%	3	The biggest football score
d)	£6,188,000	4	The fastest tennis serve
e)	32–0	5	The official distance for a marathon

Match the numbers in column *A* with the facts in column *B*.

3 **Pairwork** **Student A:** page 117 **Student B:** page 122

Reading

1 Imagine that today is 'No-Stress Day'. Read the list and answer the questions.

   a) Which suggestion is the easiest for you to do?
   b) Which suggestion is the most difficult for you to do?

ways to de-stress

1 Take off your watch.
2 Switch off your mobile phone.
3 Don't eat your breakfast on your feet – sit down and enjoy it.
4 Put on your most comfortable clothes.
5 Don't run after the bus – let it go.
6 Smell the roses.
7 Give up the gym.
8 Fall in love.
9 Only switch on your television if there's something you really want to watch.
10 Throw away or give away any clothes you haven't worn for the past two years.
11 Have a laugh.
12 Hang up your clothes when you take them off.
13 Spend ten minutes doing absolutely nothing.
14 Walk.
15 Only do the ironing if you love it.
16 Put on your favourite music and turn up the volume.

Discuss your answers with a partner.

2 Work with your partner. Add three of your own suggestions to the list.

Vocabulary

1 Complete the sentences using these phrasal verbs from the list above.

give up   hang up   put on   switch off   switch on   ~~take off~~   throw away

   a) I always *take off* my shoes before I go into my house.
   b) If I want to relax, I _____ all the lights and sit in silence.
   c) When I want to look my best, I _____ a suit.
   d) I could never _____ coffee – it's the only thing that keeps me awake.
   e) The first thing I do when I get to the office is _____ my computer.
   f) I never _____ plastic bags because they're so useful.
   g) I never do any ironing. I just _____ my clothes very carefully when they are wet.

2 Are any of the sentences true for you? Discuss with your partner.

Grammar

Phrasal verbs

Intransitive
She **sat down**.

Transitive (separable)
He **took off** his shoes.
He **took** his shoes **off**.
He **took** them **off**.

Transitive (not separable)
They **ran after** the bus.
They **ran after** it.

1 Work with a partner. Look at the three phrasal verbs used in these sentences (*take off, run after* and *sit down*) and answer the questions.

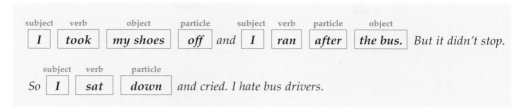

subject	verb	object	particle		subject	verb	particle	object	
I	took	my shoes	off	*and*	I	ran	after	the bus.	*But it didn't stop.*

	subject	verb	particle	
So	I	sat	down	*and cried. I hate bus drivers.*

a)   Which phrasal verb does not take an object? (INTRANSITIVE)
b)   Which phrasal verb can have the object between the verb and the particle? (TRANSITIVE – SEPARABLE)
c)   Which phrasal verb always has the object after the particle? (TRANSITIVE – NOT SEPARABLE)

2 When the object is a pronoun such as *it, them, her,* where do you always put it when the phrasal verb is: a) separable? b) inseparable?

3 Put the words in the correct order to make answers to the questions. Look the phrasal verbs up in a dictionary if you are not sure.

a)   What shall I do with this banana skin? (away / throw / it)   *Throw it away.*
b)   What shall I do with this mess? (it / up / clear)
c)   What shall I do with my trousers? (hang / up / them)
d)   What shall I do about this problem? (it / deal / with)
e)   What shall I do with this application form? (fill / in / it)
f)   What shall I do about my party? Nobody can come. (it / call / off)

4   Grammar *Extra* 5, Part 2 page 134. Read the explanation and do the exercises.

Listening & Speaking

1 You are going to listen to a radio programme about laughter clubs. Do you think the statements (*a–e*) are true or false?

a)   Young children laugh much more than adults.
b)   Laughter clubs started in the USA.
c)   Laughter releases happy chemicals called endorphins.
d)   Laughing is good for the heart.
e)   In laughter clubs, people laugh at funny stories.

🌐 2.08 **Listen and check your answers.**

2 Face your partner. Take it in turns to try to make each other laugh.

3 Work with your partner. Discuss the following questions.

a)   What kind of thing makes you laugh?
b)   How do you feel after a good laugh?
c)   When was the last time you laughed so much you couldn't stop?

Useful phrases

1 🌐 2.09 **Listen to the three conversations (*a–c*). Which sports are these people learning?**

a) Sally's learning to _____ .

b) Jimmy's learning to play _____ .

c) Rebecca's learning to play _____ .

2 **Match each person in Exercise 1 with a set of instructions *1, 2* or *3*.**

1
Throw the ball in the air.
Don't look at me.
Look at the ball.
Pick up your racket.
Try again.

3
Kick the ball.
Don't throw the ball.
Don't pick it up.
Don't touch the ball with your hand.
Use your foot.

2
Stand up on the board.
Hold on.
Don't let go.
Be careful.
Don't go too fast.

3 **Complete the first conversation in Exercise 1 by replacing the highlighted phrases (*1–6*) with the useful phrases in the box.**

Be careful!   Be patient.   Come back!   ~~Don't be horrible~~.
Don't worry.   Try again.

Paul: OK, are you ready?

Sally: Yes.

Paul: Right. Stand up on the board.

Sally: OK. Oohhhh!

Paul: Ha ha ha!

Sally: (1) Be nice. *Don't be horrible.*

Paul: Oh, sorry. OK. (2) Don't give up. Good! Great. Hold on. Don't let go.

Sally: Ohhhh! It's too difficult. I can't do it.

Paul: Don't be silly. Of course you can do it. (3) Don't be impatient. Come on, try again.

Sally: I look stupid.

Paul: (4) Relax. Everyone looks stupid the first time. Now, stand up on the board.
 That's it. (5) Take care! Good. Well done. Now, don't go too fast, Sally. Sally!
 (6) Don't go too far!

Sally: Wheeee!

Listen to the conversation again and check. Practise the conversation with a partner.

Vocabulary *Extra*

Sport

1 Complete the table. Use the pictures of equipment to help you.

Sport	Person	Place	Equipment
athletics	an athlete	an athletics track	shorts, a running vest, (1) *running shoes*
skiing	a skier	a ski resort	skis, ski boots, ski poles, (2) _____
football (soccer)	a footballer	a football pitch	a football, shorts, a football shirt, (3) _____
golf	a golfer	a golf course	golf balls, (4) _____
swimming	a swimmer	a swimming pool	a swimming costume, (5) _____ , (6) _____
tennis	a tennis player	a tennis court	tennis balls, (7) _____ , (8) _____

swimming trunks

golf clubs

football boots

running shoes

a net

a helmet

a tennis racket

goggles

2 Add more words or sports to the table in Exercise 1. Use your dictionary.

Focus on verbs used with sports

1 Underline the most appropriate alternative in each of these sentences.

a) I **do** / play / practise some exercise two or three times a week. It keeps me fit.
b) I've never **been** / played / practised windsurfing. I can't swim.
c) I'd like to **play** / go / practise snowboarding. I love the mountains.
d) The last time I **did** / went / practised some sport was on holiday.
e) I **did** / played / practised a lot of football when I was a child. Now I just watch it on TV.
f) I'm not very good at tennis because I don't have time to **do** / go / practise.

How many of the sentences are true for you? Compare with a partner.

2 Complete the verb phrases with *do*, *go* or *play*. Use your dictionary and add more sports to each list.

a) _____ cycling	b) _____ athletics	c) _____ basketball
fishing	judo	golf
swimming	_____	rugby
windsurfing		tennis
_____		volleyball
		_____

6 Job

Grammar Permission and obligation (*can / have to*). Present perfect and past simple
Vocabulary Jobs. Collocations (work). *should*. Office equipment
Useful phrases Presenting yourself

Listening

1 🌐 2.10 **Listen to four people giving answers to the same question. What was the question?**

▲ Mark, a company director

▲ Lucy, a surgeon

▲ Frank, a teacher

▲ Mia, a model

2 **Listen again and tick the jobs that each person mentions.**

Mark: a soldier ✓ an engineer ☐ a DJ ☐ a company director ☐

Lucy: a surgeon ☐ a ballet dancer ☐ a doctor ☐ a tour guide ☐ a butcher ☐

Frank: a farmer ☐ a vet ☐ a pilot ☐ a snowboarder ☐ a teacher ☐

Mia: an archaeologist ☐ an au pair ☐ a model ☐ a telesales person ☐

What did you want to be when you were a child?

Speaking

1 **Work as a class. Write the names of all the jobs that you, your parents and your grandparents have done.**

2 **Work in small groups. Look at all the jobs you have written down in Exercise 1 and discuss these questions.**
   a) In which job can you earn the most money?
   b) In which job do you get the most holidays?
   c) Which job do you study longest for?
   d) In which job do you need the most training?
   e) Which job is the most stressful?
   f) Which job is the most useful to society?

Reading

1 You are going to read about the model and snowboarder, Charlotte Dutton. Look at these words and phrases. Do you associate them with modelling or snowboarding?

> crash helmet   designer clothes   freezing   muscles   Paris   slim   strong
> warm, baggy clothes

Read the article and check your ideas.

Charlotte Dutton
FROM MOUNTAINS TO MODELLING

CHARLOTTE DUTTON has two jobs. Half the year she's a top model in Europe, and the other half she's a professional snowboarder in Canada.

'I love modelling and snowboarding,' she says, 'but I have to be two different people! You need muscles to be a snowboarder, but you have to be slim to be a
5   model. When I'm modelling I can't eat anything fattening. But in the mountains it's freezing, so you have to eat protein, cakes and chocolate. For the jumps and turns, you have to be strong. Snowboarding is sometimes dangerous, and I often fall. But I have to be careful because I can't break my leg and then go to Paris to model the best skirts. It's funny – half the year I have to wear warm, baggy clothes and a crash
10 helmet. Then I go to Europe for a season, and I have to wear beautiful designer clothes.'

Does she want to be a top international model or an Olympic snowboarder? The answer is she wants to be both ... but when she's much
15 older, she dreams of living in a bakery and eating cakes all day!

2 Imagine you could do two jobs. Which jobs would you like? Tell a partner.

Grammar

*can/can't
have to/don't have to*

can = It's permitted.
can't = It isn't permitted.
You **can** get married at 16 but you **can't** buy alcohol until you are 18.

have to = It's necessary.
don't have to = It isn't necessary.
You **have to** wear a helmet on a motorbike but you **don't have to** wear one on a bicycle.

1 Match the beginnings and ends of these sentences so that they make sense.

a) A snowboarder   can get up late.
b) A club DJ   has to have very clean hands.
c) A flight attendant   has to wear a crash helmet.
d) A tour guide   can't eat fattening food.
e) A model   has to know a lot of history.
f) A cook   doesn't have to pay for flights.

2 Match the underlined part of each sentence (*a–d*) with the correct meaning (*1–4*).

a) <u>I can</u> arrive at any time.   1   It's necessary for me to …
b) <u>I can't</u> wear jeans.   2   It isn't OK for me to …
c) <u>I have to</u> use a computer.   3   It isn't necessary for me to …
d) <u>I don't have to</u> wear a uniform.   4   It's OK for me to …

Think about your work or school. Which sentences are true for you?

3   Grammar *Extra* 6, Part 1 page 136. Read the explanation and do the exercises.

Reading

1 Work with a partner. Discuss the bad experiences you could have in these jobs.

> an actor   an au pair   a factory worker   a vet   a waiter

🔘 **2.11** Read the article. Compare your ideas with the stories Polly and Leo tell. Were any of your ideas similar?

Nightmare jobs

Polly: a vet

What's the worst thing that has ever happened in your job?
Probably the dog that
5 bit me. It wasn't a big
one – I don't mind the
big ones. The small ones are the worst. It
gave me a very nasty bite.

Have you ever done any other jobs?
10 Yes, I did various jobs when I was a student.
One summer I did fruit-picking in France,
Spain and Greece.

What's the worst job you've ever done?
I worked as an au pair for a rich family in
15 New York. I never had a day off and I had to
do everything – cooking, cleaning, shopping –
and look after their horrible children. I left
after two weeks and managed to get a job as
a waiter in an Italian restaurant.

Leo: an actor

20 **What's the worst thing that's ever happened in your job?**
So many bad things have happened – but I think my worst
moment was when I read my first bad review in the newspaper.
They wrote terrible things about me, and I was so upset. Now
I don't read my reviews any more.

25 **Have you ever done any other jobs?**
Oh yes, it's hard to make a living as an actor. So I've done lots of
part-time jobs over the years. For example, I've worked in a shop,
sold ice cream on the beach and handed out publicity
flyers in the street.

30 **What's the worst job you've ever done?**
The worst job I've ever done
was at an egg-packing factory.
Working conditions are terrible
– you stand for hours at the end
35 of a conveyor belt, putting eggs
into boxes. You can't have a break,
and if you want to go to the toilet, you
have to ask for permission. And worst
40 of all, the smell was disgusting – I've
never eaten an egg since then.

2 Answer the questions from memory. Read again and check your answers.

a) Who's done lots of part-time jobs?
b) Who's been fruit-picking?
c) Who's looked after horrible children?
d) Who's sold ice cream on the beach?
e) Who's worked in a factory?
f) Who's worked as a waiter?

3 Ask questions and try to find somebody who has had the experiences above.

Vocabulary

1 Add another collocation to each of the sets below using words and phrases from the article above.

a) to have ⎡some time⎤ / ⎡two weeks⎤ / ⎡*a day*⎤ off (line 15)

b) to ⎡find⎤ / ⎡lose⎤ / ⎢_____⎥ a job (line 18)

c) to make a ⎡decision⎤ / ⎡money⎤ / ⎢_____⎥ (line 26)

d) a ⎡well-paid⎤ / ⎡full-time⎤ / ⎢_____⎥ job (line 27)

e) to have a ⎡nap⎤ / ⎡rest⎤ / ⎢_____⎥ (line 37)

f) to ask for ⎡advice⎤ / ⎡a pay-rise⎤ / ⎢_____⎥ (line 39)

2 Use any collocations from Exercise 1 to write six sentences about yourself.

The last time I had some time off was at Christmas.
I'd like to find a better job.

Grammar

Present perfect

I've
You've   worked
He/She/It's   seen
We've   been
They've

I've = I have
He's = He has

Have you ever **worked**
in a bar?
Yes, I **have**.
No, I **haven't**.

(*ever* = at any time
'up to now')

1 Look at these two sentences from the article on page 50 and answer the questions below.

1 *'Yes, I did various jobs when I was a student.'*
2 *'So I've done lots of part-time jobs over the years.'*

a) Which sentence refers to a completed action in 'finished' time. What tense is used?
b) Which sentence refers to a completed action in time 'up to now'. What tense is used?

2 Complete the table with the time expressions in the box.

| a few moments ago | in 2005 | in the last two weeks | last week | never |
| over the years | recently | this week | today | when I was a student | years ago |

'Finished' time	Time 'up to now'
a few moments ago	*in the last two weeks*

3 Complete the sentences with time expressions from Exercise 2, or some of your own. Write true sentences using the appropriate tense for the verb in brackets.

a) I (buy) _____ a great CD ...   *I bought a great CD last week.*
b) I (not go) _____ to the beach ...
c) I (meet) _____ some interesting people ...
d) I (spend) _____ a lot of money ...
e) I (not see) _____ any good films ...
f) I (do) _____ a lot of silly things ...
g) I (read) _____ *The Da Vinci Code* ...
h) I (lose) _____ my keys ...

4 Pairwork **Student A:** page 117 **Student B:** page 122

5 Grammar *Extra* 6, Part 2 page 136. Read the explanation and do the exercises.

Pronunciation

1 Complete the table with the past participles of these irregular verbs. Underline the past participle in each group with a different vowel sound.

Infinitive	Past participle
a) say read feed be	*said read fed <u>been</u>*
b) know buy fly grow	
c) ring sing bring hang	
d) drink teach think fight	

2 🌐 2.12 Listen, check and repeat.

Speaking

1 Work with a partner. Make questions from the following prompts.

a) best or worst / party / ever go to
    What's the best party you've ever been to?
b) best or worst / holiday / ever go on
c) best or worst / meal / ever eat

d) best or worst / joke / ever hear
e) best or worst / car / ever go in
f) best or worst / T-shirt / ever wear
g) best or worst / bed / ever sleep in

2 Choose three questions from Exercise 1 and ask your partner. Find out as much as you can.

'What's the best holiday you've ever been on?' 'When I went to Australia.' 'When did you go?'

Listening

1 Look at the photo of Mr Reynold. You are going to listen to a radio interview with him. Work with a partner and discuss possible answers to these questions.

a) What sort of company does Mr Reynold work for?

b) When did he start working for the company?

c) How old is he now?

🔘 2.13 **Listen and check your ideas.**

2 Listen again and decide if these statements are true or false. Correct the false statements to make them true.

a) Mr Reynold never forces anybody <u>to retire</u>. *True.*

b) The oldest <u>employee</u> at Reynold's is 97. *False. He's 87.*

c) Reynold's pays <u>a decent salary</u>.

d) Employees get five weeks' <u>paid holiday</u>.

e) All the staff are over the <u>retirement age</u>.

f) Mr Reynold's secretary Edith had to <u>resign</u> because she wanted to get married.

g) Mr Reynold's brother is going to <u>run</u> the business from next year.

Vocabulary

1 Use appropriate words and expressions underlined in Exercise 2 above to complete these statements.

a) Everybody should get six weeks' *paid holiday* a year.

b) Nurses, teachers and police officers don't get _____ . They should get more money.

c) The official _____ should be the same for men and women.

d) If you don't want _____ you should be able to continue working.

e) Managing directors who _____ large corporations shouldn't earn such large salaries.

f) Politicians who tell lies should _____ .

2 Tick the ending that best describes the meaning of *should* in the statements in Exercise 1.

You use *should* when you think something is …

| a funny idea. ☐ |
| a good idea. ☐ |
| a strange idea. ☐ |

3 Work in small groups. Do you agree or disagree with the statements in Exercise 1?

Writing

1 Read this letter of application for a job at Reynold's Department Store. Use the words and expressions in the box to improve the parts of the letter that are highlighted.

> enclosed ~~Sir or Madam~~ a new challenge look forward to hearing
> would like to apply for reached retirement age

Reynold's Department Store
100–105 Wimbourne Rd
Bournemouth
BH2 6TG

45 Walpole Rd
Bournemouth
BH1 4EH

6th March 2008

Dear (1) Reynold *Sir or Madam*

I saw your advertisement for a position as sales assistant in your garden furniture department and I (2) want the job.

I am an experienced shop assistant and I have worked in many different departments. Please see my curriculum vitae, (3) in the same envelope , for more details.

I started working in shops when I was twenty-one, forty-five years ago. I left my last job six years ago when I (4) got too old , but I get terribly bored at home. I feel I am ready for (5) new things now .

I would be available for an interview at any time, even at short notice.

I (6) can't wait to hear from you.

Yours faithfully,

Enid Smith

Enid Smith (Miss)

2 Write your own letter of application for your dream job.

Speaking: anecdote

1 🔊 2.14 Listen to Kim talking about her friend's job. Underline the answers she gives.

a) 'What's his or her name?' 'Her name's **Hannah** / Ann.'
b) 'What does she do?' 'She's a **train driver / personal trainer**.'
c) 'Who does she work for?' '**She works for a local sports centre /
   She's self-employed**.'
d) 'What time does she start work?' 'At **7.00 / 8.30** a.m.'
e) 'How much does she earn?' 'She gets **£35 / £25** an hour.'
f) 'What does she love about her job?' '**She helps people to get fit /
   She travels a lot**.'
g) 'Would you like to do your friend's job? Why?' '**Yes, because she doesn't have to
   work in an office / No, because she has to get up early**.'

2 You're going to tell your partner about somebody you know who has a good job.

- Ask yourself the questions in Exercise 1.
- Think about *what* to say and *how* to say it.
- Tell your partner about the person's job.

▲ Hannah

Useful phrases

1 🔊 **2.15 Listen to four people presenting themselves to the *Quit Smoking* group. Underline the correct information.**

Layla
'I work for a big company and we produce **sports clothes** / <u>audio equipment</u> / **bicycles**. I'm responsible for **sales and promotion** / **quality control** / **advertising**.'

Mike
'At present I'm **working for my father** / **unemployed** / **training to be an engineer**. I'm looking for a job in **publishing** / **the theatre** / **tourism**.'

Jack
'I work as a bodyguard and I'm based **in the south** / **at head office** / **in London**. My job involves **a lot of foreign travel** / **import and export** / **sitting at my desk all day**.'

Elsie
'I run **the photography department** / **the accounts department** / **my own company**. I'm in charge of **a department** / **marketing** / **taking photographs**.'

🔊 **2.16 Listen, check and repeat the useful phrases.**

2 **Three people arrive late for the group. Read the notes and use words from Exercise 1 to complete their presentations.**

- Sarah
- Receptionist, *Cutters Hairdressers*
- Responsible for appointments and accounts

'Hi, I'm Sarah. I work (1) *as a* receptionist (2) _____ *Cutters Hairdressers*. I'm in (3) _____ of appointments and accounts.'

- Charles
- Tour guide, *City Tours*
- Takes tourists around London
- Wants to be hotel manager

'I'm Charles. I'm a tour guide and I work (4) _____ *City Tours*. My job (5) _____ taking tourists around London. At present, I'm (6) _____ for a job (7) _____ hotel management.'

- Andrew
- Director of *Fine Wines*
- Make red and white wine.
- In south-east England

'My name's Andrew. I (8) _____ a company called *Fine Wines*. We (9) _____ red and white wine. We're (10) _____ in south-east England.'

🔊 **2.17 Listen and check your answers.**

3 **Write a short presentation of yourself. Use true information or invent information based on your ideal job. Use three or more useful phrases from Exercise 1.**

Vocabulary *Extra*

Office equipment

1 Match the pictures with the words.

- [16] a bin
- [ ] a briefcase
- [ ] a calculator
- [ ] a desk lamp
- [ ] a filing cabinet
- [ ] a folder
- [ ] a hole punch
- [ ] a keyboard
- [ ] a mouse
- [ ] a note pad
- [ ] paper clips
- [ ] a photocopier
- [ ] Post-its®
- [ ] a printer
- [ ] a screen
- [ ] a stapler

2 Work with a partner. Cover the words and look at the pictures. Ask and answer questions.

'What's number 1?'
'A printer.'

'What are number 2?'
'Paper clips.'

Focus on *work* and *job*

1 Work with a partner. Complete the following questions with *job* or *work* and then ask each other the questions.

a) Have you ever had a part-time _____ ?
b) Would you like to _____ abroad ?
c) Do you know anybody who has a dangerous _____ ?

2 Make more questions by replacing the highlighted words in Exercise 1 with appropriate alternatives from the box.

| applied for | badly-paid | boring | from home | in marketing | looked for | lost | outdoors |
| resigned from | stressful | well-paid | | | | | |

Ask and answer six more questions with your partner.

Review B

▶ Grammar *Extra* pages 132–137

Grammar

1 Put the adverbs of frequency in the correct position.

a) We get up at 7.00 a.m. (always)
We always get up at 7.00 a.m.

b) You get to class on time! (never)

c) We eat meat. (occasionally)

d) They are at home on Sunday evenings. (often)

e) Yuko goes out in the evening. (hardly ever)

Rewrite each sentence to make it true for you.

a) *I never get up at 7.00 a.m.*

2 Put the words in the correct order.

a) this / My / pen / bought / me / son
My son bought me this pen.

b) lend / you / mobile / Could / your / me ?

c) children / gave / They / their / their / money / to

d) my / a / dad / making / cake / for/ I'm

e) email / you / send / an / Did / them ?

3 Put the words in the box in the correct column.

agree avoid can't stand choose decide don't mind enjoy forget like love need spend time want would like

Verbs + *ing*-form	Verbs + *to*-infinitive
avoid	*agree*

4 Complete the sentences with the comparative or superlative form of the adjectives in the box.

cheap expensive ~~fit~~ good-looking noisy sensitive

a) Jim runs and swims. He's the *fittest* man I know.

b) Jo is crying again. She's much more _____ than I thought.

c) This old car costs only £2,000! It's not as _____ as that new one.

d) Matt is so handsome – he's the _____ man in the class!

e) I have £20. Which is the _____ suit in the shop?

f) Be quiet, Guy! … Why are you so much _____ than Ali?

5 Complete the text with the present simple or present continuous form of the verbs.

I (1 love) *love* shopping and I especially (2 like) _____ shopping for clothes! So I (3 have) _____ a lot of clothes. My boyfriend (4 not understand) _____ . He (5 have) _____ four pairs of trousers, two pairs of shoes and ten T-shirts. Of course I never (6 wear) _____ most of my clothes. So at the moment I (7 try) _____ to wear my old clothes and I (8 not buy) _____ any more new clothes. I (9 save) _____ money, but I (10 look) _____ terrible!

6 Underline the correct words.

'OK, everybody. Mr Smith says the exam starts at 10.00, but we all (1) **have to** / **can't** arrive ten minutes before then. He says we (2) **have to** / **don't have to** register at the desk before the exam. We (3) **can** / **have to** take money, mobiles, pens and pencils into the exam room with us, but we (4) **can** / **can't** take any large bags. Oh, and we (5) **have to** / **can't** turn off our mobiles.'

7 Complete the conversation with the past simple or present perfect forms of the verbs.

A: Hi. I'm interested in the shop assistant job.

B: (1 you work) *Have you worked* in a shop before?

A: No, but I (2 do) _____ lots of shopping!

B: Oh. (3 you have) _____ any other jobs?

A: Yes, I (4 be) _____ a waitress, and last year I (5 work) _____ as an au pair in Paris. I (6 go) _____ to Paris after I (7 leave) _____ school. Wonderful shopping!

8 Spot the mistake! Cross out the incorrect sentence.

1 a) ~~I like always to read on trains.~~
   b) I always like to read on trains.

2 a) He bought me a very nice book.
   b) He bought for me a very nice book.

3 a) Do you want to go out tonight?
   b) Do you want go out tonight?

4 a) Athens is more older than Paris.
   b) Athens is much older than Paris.

5 a) It's too late for TV now. Please turn it off.
   b) It's too late for TV now. Please turn off it.

6 a) I've seen that new show on TV last week.
   b) I saw that new show on TV last week.

Vocabulary

1 Put the words in the correct group.

a) a box of *chocolates, tissues*

b) a bunch of …

c) a can of …

d) a packet of …

e) a bottle of …

chocolates ▲

▲ beans

▲ biscuits

▲ perfume

▲ keys

▲ petrol

▲ crisps

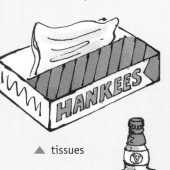
▲ tissues

wine ▶

▲ flowers

2 Underline the odd word out in each group.

a) <u>necklace</u> cotton leather silk

b) patterned plain boots striped

c) earrings gloves shirt woollen

d) checked jacket shoes vest

3 Match the beginnings and endings to make questions.

a) How long   1 do you watch films in English?

b) How far   2 do you know your teacher?

c) How many   3 money did you spend today?

d) How often   4 pairs of gloves do you have?

e) How much   5 is it from your house to the shops?

f) How well   6 does it take you to get home
                      in the evening?

Ask and answer the questions with a partner.

4 Write the numbers in words.

a) ¹/₂ *a half*

b) 0.45

c) ³/₄

d) 58%

e) $23,000,000

5 Match the beginnings and endings of the sentences.

a) Please take   1 down here?

b) What time do you get   2 your shoes off.

c) Would you like to sit 3 after her toy mouse.

d) My cat likes to run   4 up in the morning?

6 Underline the best collocation to complete the sentences.

a) I don't like working every day. I want a
    full-time / part-time job.

b) I don't earn much. I need to ask for **advice /
    a pay-rise**.

c) Leave your job or stay – you should make a
    living / decision!

d) I work all the time. I need some **day / time** off.

e) Juan isn't working at the moment. He **found / lost**
    his job last week.

Pronunciation

**1 Look at some words from Units 4–6. Say the words
and add them to the table.**

> ~~adult~~ ~~advice~~ afford au pair avoid
> flowers ~~horrible~~ interested mobile
> packet present quality receive
> talented valuable

A: ☐☐	B: ☐☐	C: ☐☐☐
adult	*advice*	*horrible*

2 Underline the stressed syllable in each word.

🔵 2.18 **Listen, check and repeat.**

Reading & Listening

1 **Read about Kate and Helena. Are these statements true or false?**

a) Kate is older than Helena.
b) Kate and Helena are both successful.
c) Kate and Helena both like to keep fit.
d) Kate and Helena do the same job.
e) Kate and Helena wear the same sort of clothes.

2 **Read the article again and answer the questions.**

a) Who earns more money?
b) How does Kate exercise?
c) How often does Helena go to the gym?
d) Do Kate and Helena both have to dress smartly at work?
e) Is their relationship good?
f) Has their relationship always been good?
g) Which sister is a good listener?

As different as
chalk and cheese

Sisters Kate and Helena Stewart talk about each other and how they get on together

Kate: 'Helena and I have always been very different. She's a typical older sister – she's four years, four months and four days older than me. She's ambitious, but I'm more relaxed about life and work.

5 Helena is the director of a small but successful company. She earns a lot of money and drives a beautiful car, but her job is more stressful than mine.

Helena has always been very sophisticated – you would never see her in a T-shirt – and normally buys
10 designer clothes. She loves keeping fit and spends her free time in the gym. Walking to work and climbing the stairs is my exercise. I find it more interesting than the gym, and cheaper, too.

The best thing about Helena is her kindness. She
15 always buys beautiful presents for everyone and never thinks about how much they cost. We've become much closer in the last five years but we're still completely different people.'

Helena: 'My relationship with Kate hasn't always
20 been easy. When we were younger I had to look after her because I was her older sister. These days it's different. She's more confident, and our relationship is easier. She's been very successful in her work and her life. She works for a TV company as a researcher. She
25 doesn't earn as much as I do, but I think she's happier. She doesn't have to go to the office every day, like I do.

Kate isn't very interested in looking smart. She usually wears jeans and a T-shirt – she can wear anything she likes at work. She isn't very fit, either.
30 I like to work out at the gym four times a week, but Kate hates the gym. She never goes.

Kate is a great listener. If I have a problem I know I can always talk to her. Kate is very different from me, but she's my sister and I love her.'

3 🔊 **2.19 Listen to Tom and Patsy and answer the questions.**

a) How are Tom and Patsy related?
b) How does Patsy feel about Tom?

4 **Listen again and underline the correct answers.**

a) Patsy is **older** / **younger** than Tom.
b) **Patsy** / **Tom** is not very fashionable.
c) Patsy **always** / **never** buys clothes for Tom.
d) Patsy **usually** / **never** watches sport on TV.
e) Tom **likes** / **doesn't like** sitting in the garden.
f) Patsy thinks Tom is **very serious** / **very funny**.

▲ Tom   Patsy ▶

Writing & Speaking

1 **Read the description. Tick the questions that are answered.**

a) What's his name?
b) How are you related?
c) What's the age difference between you?
d) Do you have the same interests?
e) Do you wear the same sort of clothes?

f) What does he do?
g) Does he have any annoying habits?
h) What are his best points?
i) What do you think he's doing now?

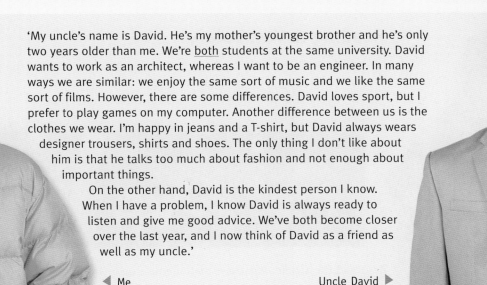

'My uncle's name is David. He's my mother's youngest brother and he's only two years older than me. We're <u>both</u> students at the same university. David wants to work as an architect, whereas I want to be an engineer. In many ways we are similar: we enjoy the same sort of music and we like the same sort of films. However, there are some differences. David loves sport, but I prefer to play games on my computer. Another difference between us is the clothes we wear. I'm happy in jeans and a T-shirt, but David always wears designer trousers, shirts and shoes. The only thing I don't like about him is that he talks too much about fashion and not enough about important things.
On the other hand, David is the kindest person I know. When I have a problem, I know David is always ready to listen and give me good advice. We've both become closer over the last year, and I now think of David as a friend as well as my uncle.'

◀ Me   Uncle David ▶

2 **Find the words/phrases from the box in the text and underline them.**

> ~~both~~   whereas   however   but
> on the other hand

Complete the rules using the words/phrases in the box.

Expressing similarity

a) You use *both* when you want to say the same thing about two people or things.

Expressing contrast

b) _____ and _____ are often used to contrast ideas within the same sentence.
c) _____ and _____ are often used to contrast ideas in two different sentences.

3 **Underline the correct expressions in these sentences.**

a) I like playing football. **However / Whereas**, my brother prefers tennis.
b) I like playing football, **however / whereas** my brother prefers tennis.
c) I can't stand watching sports. **But / On the other hand**, I love playing them.
d) I can't stand watching sports **but / on the other hand** I love playing them.

4 **Write the words in the correct order.**

a) both / dancing / love / We
b) have / both / We / America / to / been

Work with a partner. Are the sentences true for you?

5 **You're going to tell your partner about a member of your family and compare yourself with him/her.**

- Choose some questions in Exercise 1 that you can answer.
- Think about what you're going to say and the language you will need.
- When you're ready, take it in turns to tell each other about a member of your family.

6 **Write a comparison between yourself and a member of your family. Try to answer as many of the questions in Exercise 1 as you can. Use the expressions in Exercise 2 to describe contrast and similarity.**

▶ 🎵 **2.20** **Song:** *Suspicious Minds*

7 Eco

Grammar Subject questions. Dynamic and stative meanings. Future forms
Vocabulary Climate change. Opinions. *have* and *have got*
Useful phrases On the telephone

Reading & Vocabulary

1 **Work with a partner. Look at the photographs and discuss the questions.**

a) What do you think is happening?
b) Do people worry about climate change in your country?

2 **Read the article. Are these statements true or false?**

a) World leaders participated in protest marches and demonstrations.
b) The protestors carried banners and shouted political messages.
c) A group of protesters on bicycles went to 10 Downing Street.
d) They delivered a letter asking world leaders to do something immediately about the economy.
e) Trafalgar Square was extremely crowded and very busy in the afternoon.
f) A small group of protesters separated from the peaceful demonstrators and went shopping.

Climate change march

In London today, 20,000 people took part in protest marches and demonstrations as world leaders were meeting for climate change talks. The event was organised by the Campaign Against Global Warming.

The day started early outside the US embassy with poetry readings and speeches.
5 Protestors then marched slowly to Trafalgar Square, carrying banners and shouting slogans .

A group of protesters on bicycles made their way to 10 Downing Street and delivered a letter to the Prime Minister demanding urgent action on climate change.

By three o'clock in the afternoon, Trafalgar Square was swarming with people and
10 buzzing with activity . There was a carnival atmosphere with music provided by a samba band, a New Orleans jazz band and Scottish pipers.

Most of the protesters marched peacefully, but a small group of people broke away from the peaceful demonstrators. They smashed shop windows and tried to set fire to a supermarket. Five people were arrested.

3 **Look at the highlighted phrases in the article. Find phrases with similar meanings in the sentences (*a–f*) in Exercise 2.**

took part in = *participated in*

4 **What evidence of climate change have you noticed in your country? What are you and your family, your local government, your national government doing about it? Discuss with your partner.**

Listening & Vocabulary

1 🌐 **2.21 Listen to interviews with four protestors at the Climate change march. Match each person with an opinion (1–4).**

▲ Jo, 26   ▲ Jake, 14   ▲ Debbie, 37   ▲ Ronny, 27

1 'I'm in favour of protecting wild animals.'
2 'I'm against food imports.'
3 'I'm against big cars in the city.'
4 'I believe in responsible tourism.'

2 **Complete the sentences below with the words and phrases in the box.**

> against   ~~anti~~   believe   don't feel   in favour   really care   support

a) I'm not *anti*-cars – I just think more people should use public transport.
b) I don't _____ about people. They can look after themselves.
c) I'm _____ of small family-run companies.
d) I _____ in responsible tourism.
e) I'm _____ cars in the city centre.
f) I _____ local farmers.
g) I _____ strongly about politics.

Which statements do you agree with? What other things do you feel strongly about? Discuss with your partner.

Grammar

Subject questions

subject   object
John hates **cars.**

Subject question:
Who hates **cars**?

Object question:
What does **John** hate?

1 **Look at the sentence and the questions (1 and 2) below. Answer questions (a–c).**

subject   **verb**   **object**
Jo   *believes in*   *responsible tourism.*

1 *Who believes in responsible tourism?*   2 *What does Jo believe in?*

a) What is the subject of the main verb in question 1?
b) What is the subject of the main verb in question 2?
c) In questions where *Who* (*Which, What* or *Whose*) is the subject of the verb, do you use *do, does* or *did*?

2 **Write questions for the missing subjects or objects.**

a) Mahatma Gandhi believed in **[object]**. *What did Mahatma Gandhi believe in?*
b) **[subject]** said, 'I have a dream' in a famous speech. *Who said, 'I have a dream' in a famous speech?*
c) 'Slogan' means **[object]**. *What …*
d) **[subject]** has a boat called 'Rainbow Warrior'. *Which organisation …*
e) Thirty-six million people protested against **[object]** in 2003. *What …*
f) **[subject]** fought against apartheid for over fifty years. *Who …*

Ask your partner the questions. Choose answers from the box below.

> Greenpeace   Martin Luther King   Nelson Mandela   non-violent protest
> political message   the Iraq war

Pronunciation

1 Look at some words ending in *tion*. Say the words and add them to the table.

| demonstration | destruction | education | explanation | globalisation |
| modernisation | organisation | pollution | revolution | solution |

A: ☐☐☐	B: ☐☐☐☐	C: ☐☐☐☐☐
	demonstration	

2 🔊 2.22 **Listen, check and repeat.**

Grammar

Dynamic and stative meanings

Dynamic meanings
(something 'happens')
He **has lunch** at 1.00 p.m.
He**'s having lunch** now.
Note: use simple or continuous forms.

Stative meanings
(nothing 'happens')
I **believe** in democracy.
We **want** to help.
Note: use simple forms only.

Some verbs (*have*, *look*, *think*) can have both meanings.

1 Look at the verbs in these extracts from the interviews on page 61. Answer the questions.
'I'm having fun with my friends.'   *'They're polluting our rivers.'*
a) Do the verbs describe actions or states?
b) What is the name of the tense used in each extract?

2 Rewrite these sentences by putting the verb in brackets in the present continuous.
a) A phone (ring) _____ . *A phone is ringing.*
b) A teacher in another class (talk) _____ .
c) The traffic (make) _____ a lot of noise.
d) A clock (tick) _____ .
e) Birds (sing) _____ .
f) Rain (fall) _____ .
g) A student (laugh) _____ .
h) People (chat) _____ .

Listen in silence for fifteen seconds and tick the actions that are happening now. Note down other things that are happening now.

3 Look at the verbs in two more extracts from the interviews. Answer the questions.
'I want to help polar bears.'   *'I have a car.'*
a) Do the verbs describe actions or states?
b) What is the name of the tense used in each extract?
c) Is it possible to use a continuous tense with verbs when they describe a state?

4 Look at the verbs in brackets. Do they describe an action or a state? Complete the sentences with the present simple or the present continuous.
a) Sue (think) *is thinking* of going out this evening.
b) Rosa (think) *thinks* politics is boring.
c) Marta (have) _____ a TV in her bedroom.
d) Julie (have) _____ difficulty with this exercise.
e) Brian (look) _____ like his father.
f) Rob (look) _____ for a new place to live.
g) Jane (like) _____ James Bond films.
h) Tony (know) _____ how to play the piano.

Replace the names with names of students in the class to make as many true sentences as you can. Ask questions to help you.
'Are you thinking of going out this evening?'
'Do you think politics is boring?'

5 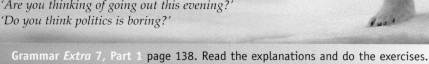 Grammar *Extra* 7, Part 1 page 138. Read the explanations and do the exercises.

Speaking

1 **Work in small groups. Discuss which of these activities are good/bad for the environment.**

a) Cycling to work/school.
b) Buying a hamburger in a plastic container.
c) Paying more for environmentally-friendly products.
d) Buying imported fruit and vegetables.
e) Using plastic bags for your shopping.
f) Buying cheap, mass-produced clothes.
g) Using public transport.
h) Travelling alone in your car.
i) Picking up litter.
j) Drinking bottled water.
k) Recycling bottles.
l) Travelling by air.

Think of any other activities that are either good or bad for the environment.

2 **Do a survey to find out how many people have done the different activities in Exercise 1 in the last two weeks. Follow these instructions.**

- Prepare the question you are going to ask for each activity.
  a) Have you cycled to work/school in the last two weeks?
- Decide which person in the group is going to ask each question.
- Go round the class. Ask your question(s) and note down the answers.
- In your groups, write down the results of the survey for each activity.

Activities	Yes	No
cycled to work/school	✓✓✓	✗✗✗✗✗✗✗✗✗✗✗✗
bought a hamburger in a plastic container	✓✓✓✓✓✓✓✓✓✓	✗✗✗✗✗

Writing

100% Everybody
↑ Most people
  A large number of people
  Several people
  A small number of people
↓ (Only) a few people
0% Nobody

1 **Read a survey report for Greensville, USA. Complete the report with one of the following phrases.**

| very green   not very green |

SURVEY REPORT

How **green** are you?

Eco Magazine travelled to Greensville, USA, where they interviewed 1,000 people for a new survey. The aim of the survey was to find out how green the people of Greensville are.

According to the survey, <u>only a few people</u> have used public transport in the last two weeks, but <u>everybody</u> has travelled alone in their car. <u>Nobody</u> has cycled to work. <u>Several people</u> have bought imported fruit and vegetables, and <u>most people</u> have bought a hamburger in a plastic container. However, <u>only a few people</u> have picked up litter.

<u>A large number of people</u> have drunk bottled water in the last two weeks, <u>but only a few people</u> have recycled their bottles.

The survey found that <u>nobody</u> has paid more for something because it is environmentally friendly.

<u>Everybody</u> has used plastic bags for their shopping, and <u>several people</u> have bought cheap, mass-produced clothes.

Finally, <u>a small number of people</u> have travelled by air in the last two weeks.

The results of the survey suggest that the people of Greensville, USA, are _____ .

2 **Write a survey report for your class. Replace the underlined expressions in the Greensville report with information from your own survey in Speaking Exercise 2 above. Change other parts of the report if necessary.**

Reading & Listening

1 Read this list of different duties that people volunteer to do in developing countries.
Which duties do you feel you could do / couldn't do? Compare with a partner.

a) work in an orphanage
b) teach children to read
c) look after sick animals
d) visit people in hospital
e) teach English
f) help to construct houses, bridges, roads
g) do housework and help in people's homes
h) plant trees and do organic farming

Read the website information and match the projects (*1* and *2*) with the duties (*a–h*).
Which duties does the information not mention?

http://www.originalvolunteers.com/

Home   Search   Shop   Bookmarks

WELCOME TO
ORIGINAL
VOLUNTEERS

- **Change your life.**
- **Do something important.**
- **Learn new skills, gain self-confidence and make friends for life.**

1 Northern India

Volunteers live with a local family.

DUTIES: You help in people's homes, plant trees and do organic farming. You can also try learning Hindi.

FREE TIME: You can go to festivals and go trekking in the Himalayas.

2 Ghana

Volunteers help at an orphanage.

DUTIES: You play with the children and teach them to read.

FREE TIME: You can visit the wonderful beaches or see the elephants in the National Park.

2 🔊 2.23 **Listen to Helen and her friend. Which project is Helen going to join?**

3 **Tick the things Helen says she's going to do.**

a) change her life ✓
b) get a better boyfriend
c) do something important
d) work with animals
e) work in an orphanage
f) get a good salary

Which of the two projects would you like to do? Tell your partner.

Grammar

Future: (*be*) *going to*

Future plans and intentions

How **are you going to** lose weight?

I'm going to do more exercise.

I'm not going to eat so much bread.

1 **Correct the mistakes in these sentences from the conversation.**

a) 'I going to change my life.'
b) 'I'm not go to work with animals.'
c) 'How much are they going pay you?'

2 **Complete the sentence with the words *future* and *past* to describe the use of (*be*) *going to*.**

You use (*be*) *going to* when you talk about a decision you made in the (1) _____ to do something in the (2) _____ .

3 **Write questions about the future with (*be*) *going to*.**

a) drive home / after the lesson ?
   Are you going to drive home after the lesson?
b) watch TV / this evening ?
c) learn another foreign language / one day ?
d) buy any new clothes / this weekend ?
e) do anything interesting / next week ?
f) travel abroad / next year ?

Ask your partner the questions.

Listening

1 🔘 2.24 Listen to a conversation between Helen and her mother about Helen's arrangements for her trip to Ghana. Underline the correct word.
a) Helen is **confident** / **depressed** / **surprised**.
b) Helen's mum is **angry** / **embarrassed** / **worried**.

2 Listen again and underline the correct information.
a) Helen is arriving in Accra at 10.00 **a.m** / **p.m.**
b) Bob White is taking her to her **school** / **accommodation**.
c) She's staying with a **Ghanaian** / **Nigerian** family.
d) She's starting work on **Wednesday** / **Monday**.
e) She's working in a **big** / **small** town near Accra.
f) She's coming back in time for her **mum's** / **dad's** birthday.

In what situations do your parents worry about you?

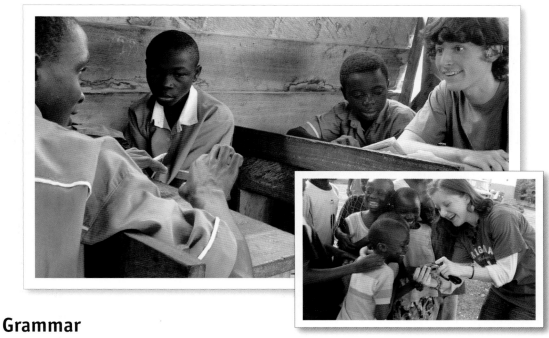

Grammar

Future: present continuous

Future arrangements

He**'s arriving** tomorrow.

She **isn't coming** with him tonight.

Where **are** you **meeting** them next week?

1 The sentences (a–f) in Listening Exercise 2 all use the present continuous to talk about the future. Is the following explanation true or false?

You can use the present continuous with a future time expression to talk about future arrangements.

2 In many situations (be) *going to* and the present continuous are both possible. Put a tick if both options are possible. Put a cross if the present continuous is *not* possible.
a) I'm **going to meet** / **meeting** a friend after the lesson. ✓
b) I'm **going to start** / **starting** guitar lessons one day. ✗
c) My friends are **going to come** / **coming** round this evening.
d) I'm **going to see** / **seeing** my grandparents this weekend.
e) I'm **going to read** / **reading** a novel in English one of these days.
f) I'm **going to win** / **winning** my tennis match this weekend!
g) I'm **going to play** / **playing** football on Monday.
h) I'm **going to learn** / **learning** Chinese one day.

Are any of these sentences true for you?

3 Pairwork **Student A:** page 118 **Student B:** page 123

4 Grammar *Extra 7*, Part 2 page 138. Read the explanations and do the exercises.

Useful phrases

1 Matt Walker (*M*) is phoning a big chemicals company. Underline the most appropriate expressions to complete his conversation with the receptionist (*R*).

R: Good morning. Regal Chemicals.

M: (1) **I want to speak to the Managing Director.** / <u>**Could I speak to the Managing Director, please?**</u>

R: Do you mean Mr Carr?

M: Yes, that's right. Mr Carr.

R: (2) **Who's speaking?** / **Who are you?**

M: My name's Matt Walker.

R: Hold on, please, and (3) **I'll try to put you through.** / **I'll get him.** ...
     Hello. (4) **He's not there.** / **I'm afraid Mr Carr is out at the moment.**

M: Oh. Do you know when he'll be back?

R: I'm not sure. (5) **Would you like to leave a message?** / **You can leave a message.**

M: Yes, please.

R: Right. (6) **Wait.** / **Hold on a moment, please.** OK, what would you like to say?

M: Please tell Mr Carr that REGAL CHEMICALS IS POLLUTING THE ATMOSPHERE AND DESTROYING THE PLANET. THE CAMPAIGN AGAINST GLOBAL WARMING ...

🔘 2.25 **Listen and check your answers.**

2 🔘 2.26 **Listen and repeat the useful phrases.**

a) Could I speak to the Managing Director, please?
b) Who's speaking?
c) I'll try to put you through.
d) I'm afraid Mr Carr is out at the moment.
e) Would you like to leave a message?
f) Hold on a moment, please.

3 Work with a partner. Practise the conversation. Take it in turns to be Matt and the receptionist.

Vocabulary *Extra*

Environmental problems and solutions

1 Match the pictures with the phrases.

- [3] a <u>bott</u>le bank
- [ ] a <u>car</u>bon <u>foot</u>print
- [ ] environ<u>ment</u>ally-<u>friend</u>ly <u>prod</u>ucts
- [ ] glo<u>bal warm</u>ing
- [ ] mass-pro<u>duced</u> clothes
- [ ] or<u>gan</u>ic <u>veg</u>etables
- [ ] a <u>plas</u>tic con<u>tain</u>er
- [ ] <u>pub</u>lic <u>trans</u>port
- [ ] re<u>new</u>able <u>en</u>ergy

2 Work with a partner. List the expressions from Exercise 1 under the following headings.

Problems	Solutions
global warming	*organic vegetables*

Add your own ideas to each list.

Focus on *have / have got*

1 Complete the sentences using *do, don't, got, have, haven't.*

a) '*Do* you have a car?' 'Yes, I _____ .' 'No, I _____ .'
b) '*Have* you _____ a car?' 'Yes, I _____ .' 'No, I _____ .'

Complete the sentence with *have/has* and *have/has got.*

When (1) _____ means to own or possess, you can also use (2) _____ .

2 Write questions using *have / has got.*

a) you / any brothers and sisters?
   Have you got any brothers and sisters?
b) you / more than one credit card?
c) you / a pet?
d) you / a headache?
e) your mother / the same eyes as you?
f) your father / any hobbies?

Ask and answer the questions with your partner.

3 Look at some uses of *have.* Tick the sentences where *have/has* can be replaced by *have/has got.*

a) Do you have a laptop? ✓
b) I always have lunch at home.
c) My mother has short, grey hair.
d) I don't have an MP3 player.
e) Do you have any children?
f) Are you having a birthday party this year?

Rewrite the sentences you have ticked with *have got.*

a) *Have you got a laptop?*

8 Education

Grammar Permission and obligation (*could / had to*). *should* and *must* for advice
Vocabulary Education and training
Useful phrases Giving your opinion

Reading

1 **You are going to read about a trainee geisha. Before you read, look at the sentences below and decide if you think they are true or false.**

a) A lot of women in Japan today want to become geishas.
b) A geisha has to have a different kimono for every month of the year.
c) To become a geisha you have to study for many years.
d) A geisha has to sing and dance for her customers.
e) A geisha can't speak to her customers.
f) A trainee geisha can go to high school.
g) A geisha doesn't have to stay single.

2 **Read the article and check your ideas in Exercise 1.**

TRAINING TO BE A

Geisha

The white face, the dark eyes and hair, the blood red lips – both the Japanese and foreigners are fascinated by these beautiful and mysterious women. Makiko is training to be a geisha. Not many girls want to become geishas in Japan today. Makiko's parents wanted her to go to university,
5 study medicine and become a doctor. But Makiko's grandfather paid for her training and bought the kimonos she needed. It's very expensive to become a geisha. You have to have a different kimono for each month of the year, and today a kimono can cost three million yen, that's about $25,000.

It's a hard life for a trainee geisha. She has to leave her family and move
10 into a special boarding house called a 'maiko house'. Here, she has to learn traditional Japanese arts such as playing instruments, the tea ceremony, flower arranging, singing and dancing. She has to take a lot of difficult tests and exams. Only the best will pass all the tests and become geishas many years later.

We asked Makiko to describe exactly what a geisha does.
15 'A geisha has to serve customers and also entertain them. She has to sing and dance, and make conversation.'

Does she enjoy her life as a trainee geisha?

'I love it, but it's hard work. Sometimes I get tired of wearing the kimonos and I want to put on a pair of jeans and go to high school like a normal teenager. But I can't have a
20 normal life now. I don't mind. I feel very lucky.'

And what about later – can she have a family?

'Of course. A geisha can have relationships like anybody else and she can get married when she chooses.'

In Japan today there are fewer than a thousand geishas, but they play an important
25 role in preserving Japanese culture and history.

3 **What did your parents/grandparents want you to study at school? Did you follow their advice? Tell a partner.**

'My parents wanted me to study science and become a doctor. I preferred languages and now I'm a teacher.'

Vocabulary

1 Complete the following statements using words from the article on page 68.

a) More and more people are *training* to be computer programmers. (line 3)

b) Not many people want to _____ teachers nowadays. (line 3)

c) If you _____ medicine, it takes seven years before you qualify as a doctor. (line 5)

d) It can _____ a lot of money to go to university. (line 8)

e) When they go to university, most students leave home and _____ into student accommodation. (line 9)

f) If you fail your end of year exams, you can usually _____ them again a few months later. (line 12)

g) You have to _____ an entrance exam if you want to go to university. (line 13)

h) University students play an important _____ in the future of the country. (line 24)

2 Work in small groups. Are the statements in Exercise 1 true for your country.

Pronunciation

1 🔊 2.27 Listen and repeat the school subjects in the table. Notice the stress.

1: ☐	2: ☐☐	3: ☐☐☐	4: ☐☐☐☐	5: ☐☐☐☐☐
Art Maths	English History Music Physics	Chemistry Literature Politics Geography	Biology Philosophy Technology	Economics

2 Work with a partner. Discuss which subjects in Exercise 1 are/were …

a) the hardest/easiest to learn.   b) the most boring/interesting.   c) the least/most useful.

Speaking: anecdote

1 🔊 2.28 Listen to Andy talking about his favourite school subject. Underline the answers he gives.

a) 'What was your favourite subject at school?' '**Maths** / **Art**.'

b) 'Why did you particularly like this subject?' '**It was easy** / **I was good at it**.'

c) 'What was the teacher's name?' '**Miss Lewis** / **Mr Lewis**.'

d) 'What did she look like?' 'She **had long black hair and wore bright colours** / **looked like a teacher**.'

e) 'Why were her lessons special?' 'They were **fun** / **interesting and varied**.'

f) 'How many hours did you have a week?' 'We had **three** / **six** hours a week.'

g) 'Did you learn anything which is useful to you today?' 'Yes, I **still love taking photos** / **make a living as a photographer**.'

2 You're going to tell your partner about your favourite school subject.

- Ask yourself the questions in Exercise 1.
- Think about *what* to say and *how* to say it.
- Tell your partner about your favourite school subject.

Reading

1 Look at the quotes from three men in the Bennett family. They are talking about their fathers. Try to match each quote with the man who said it.

a) The grandfather   1 'I've always had a very close relationship with my dad.'

b) His son   2 'My father was always at work.'

c) His grandson   3 'We had to obey him without question.'

🔊 **2.29** **Read the article and check your ideas.**

Three generations

Gordon – the grandfather (72)

'I think my son and my grandson have a lovely relationship – it wasn't like that when I was a boy. My father was a very strict man, we
5 had to obey him without question.

I had to walk five kilometres to school. There was no other way of getting there. At home we didn't have a television, so we had
10 to make our own entertainment. I spent all my free time outside playing football.

But we couldn't play football on Sundays because we had to go to
15 church.

I left school when I was fourteen and went to work in a bakery. That's where I met Mabel.

We couldn't bring girlfriends
20 home in those days. We had to meet in public places. I suppose that's why so many people got married young. I was only nineteen, and Mabel was eighteen.'

Tony – his son (48)

'When I was growing up, my father was always at work, and when he came home, we couldn't disturb him, because he was tired.
5 Because my father left school very early and regretted it afterwards, he wanted me to do well at school. I had to do my homework every night and I could only watch television at the
10 weekend.

When I was eighteen I got a place at university. My parents didn't have to support me financially, because the government gave me a grant to study.
15 I didn't go home very often, even during the holidays. I preferred spending time with my friends, especially my girlfriends. In my last year of university I met Louise, and
20 we got a place together. We had to get married when Louise found out she was pregnant.'

Scott – his grandson (19)

'I've always had a very close relationship with my dad and I don't have to hide anything from him.

When I was at school, I had a
5 lot of freedom. When I went out, I didn't have to come home at a certain time – my parents trusted me.

I'm at college now, and my
10 parents have to pay for my studies, but I have to work in the evenings to pay for any luxuries I want.

I think it's wrong that my parents have to pay for my studies.
15 I think colleges and universities should be free for everybody.

My girlfriend often stays with me at my parents' house, and I sometimes go and stay at her
20 parents'. Both our parents think we should get married one day, but we're definitely not in a hurry.'

2 Read the article again and answer the questions.

a) Why did Gordon have to walk to school?

b) Why couldn't Gordon play football on Sundays?

c) Why could Tony only watch television at the weekend?

d) Why didn't Tony's parents have to pay for his university education?

e) Why did Tony have to get married to Louise?

f) Why does Scott have to work in the evenings?

3 In what ways has life changed in your family over the generations? Tell your partner.

'My grandmother had to leave school at fourteen. Women couldn't go to university in those days.'

Grammar

could and *had to*

Permission
I **could** only watch TV on Sundays.
We **couldn't** swear.
Could you bring girlfriends home?

Obligation
He **had to** walk to school.
They **didn't have to** come home early.
Did you **have to** pay for your studies?

1 Complete the following table with the different forms of *can* and *have to*.

	Permission: *can*		Obligation: *have to*	
	Permitted	**Not permitted**	**Necessary**	**Not necessary**
Present	You (1) *can*	You (3) _____	You (5) _____	You (7) _____
Past	You (2) _____	You (4) _____	You (6) _____	You (8) _____

2 Complete the questions and answers about the article on the Bennett family.

a) '*Did* Gordon *have to* obey his dad without question?' 'Yes, he *did*.' 'No, he *didn't*.'
b) '*Did* Gordon *have to* go to church on Sundays?' 'Yes, he _____.' 'No, he _____.'
c) '*Could* Gordon bring his girlfriends home?' 'Yes, he _____.' 'No, he _____.'
d) '_____ Tony _____ do his homework every night?' '_____.' '_____.'
e) '_____ Scott come home at any time?' '_____.' '_____.'
f) '*Does* Scott have to hide things from his dad?' '_____.' '_____.'

🌐 **2.30 Listen, check and repeat.**

Refer to the article on page 70 and answer the questions.

3 Ask a partner similar questions to the ones in Exercise 2.
'Did (Do) you have to obey your dad without question?'

4 Pairwork **Student A:** page 118 **Student B:** page 123

5 Grammar *Extra* 8, Part 1 page 140. Read the explanations and do the exercises.

Listening

1 🌐 **2.31 Listen to a conversation between Gordon (the grandfather) and Scott (his grandson) in Scott's car. Which of the following topics do they talk about?**

▲ road travel   ▲ money   ▲ military service   ▲ appearance   ▲ politics   ▲ air travel

2 Write sentences to summarise the differences between 'then' and 'now', according to the conversation. Use an appropriate form of *have to* or *can*.

a) wear a seatbelt
   Now: You have to wear a seatbelt.
   Then: You didn't have to wear a seatbelt.
b) wear a helmet
c) use cash
d) do military service
e) have long hair
f) wear earrings

Listen again to check your answers.

3 Which differences between 'then' and 'now' in Exercise 2 are true for your country? What other differences can you think of? Discuss with your partner.

Reading & Listening

1 Your friend is going to meet his girlfriend's parents for the first time. Look at the advice (*a–f*). Which piece of advice do you think is the most important?

a) Make a good first impression
b) Tell the truth
c) Wear the right clothes
d) Avoid controversial topics of conversation
e) Do some research
f) Be prepared to answer questions

2 Read the article. Label the paragraphs (*1–6*) with the pieces of advice (*a–e*) from Exercise 1. What other advice can you think of?

Meet the PARENTS

1 *e) Do some research*

Find out information about the parents before you meet them. Do you have anything in common with them? Have they been on holiday recently? You should ask your girlfriend/boyfriend about her/his parents' hobbies, interests and favourite topics of conversation.

2 _____

It's fine to wear your old jeans and Nirvana T-shirt most of the time, but you should make an effort when you meet the parents. However, you shouldn't go to the opposite extreme: don't wear your 'job interview' clothes. You should be clean and tidy, but not too formal.

3 _____

First impressions are very important. You should greet them with a smile and a firm handshake for Dad, and a quick kiss (on the cheek) for Mum. You mustn't call them by their first names. Wait until they give you permission.

4 _____

You should be honest about what you do. If you're an IT technician, you shouldn't say you're a research scientist, information architect or web millionaire. If you're unemployed, you should tell them about your plans for a brilliant career.

5 _____

You probably don't share the same opinions or tastes about most things, so you must avoid subjects such as politics or religion. You can ask them about what your girlfriend or boyfriend was like as a child – parents love talking about their little prince or princess.

6 _____

You should think of a good answer to the question: What are you going to do in the future?

3 🔵 2.32 Listen to a young man meeting his girlfriend's parents for the first time. Tick the advice in the article that he follows. Put a cross next to the advice that he doesn't follow.

e)   Do some research ✗

How do you think the evening continued?

Vocabulary

1 Complete these sentences using words from the article above.

a) I don't have anything in *common* with my parents. (paragraph 1)
b) I always make an _____ to stay in touch with old friends. (paragraph 2)
c) My bedroom is always clean and _____ . (paragraph 2)
d) It's more important for me to be happy than to have a brilliant _____ . (paragraph 4)
e) I _____ the same opinions and tastes as my best friend. (paragraph 5)

2 Are any of the sentences in Exercise 1 true for you? Compare with a partner.

Grammar

should and must

I		
You		
He	should	
She	shouldn't	stay.
It	must	go.
We	mustn't	
They		

1 Match the phrases (*a–d*) in bold with the meanings (*1–4*).

a) **You should** be honest about what you do.
b) **You shouldn't** say you're a research scientist.
c) **You must** avoid subjects such as politics or religion.
d) **You mustn't** call them by their first names.

1 It's a bad idea.
2 It's a *very* good idea.
3 It's a *very* bad idea.
4 It's a good idea.

Choose the correct alternative in this sentence.

When you are giving advice, *must* is **stronger** / **weaker** than *should*.

2 Look at the situations and complete the sentences. Use *must* or *mustn't*, *should* or *shouldn't* and a verb in the box.

~~do~~	do	forget	hold	speak	watch

a) One friend to another friend: 'You *should do* more exercise.'
b) A doctor to a patient: 'You _____ more exercise!'
c) A father with his four year-old child in town: 'You _____ my hand!'
d) A sister to her sister: 'You _____ Mum's birthday this year!'
e) An English teacher to her students: 'You _____ English in class.'
f) A mother to her teenage son: 'You _____ so much television. It's bad for you.'

Have you heard similar sentences recently? What was the situation? Tell a partner.

3 Grammar *Extra* 8, Part 2 page 140. Read the explanation and do the exercises.

Reading & Speaking

1 Work with your partner. Use the words in the box to complete the advice below.

~~clothes~~	directions	funny	pay	shoes	silent	stomach	time	women	work

HOW TO BE THE
Perfect girlfriend

a) You should make an effort with your *clothes* and you shouldn't cut your hair: a man likes his girlfriend to look feminine.

b) The way to a man's heart is through his _____ . You should cook for him, and if he's really hungry, don't give him salad.

c) You must listen to him. He likes explaining how things _____ .

d) You shouldn't ask him to help you choose a pair of _____ . He only has three pairs, and he thinks that's enough.

e) You mustn't try to give him _____ . Christopher Columbus didn't need them!

HOW TO BE THE
Perfect boyfriend

a) You must arrive on _____ for dates – women hate it when you keep them waiting.

b) You should _____ when you go out. Women want to be equal, but not that equal!

c) You should be _____ . You may be good-looking, well-dressed and have the brains of Einstein, but if you can't make her laugh, forget it.

d) You should remain _____ . They want to do all the talking – even if you stop listening, pretend to be fascinated.

e) You mustn't talk about other beautiful _____ , even famous ones. She'll remember, and years later, when you make a comment about her cooking, she'll tell you to get Julia Roberts to make your lunch.

2 🔊 2.33 **Listen and check your ideas. Do you agree with the advice? Discuss your real opinions about what makes a successful date.**

Useful phrases

1 🌐 2.34 **Listen to a conversation between two women. Look at the topics below and tick the ones they talk about.**

a) Looking after children
b) Taking care of the elderly
c) Marriage
d) Leaving home
e) Education

2 **Complete the following sentences from the conversation in Exercise 1 with *I think* or *My daughter thinks* or *I don't think*.**

a) '_____ mothers should stay at home and look after the children.'

'Oh yes, I agree.'

b) '_____ children need their mothers at home.'

'Absolutely.'

c) '_____ fathers should stay at home and look after the children.'

'Oh no, I don't agree with that.'

d) '_____ couples should live together before they get married.'

'Oh, I'm not so sure.'

e) '_____ children should leave home when they're eighteen.'

'Well, it depends.'

Listen to the conversation again and check your answers.

3 🌐 2.35 **Listen and repeat the highlighted useful phrases in Exercise 2.**

4 **Look at the useful phrases for agreeing and disagreeing from Exercise 2. Arrange them in the right order on this line.**

Agree ✕——✕———————————————✕———✕———————————✕ Disagree
Oh yes, I agree.

5 **Rewrite the statements from Exercise 2 with *I think* or *I don't think* to show your own opinions. Discuss your ideas with a partner.**

Vocabulary *Extra*

Stages of education

1 Match the photos with the descriptions of the stages of state education in England and Wales.

[7] Age 3–5. Most children go to nursery school .

[ ] Age 5. All children start primary school .

[ ] Age 11. Everybody goes to secondary school .

[ ] Age 16. Pupils can leave school and get a job or do a vocational course (e.g. car mechanics, hairdressing or secretarial studies, etc.).

[ ] Age 16–18. Many pupils stay on at school , apply for a place at university or college and take their A-level* exams .

[ ] Age 18. Some students take a gap year before they go to university .

[ ] Age 18+. Students study subjects such as law, medicine, sociology, etc. at university .

[ ] Age 21+. Students get a degree when they finish the course and pass the final exams (finals).

* *A-levels = Advanced levels*

2 Are the stages and ages the same or different in your country?

3 Describe your own education up to now. Use as many of the highlighted phrases as possible.

I went to nursery when I was three. Then I …

▲ Secondary school

▲ Gap year

▲ Degree

▲ Vocational course

▲ A-levels

▲ Primary school

▲ Nursery school

▲ University

Focus on words used with education

1 Complete these questions with the words in the box.

apply	fail	gap	~~go~~	leave	primary	study	taken

a) Did you *go* to nursery school?

b) At what age do children start _____ school?

c) Can pupils _____ school at sixteen?

d) Is it easy to _____ for a place at university?

e) Do you know anybody who has taken a _____ year?

f) What did your parents _____ at university or college?

g) Have you ever _____ any English exams?

h) Did you pass or _____ ?

2 Answer the questions. Compare your answers with a partner.

9 Smile

Grammar Verb patterns. *for* and *since*. *been*. Present perfect simple and continuous
Vocabulary The face. Character adjectives. Parts of the body
Useful phrases Using body idioms

Reading

1 Look at this expression and discuss the questions with your partner.
- When do people say this?
- What do you say in your language?
- Do you find it easy to smile for photographs?

> **Say 'cheese'!**

2 Use five of the words from the photograph to complete the following article about smiling. Choose an appropriate singular or plural form for each word.

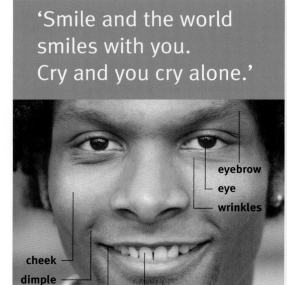

**'Smile and the world smiles with you.
Cry and you cry alone.'**

eyebrow
eye
wrinkles

cheek
dimple
mouth
tooth

According to research from the USA, we smile for many different reasons.

There's the listener/response smile. When two people are having a conversation, the listener smiles to encourage the speaker.

There's the polite smile. This is the sort of smile you make when your aunt gives you a horrible birthday present.

There's the miserable smile. For example, when you go to the dentist, and he tells you that you need to have a (1) *tooth* taken out.

Very often, these social smiles are not real: they are frequently 'fake' smiles. Fake smiles are easy to do – you just have to tighten the muscles in your (2) _____ .

But there's only one smile that is the smile of true enjoyment. This smile is extremely hard to fake. It involves the muscles at the corners of the (3) _____ and the muscles around the eyes.

When someone gives a true smile, the (4) _____ get smaller, and you see little wrinkles around the edge. The eyebrows go up and on some people, (5) _____ appear in their cheeks.

The genuine smile of enjoyment not only makes us feel good, but it makes others feel good too.

3 How many different smiles are mentioned in the article? Can you do all these smiles? Show your partner.

Vocabulary

1 Match each group of adjectives with an appropriate noun to make common collocations for description.

a) thick / thin   1 chin
b) pale / rosy   2 eyebrows
c) curly / straight / wavy 3 lips
d) full / thin   4 teeth
e) square / pointed   5 hair
f) straight / white   6 cheeks

2 Which features do you like on a man or a woman?

3 Pairwork **Student A:** page 119 **Student B:** page 124

Reading

1 **The way you smile can show what sort of person you are. Read the article below and match one of the headings (a–d) with each paragraph (1–4).**

a) Shy   b) Cheeky   c) Confident   d) Sociable

What's in a smile?

1 _____
This is the smile of a joker. The raised eyebrows and dimples in the cheeks show a good sense of humour and a warm personality. This sort of person is often a bit of a rebel – they have no respect for authority.

2 _____
The wide, toothy smile shows that this person is easygoing and friendly. They enjoy being in a crowd and are good fun to go out with. They're always looking for the next party.

3 _____
The smile is in the eyes. This is a sensitive person, and a loyal friend. This sort of person thinks before they speak and is a good listener. They don't like being the centre of attention in a crowd.

4 _____
This is a smile that says, 'I know it all.' This type of person is very sure of themselves. They like a good argument, and they usually win. They're hard-working and very ambitious. And they can be quite bossy.

Read the article again and check your answers.

2 **Think about your family, your friends, your colleagues. Can you match the descriptions (1–4) to anybody you know? Tell a partner.**

Vocabulary

1 🌐 **3.01 Listen and repeat adjectives from the text above.**

a)	ambitious	1	certain about his or her abilities
b)	bossy	2	continues to support a person in difficult times
c)	confident	3	really wants to become successful, rich, or famous
d)	easygoing	4	cares about other people's feelings
e)	loyal	5	friendly and enjoys being with other people
f)	sensitive	6	tells other people what to do all the time
g)	shy	7	relaxed, calm and not easy to upset
h)	sociable	8	nervous in the company of other people

Match each adjective with its definition.

2 🌐 **3.02 Listen to six different people talking. Choose the most appropriate adjective from Exercise 1 to describe each one.**

1 sociable

3 **Find out about your own personality! In your opinion, what is the best adjective to describe these five things? Use adjectives from the box or your own ideas.**

addictive	affectionate	aggressive	annoying	calm	deep	dirty
faithful	hot	independent	mysterious	nasty	selfish	stormy	strong

1	a dog = _____	3	a rat = _____	5	an ocean = _____
2	a cat = _____	4	coffee = _____		

🌐 **3.03 Listen to find out the meaning of what you have written. Is it accurate? Tell your partner.**

Reading

1 Read and answer the questionnaire below. Compare your score with a partner.

Optimist or pessimist
– what are you?

For each situation, choose *a, b* or *c* according to what you are most likely to say.
Then calculate your score and read what it means!

**1 You're having a long walk in the country.
It starts raining.**
a   It always rains when I go for a walk.
b   It's OK – it's not snowing!
c   Great! I really enjoy walking in the rain.

2 It's autumn.
a   I don't like autumn because it will soon be winter.
b   It's just another time of year.
c   It's a beautiful time of year.

3 It's your 40th birthday.
a   The best years of my life are over.
b   I'm getting older – so what? It happens to everybody.
c   Life begins at 40 – where's the party?!

4 You've got a cold.
a   I need to see a doctor as soon as possible.
b   I need to buy some tissues.
c   It's just a cold – it won't kill me.

5 You have to make an important life decision.
a   Whatever I decide to do, it will be the wrong decision.
b   I'm going to think carefully about my decision.
c   Whatever I decide to do, it will be the right decision.

6 You arrive home after a great holiday.
a   I don't want to go back to work.
b   I'm going to start planning my next holiday.
c   I'm looking forward to sleeping in my own bed.

HOW TO SCORE   Each time you answer *a* **score 1**.   Each time you answer *b* **score 2**.   Each time you answer *c* **score 3**.

If you scored 15–18 … ☺
YOU'RE AN OPTIMIST!

You are an optimist who always tries to see the positive side of life. You know how to enjoy yourself and you don't waste time worrying about things that may never happen. But be careful – your friends might find your optimism rather irritating at times.

If you scored 10–14 … 😐
YOU'RE A REALIST!

You are a realist. You know life has ups and downs, but you hope to have more good times than bad times in your life. But be careful – you can be too serious at times. You need to show your feelings a bit more.

If you scored 6–9 … ☹
YOU'RE A PESSIMIST!

You are a pessimist. You must try to stop having negative thoughts. You need to learn how to enjoy the good things in life and stop worrying about things that may never happen. And remember, there are many people in worse situations than you.

2 Who got the highest score in the class? Find out.

Grammar & Vocabulary

Verb patterns 3

Verbs + *ing*-form
enjoy   look forward to
stop   waste time
I really enjoy **walking** in the rain.

Verbs + *to*-infinitive
decide   hope   need
want
I need **to see** a doctor.

1 Underline the correct structure. Refer to examples in the questionnaire above, if necessary.

a) I hope **getting** / <u>**to get**</u> a new job soon.
b) I want **travelling** / **to travel** around the world.
c) I enjoy **speaking** / **to speak** English.
d) I need **spending** / **to spend** more time at home.
e) I never waste time **worrying** / **to worry** about the future.
f) I'm looking forward to **going out** / **go out** tonight.

Are any sentences true for your partner? Ask questions to find out.

2 Use the same verb structures to write more sentences that are true for you. Compare them with your partner.

I hope to finish my studies soon.

Reading & Speaking

1 Work with a partner. Imagine you are describing your country to some people from another country. What would you say about the topics in the box?

> the beaches   the capital city   the food   the historical sites   the mountains   ~~the people~~

2 Read and complete the text with words from the box in Exercise 1.

Thailand
Land of smiles

'Addictive!' This is how most visitors describe Thailand. After your first visit, you just have to go back again.

Visitors to the 'Land of smiles' have plenty to feel happy about.

- (1) *The people* are warm and welcoming. The cost of living is cheap, and the lifestyle is easygoing.
- (2) _____ is mouth-watering (and often mouth-burning!).
- (3) _____ and jungles of the north are perfect for trekking on elephant back.
- There are hundreds of islands, and (4) _____ are some of the best in the world. Some islands, like Ko Tao, are popular with scuba divers. Others, like Ko Pha Ngan, are well-known for their full-moon parties. *The Beach*, a film starring Leonardo diCaprio, was filmed on Ko Phi Phi.
- (5) _____ , Bangkok, is one of the most vibrant cities on the planet. The spectacular Royal Palace is just one of (6) _____ to visit there.

3 Think about the following places. Tell your partner about them. Give details.
a) A place where you've been on holiday and would like to return.
b) A place where you've been on holiday and would *not* like to return.
c) A place where you haven't been on holiday, but would like to.

Listening

▲ Kath and Roy

1 🌐 3.04 **Listen to interviews with people on holiday in Thailand. Complete the statements with the correct names.**
a) *Cindy* likes swimming in the sea.
b) _____ has a dog.
c) _____ goes shopping in the evening.
d) _____ wants to do a cookery course.
e) _____ both love Thai food.
f) _____ thinks Thailand is a perfect place to live.

Cindy

2 Replace the names in Exercise 1 with the names of students in the class. Make as many true sentences as you can. Ask questions to help you.

▲ Hans

Listening

▼ Becky

1 ● 3.05 **Listen to a radio programme about people who came to Thailand on holiday and stayed. What jobs do Becky and Jeff do in Thailand?**

2 **Are the following statements true or false? Listen again and check your answers.**

a) Becky came to Thailand to look for work.
b) Becky runs a bar on the beach.
c) The tsunami in 2004 destroyed Becky's bar.
d) Becky is married to a Thai man.
e) Jeff is studying Thai.
f) Jeff wants to go home.

▲ Jeff

3 **Apart from your own country, which country in the world would you like to live in? Tell a partner.**

Grammar

for, since and been

for + a period of time
for 24 hours

since + a point in time
since yesterday

been can be the past participle of *go* and *be*
I've never **been** to Oslo. (go)
He's **been** here since May. (be)

1 **Complete the two sentences about Becky with *for* or *since*.**

a) Becky <u>has been</u> in Thailand _____ 2004.
b) Becky <u>hasn't been</u> to the UK _____ a few years.

2 **Look at the diagram and complete the table so that the information is correct, counting from today.**

Yesterday		Today

● ↑
since yesterday
(a point in time)

for 24 hours
(a period of time)

since		for
yesterday	=	*24 hours*
2004	=	_____ *years*
Sunday	=	_____ *day(s)*
my last birthday	=	_____ *month(s)*
I last went abroad	=	_____
I started studying English	=	_____

Add more examples of your own to the table.

3 **Read the sentences in Exercise 1 again. Discuss the questions with your partner.**

a) What tense are the underlined verbs in?
b) In which sentence is *been* the past participle of *go*?
c) In which sentence is *been* the past participle of *be*?

4 **Make true sentences about yourself using the following prompts and an appropriate time expression with *since*, *for* or *never*.**

a) not go to London
   I haven't been to London since I was sixteen.
   I haven't been to London for years.
   I've never been to London!
b) not go to a good party
c) not go to the beach

d) not go to a rock concert
e) not go to a wedding
f) not go out for dinner
g) not go skiing
h) not go abroad

Compare your sentences with your partner.

Grammar

Present perfect simple & continuous

You can use the continuous form with most verbs
I've been studying English since 2007.

Use the simple form for verbs with stative meanings
I've had the same car for ten years.

1 Look at the table based on information from the radio programme on page 80. Which 'facts' (*1, 2* or *3*) describe *how long* each activity has continued?

1 Past facts	+	2 Present facts	→	3 Present perfect facts
Becky arrived in Thailand in 2004.	+	Becky's in Thailand now.	→	She's been in Thailand since 2004.
Jeff started working in a dive centre six months ago.	+	Jeff's working in a dive centre now.	→	He's been working in a dive centre for six months.

2 Underline the verbs *be* and *work* in column 3 of the table. Discuss the questions with a partner.

   a) Which verb describes a state?
   b) Is it in the present perfect simple or continuous?
   c) Which verb describes a continuous or repeated action?
   d) Is it in the present perfect simple or continuous?

3 Complete these sentences with the present perfect simple or continuous.

   a) I (study) *'ve been studying* English for about two years.
   b) I (be)_____ in this particular class since September.
   c) I (know)_____ my English teacher for a few months.
   d) I (have)_____ this textbook since I started the course.
   e) I (use) _____ the same English dictionary for a couple of years.
   f) I (want) _____ to learn Italian since I first visited Italy.

   Change the time expressions if necessary so that the sentences are all true for you.

4 Find out how long your partner has been doing the things in Exercise 3. Ask questions beginning *How long ...*

   'How long have you been studying English?'

5 Grammar *Extra* 9 page 142. Read the explanations and do the exercises.

Pronunciation

1 Underline the two stressed words in each line of the chants.

   A
   How long has she been cooking?
   How long has she been cleaning?
   How long has she been shopping?
   How long have you been sleeping?

   B
   How long has he been reading?
   How long has he been playing?
   How long has he been eating?
   How long have you been waiting?

2 🔵 3.06 Listen, check and repeat the chants.

Speaking

1 Write the name of ...

   a) a café or bar you <u>go</u> to
   b) a neighbour you <u>know</u>
   c) a type of music you <u>like</u>
   d) the house you <u>live</u> in

   e) a subject you <u>are</u> interested in
   f) a TV programme you <u>watch</u>
   g) a favourite possession you <u>have</u>
   h) the place you <u>work</u> or <u>study</u>

2 Use the underlined verbs in Exercise 1 and write sentences to describe *how long* each activity has continued. Tell your partner.

   'I've been going to the café 'Les Deux Magots' since 2004.'
   'I've known my neighbour, Max, for six years.'

Useful phrases

1   Work with a partner. Read conversations *a–e*. Who's getting married?

Adam: I'm going to propose to Dawn tonight.
Harry: Do you think she'll say yes?
Adam: I hope so. Keep your **arms / legs / fingers** crossed for me.

Beth: Wow! I love your ring. Are they real diamonds?
Dawn: Of course!
Beth: I bet it cost **an eye and an ear / an arm and a leg / an eye and a tooth**.
Dawn: Probably. Adam's a very generous man.

Dawn: Have you seen Adam?
Harry: Yes, he was with a beautiful blond woman.
Dawn: What?
Harry: I'm just pulling your **hair / leg / teeth**. He's over there.
Dawn: That's not funny.

Dawn: Can you give me **a hand / a finger / an arm**?
Adam: OK, what do you want me to do?
Dawn: Help me to write these wedding invitations.
Adam: Oh, OK.

Beth: What are you wearing to Dawn and Adam's wedding?
Emma: I'm not invited.
Beth: Why not?
Emma: My husband doesn't see **cheek to cheek / head to head / eye to eye** with Adam.

2   Underline the correct alternative to complete the highlighted useful phrases.

🌐 **3.07 Listen to the conversations and check your answers.**

3   Match the useful phrases (*a–e*) with their meanings (*1–5*).

a) Keep your fingers crossed for me.   1 It was expensive.
b) It cost an arm and a leg.   2 He doesn't get on well with him.
c) I'm pulling your leg.   3 Wish me luck.
d) Can you give me a hand?   4 I'm joking.
e) He doesn't see eye to eye with him.   5 Can you help me?

🌐 **3.08 Listen and repeat the useful phrases.**

4   Work with your partner. Write a conversation including at least two of the useful phrases from Exercise 3.

Vocabulary *Extra*

Parts of the body

1 Match the pictures with the words.

`14`	ankle	☐	knee
☐	bottom	☐	lip
☐	cheek	☐	nail
☐	chest	☐	neck
☐	chin	☐	shoulder
☐	elbow	☐	stomach
☐	finger	☐	thumb
☐	forehead	☐	toe
☐	heel	☐	waist
☐	hip	☐	wrist

2 Which of the nouns in Exercise 1 would you *not* expect to use in the plural when describing somebody?

bottom, chest, ...

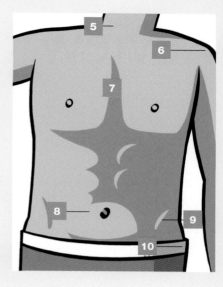

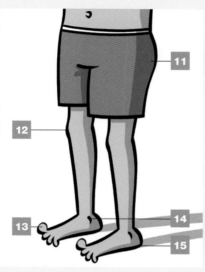

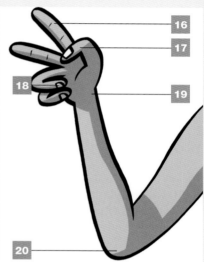

Focus on verbs + *ing*-form or *to*-infinitive (with a change in meaning)

1 Choose the correct alternative to complete the sentences.

a) Don't forget **posting / to post** those letters!
b) I don't remember **getting / to get** home last night!
c) He never forgot **kissing / to kiss** her for the first time.
d) At last it's stopped **raining / to rain**.
e) Could you remember **locking / to lock** the door when you go out?
f) I must stop **buying / to buy** some petrol on the way home.

2 Complete the table with the sentences from Exercise 1.

Using *remember, forget, stop*	Examples
1 *remember / forget* + *ing*-form: an action that somebody did. (Note: *forget* + *ing*-form is nearly always used with *never*.)	*Sentences b and c.*
2 *remember / forget* + *to*-infinitive: an action that somebody is / was supposed to do.	
3 *stop* + *ing*-form: an action that has stopped.	
4 *stop* + *to*-infinitive: the reason why somebody has stopped an action.	

Note: *begin, hate, like, love, prefer* and *start* are verbs that can take the *ing*-form or the *to*-infinitive, usually with little change in meaning.

Write your own examples to add to the table.

Review C

▶ Grammar *Extra* pages 138–143

Grammar

1 **Read the statements and then complete the questions.**

a) Al Gore made a film about global warming.
(What) *What did Al Gore make a film about?*

b) The USA is the world's biggest polluter.
(Which country)

c) The UK produces 100 million tons of litter every year. (How much)

d) Richard Branson wants Virgin Airlines to go green. (Who)

e) 730 million people travel on passenger jets every year. (How many)

f) The Alliance for Climate Protection protests against global warming. (Which organisation)

2 **Underline the correct words.**

a) He can't talk now. He **has / 's having** lunch.

b) I love cars. I **have / 'm having** two Ferraris.

c) They **believe / 're believing** in God.

d) You **look like / 're looking like** your mum.

e) We **think / 're thinking** of writing a book.

f) She **thinks / 's thinking** Beyoncé is great.

3 **Complete the sentences about the future. Use the present continuous for arrangements or *(be) going to* for intentions.**

a) I (see) *'m seeing* a friend after lunch.

b) I (visit) _____ New York one day.

c) I (go) _____ on holiday with my family next month.

d) My parents (come) _____ to my house this evening.

e) I (buy) _____ a lottery ticket this weekend.

f) I (have) _____ a meal with my friends on Friday.

Tick the statements that are true for you. Compare with a partner.

4 **Complete the sentences with the verbs in brackets in the *ing*-form or the *to*-infinitive.**

a) I enjoy (walk) *walking* in the rain.

b) I've decided (take) _____ up a new sport.

c) I'm not looking forward to (do) _____ my exams.

d) I want (go)_____ to China one day.

e) I don't often waste time (watch) _____ TV.

f) I need (spend) _____ less time at work.

Tick the statements that are true for you. Compare with your partner.

5 **Underline the correct words.**

Ben: What was your school like?

Ian: It was very strict.

Ben: (1) **Could you / <u>Did you have to</u>** wear a uniform?

Ian: Yes, we did. We (2) **couldn't / shouldn't** wear any other clothes. We (3) **should / had to** wear our uniforms all the time.

Ben: We (4) **shouldn't / didn't have to** wear a uniform at our school.

Ian: Oh, really?

Ben: Yes, but I think children (5) **could / should** wear a uniform. It's better – everyone looks the same.

Ian: Well, you (6) **mustn't / couldn't** tell anyone, but I actually enjoyed wearing my uniform!

6 **Make sentences using the present perfect simple or continuous with *for* or *since*.**

a) They're living in France. They moved there in 2005. (since)
They've been living in France since 2005.

b) We're learning the violin. We started two months ago. (for)

c) She wants to be a vet. She decided this when she was six. (since)

d) He's studying Chinese. He started a year ago. (for)

e) I know him. I met him when we were at school. (since)

f) She has a motorbike. She bought it three weeks ago. (for)

7 **Spot the mistake! Cross out the incorrect sentence.**

1 a) Who likes George Clooney?
   b) ~~Who does like George Clooney?~~

2 a) Don't worry – I believe you.
   b) Don't worry – I'm believing you.

3 a) We're visiting the USA one day.
   b) We're going to visit the USA one day.

4 a) Did you had to clean your room?
   b) Did you have to clean your room?

5 a) I'm looking forward to meeting you.
   b) I'm looking forward to meet you.

6 a) She's been here since four years.
   b) She's been here for four years.

Vocabulary

1 Complete the text with the words in the box.

> action   away   ~~buzzing~~   part   slogans
> swarming   way

Earlier today the centre of London was (1) *buzzing* with activity when a million people took (2) _____ in a demonstration. As protestors made their (3) _____ from Jubilee Gardens to Trafalgar Square, one or two small groups broke (4) _____ from the main group and made trouble. However, it was mostly a peaceful protest. The city centre was (5) _____ with people carrying banners with (6) _____ saying 'Peace!' The protestors gathered under Nelson's Column and demanded urgent (7) _____ on global peace.

2 Put the words in the correct order.

a) power / anti- / I'm / nuclear
   I'm anti-nuclear power.
b) against / in the city / using big cars / I'm
c) feel strongly / global / I / warming / about / don't
d) in favour / more money / of / I'm / for farmers
e) about / politics / really care / don't / I
f) I / wild animals / support / the protection of

Tick the statements you agree with. Compare with a partner.

3 Match the two halves of the statements.

a) 3   b) …

a) Lots of young people want …
b) More people are training to be …
c) It's not easy to pass …
d) A good education doesn't cost …
e) University students usually move …
f) Parents play an important …

1   actors and singers than ever before.
2   much money.
3   to become celebrities.
4   exams at school or university.
5   role in their children's education.
6   into student accommodation.

Tick the statements that are true for your country. Compare with your partner.

4 Complete the conversation with the words in the box.

> avoid   career   common   ~~effort~~   opinions
> tidy

Teacher: Now listen, Rose. I'd like to see you make more of an (1) *effort*. You know, you have a brilliant (2) _____ ahead of you.
Rose: Yes, Miss.
Teacher: Rose, I think you and I have a lot in (3) _____ .
Rose: Yes, Miss.
Teacher: I was like you when I was your age. We share the same (4) _____ , don't we?
Rose: Yes, Miss.
Teacher: OK, please try to (5) _____ getting into trouble – and please keep your desk clean and (6) _____ .
Rose: Yes, Miss.
Teacher: Good. I've enjoyed our little chat.
Rose: Yes, Miss.

5 Complete the description with the words in the box.

> ~~curly~~   full   rosy   square   thick   white

Tony is a tall man with short, (1) *curly* hair and blue eyes. He has fairly (2) _____ eyebrows and (3) _____ lips. He probably works outside, because his cheeks are (4) _____ . He's very handsome and has a (5) _____ chin and (6) _____ teeth.

6 Complete the character adjectives.

a) *ambitious*
b) b__ssy
c) c__nf__d__nt
d) __ __syg__ __ng
e) __nd__p__nd__nt
f) l__y__l
g) myst__r__ __ __s
h) s__lf__sh

Pronunciation

1 Look at some words from Units 7–9. Say the words and add them to the table.

> ~~affectionate~~   ~~against~~   believe   biology
> ~~confident~~   ~~curly~~   degree   democracy
> earlier   eyebrows   forehead   pointed
> responsible   sociable   support   tourism

A: ☐☐	B: ☐☐	C: ☐☐☐	D: ☐☐☐☐
curly	*against*	*confident*	*affectionate*

2 Underline the stressed syllable in each word.

🔘 3.09 **Listen, check and repeat.**

Reading & Listening

1 🌐 **3.10 Read the article about Phil and Hazel Green.**

The Greens

go green

Phil Green 'A few years ago I lost my job, and my life changed completely. I became interested in green issues, and I started worrying about climate change. Then last summer I decided
5 I really wanted to do something to help the planet. I talked to Hazel and the children, and we decided to go green.
   Since then we've made some big changes to our life. First, we sold our cars – we had two.
10 That wasn't a problem because we live in a town and there's good public transport. Anyway, I've always liked walking and we've all got bikes now. We've stopped eating meat, and started eating more vegetables. We don't go to the
15 supermarket, but we buy and eat food from local farmers, and I grow a lot of our vegetables in the garden. It's great! We've saved a lot of money because we don't buy things we don't need. Next week I'm getting some hens, so we can
20 have our own eggs. I can't wait!'

Hazel Green 'When Phil asked me to make some changes to our life, I was a bit nervous. But I knew that he was serious about it, so I said yes. Since then, life has been hard work. Of course,
25 I'm worried about what's happening in the world, but we had a very nice, comfortable, easy life before.
   When Phil said we had to sell my car, I cried. I hate walking everywhere and I don't like
30 public transport. But I miss my holidays most. We always flew to warm places like Italy or Thailand, but this year we took the train to the south coast of Wales. It rained all week. It was horrible. We eat very healthily now, though.
35 Before, I didn't think about where our food came from, but now I've learned to cook some very interesting vegetables.
   I'm a teacher and, you know, a lot of my students are very worried about the environment.
40 I try to teach them what they can do to help protect the planet.
   But I want to enjoy life, too! So, now we've decided that we can fly somewhere once a year. We're going to Spain next year. I'm really looking
45 forward to having a holiday in the sun.'

Who do you think said these things: Phil or Hazel?

a) 'I miss my car.'
b) 'I love my new life.'
c) 'I think we made the right decision, but it's difficult.'

2 **Read the article again and answer the questions.**

a) When did Phil and Hazel decide to go green?
b) Who likes walking?
c) Where does the family's food come from now?
d) Why have they saved money?
e) What does Hazel miss most about her old life?
f) Who works in a school?
g) Where did the family go on holiday this year?

3 **Work with a partner. What do you think about Phil and Hazel's changes? Could you make similar changes in your life?**

4 🌐 **3.11 Listen to the Green children, Kyle and Naomi. Underline the correct information.**

a) Kyle and Naomi think that climate change **is / isn't** a problem.
b) Kyle and Naomi think that it **is / isn't** important to make changes to our lives.

5 **Listen again. Are these statements true or false?**

a) Before he lost his job, Phil was a pilot. *False.*
b) Kyle says his dad changed after he lost his job.
c) Naomi didn't want to make changes to her life.
d) Kyle says he would like to get a car when he's older.
e) Naomi's friends think she's bossy.
f) Kyle's friends think climate change isn't a problem.

Writing & Speaking

1 Read the email from Meg to her friend, Joe. There is one word missing in each line. Find the missing words in the box and put them in the correct places in the email.

be	but	can	for	forward	going	have	holiday	~~last~~	'm	my
should	tell									

Hi Joe,

① Guess what! I bought a lottery ticket ^last week, and I won £3 million!!! I so excited.

② I'm going to make some big changes in my life, starting with job. I'm leaving today! I've decided I'm going to go to university. I've always wanted to be a doctor, my parents couldn't pay for my studies. Now I finally do it!

③ I'm going to split up with Kenny tomorrow. We nothing in common, and he doesn't like my friends. I don't want a boyfriend now. I'm going to too busy with my studies!

④ And I'm moving out of my sister's flat tomorrow. I'm looking to that. She's so bossy! I'm going to buy a house of my own. Do you think I give some money to my sister?

⑤ But it's not all me, me, me! I want to do something worthwhile too. I'm to give some money to Greenpeace. But first I'm planning a in a warm place. Do you want to come to Thailand with me, Joe? I'll pay your ticket!

You mustn't Kenny I won this money.

Love,

Meg

2 Match the headings to the paragraphs (1–5) in the email.

a) Living arrangements – *Paragraph 4*
b) Travel plans and other ideas
c) Job and studies
d) Announcing your news
e) Relationships

3 Imagine you've won £1 million. What changes are you going to make to your life? Think about the things in the headings (*a–e*) in Exercise 2.

4 Tell a partner about the changes you are going to make to your life.

'I'm going to buy a new flat for my parents and me.'

5 Write an email to a friend about the changes you are going to make to your life. Use the headings in Exercise 2 to organise your email.

▶ 🎵 3.12 **Song:** *Money*

10 Lifestyle

Grammar *will*. Future time clauses after *when, if, as soon as. used to*
Vocabulary Collocations. Food and cooking. Cars and driving
Useful phrases Idioms with food

Reading & Vocabulary

1 **Work with a partner. Look at the photo of Chiako and guess the answers to the following questions.**

a) What time does she get up in the morning?
b) How old is she?
c) Where does she come from?
d) What kind of diet does she have?
e) Does she have a stressful life?

Read the text and find out if you guessed correctly.

How not to die before you get old

Chiako is active and healthy. She gets up at 7.00 a.m. every day and goes for a brisk walk. Three times a week she plays gate-ball – a popular national sport – with her friends. There is nothing unusual about this, except that Chiako is 102 years old. She is not alone – there are hundreds of centenarians who lead healthy lives like this in Okinawa.

5   Okinawa is a group of Japanese islands between Japan and Taiwan. Near a beach, there is a large stone with the following proverb engraved on it: 'At 70 you are still a child; at 80 you are just a youth; and at 90, if the ancestors invite you into heaven, ask them to wait until you are 100, and then you might consider it.'

    Okinawans manage to stay slim in old age by eating a low-calorie diet which consists
10 of three quarters plant food and one quarter animal food. They eat seven servings of fruit and vegetables every day and they stop eating when they are 80% full. They also keep physically active the natural way by dancing, doing martial arts, walking and gardening. In other words, they do the things they enjoy.

    Okinawans have developed a stress-resistant personality. Nobody is in a hurry,
15 timetables are non-existent, and there is always tomorrow. Hundreds of people, both young and old, go to the beach every day to watch the spectacular sunsets. In Okinawa there is always time to watch the sun set.

    As well as large extended families, Okinawans have strong networks of friends. When someone is ill and doesn't come to work, a neighbour will always knock on their door to
20 find out how they are.

    There's no magic pill. If you keep fit, if you have good friends, a healthy diet and a stress-free lifestyle, you will live longer. It's as simple as that!

2 **Complete these collocations with words from the article.**

a) How often do you go for a *brisk* walk?
b) Do you think you l_____ a healthy life?
c) Do you know anybody who does martial a_____ ?
d) Do you feel that you are always in a h_____ ?
e) When was the last time you watched a spectacular s_____ ?
f) Do you have a large extended f_____ ?
g) Do you have a strong n_____ of friends?
h) What's your favourite way to k_____ fit?

Ask your partner the questions. Is your lifestyle similar or different from the lifestyle in Okinawa?

Listening & Grammar

1  **3.13 Listen to a woman phoning for information about a health spa called the New Life Centre. Answer the questions.**

a) Why does she want the information?

b) Do you think her husband will like her idea? Why? / Why not?

2 Complete the questions and answers about the activities at the New Life Centre.

a) 'Will he take a fitness test?'   'Yes, he will.'   'No, he won't.'

b) 'Will he do yoga?'   'Yes, he will.'   'No, he won't.'

c) '_____ he have a cigarette?'   'Yes, he _____.' 'No, he _____.'

d) '_____ he have a sauna and a jacuzzi?' '_____.'   '_____.'

e) '_____ he go for a four-hour walk?'   '_____.'   '_____.'

f) '_____ he have time to relax in the afternoon?' '_____.'   '_____.'

🌐 **3.14 Listen, check and repeat.**

3 Work with a partner. Ask and answer the questions in Exercise 2.

Are there any health spas in your country? Would you like to go to one? Why? / Why not?

Grammar

1 Look at these sentences from the Listening section above and answer the questions.

Conjunction	+	Subordinate clause	+	Main clause
As soon as	+	he arrives	+	he'll take a fitness test.
If	+	he has a cigarette	+	he'll be in big trouble.
When	+	he finishes the week	+	he'll feel like a new man.

a) Do the sentences refer to past, present or future time?

b) Which verb form is used in the main clause?

c) Which verb form is used in the subordinate clause?

Which of the conjunctions suggest …

d) it is *possible* that one action will follow another action?

e) it is *certain* that one action will follow another action at some time?

f) it is *certain* that one action will *immediately* follow another action?

2 Underline the correct verb forms.

a) If there's nothing good on TV this evening, I **go** / **'ll go** out.

b) I'm going to go straight home as soon as the lesson **will finish** / **finishes**.

c) When I**'ll go** / **go** on holiday next summer, I'll send all my friends postcards.

d) I'm going to retire as soon as I**'m** / **'ll be** sixty.

e) When I**'ll have** / **have** enough money, I'm going to buy some new clothes.

f) If I get up early tomorrow, I think I **go** / **'ll go** for a run.

How many sentences are true for you? Rewrite the sentences so that they are all true for you.

3 Grammar *Extra* 10, Part 1 page 144. Read the explanations and do the exercises.

---

will

I'll

You'll

He'll   come back.

She'll   be OK.

It'll   go away.

We'll

They'll

Will you see her?

Yes, I **will**.

No, I **won't**.

(*'ll* = will

won't = will not)

Future time clauses

conjunction – *if*, *when*, *as soon as*

subordinate clause = present form

main clause = future form

If **I go**, **will you come too**? As soon as **they arrive**, **we'll start**.

You can also put the main clause first. **I'm going to buy a car** when **I pass my test**.

Vocabulary

1 Look at the photos of Nick's food shopping. Then look at his shopping list. Which five items did he forget to buy?

FRUIT AND VEGETABLES
lemons, oranges, cherries,
grapes, peaches, mushrooms,
tomatoes, lettuce, spinach,
carrots, cauliflower,
aubergine, red peppers,
cucumber, onions, garlic
MEAT AND FISH
a chicken, sausages,
a trout, prawns, sardines
OTHER
tea, soup, nuts, beans

2 Look at the shopping list again and complete the task.

* Circle the items of food you have eaten in the last three days.
* Underline the items you really like.
* Cross out the items you don't like very much.

Compare with a partner. What items of food are *always* on your shopping list?

Pronunciation

1 🌐 3.15 Listen and repeat the words in column *A* and column *B*. Notice the vowel sounds in red.

A		B	
a)	lettuce	1	nut
b)	onion	2	tomato
c)	banana	3	spinach
d)	sardines	4	beans
e)	orange	5	lemon
f)	aubergine	6	cauliflower

2 🌐 3.16 Match a word from column *A* with a word from column *B* according to the red vowel sounds. Listen and check your answers.

Which word do you find the most difficult to say?

Reading & Vocabulary

1 Read this extract from a website about bananas. Tick the dishes you would like to try. Put a cross next to the ones you wouldn't like to try.

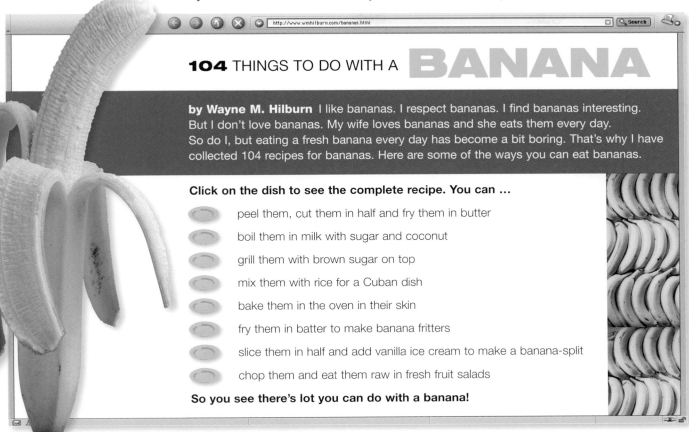

104 THINGS TO DO WITH A **BANANA**

by Wayne M. Hilburn I like bananas. I respect bananas. I find bananas interesting. But I don't love bananas. My wife loves bananas and she eats them every day. So do I, but eating a fresh banana every day has become a bit boring. That's why I have collected 104 recipes for bananas. Here are some of the ways you can eat bananas.

Click on the dish to see the complete recipe. You can ...

- peel them, cut them in half and fry them in butter
- boil them in milk with sugar and coconut
- grill them with brown sugar on top
- mix them with rice for a Cuban dish
- bake them in the oven in their skin
- fry them in batter to make banana fritters
- slice them in half and add vanilla ice cream to make a banana-split
- chop them and eat them raw in fresh fruit salads

So you see there's lot you can do with a banana!

2 Read the list of dishes again and note down words which describe ...

a) different ways of preparing food (*peel, …*)
b) different ways of cooking food (*boil, …*)
c) one word meaning *not cooked*

3 Write down the name of your favourite dish. Think about these questions.

- What ingredients do you need?
- How do you prepare the ingredients?
- How do you cook the ingredients?

Tell a partner about your favourite dish.

Speaking: anecdote

1 🔊 3.17 Listen to Josh talking about the fittest/healthiest person he knows. Underline the correct information.

a) 'Who is the fittest/healthiest person you know?' 'My **uncle** / **cousin**.'
b) 'How old is he?' 'He's **36** / **26**.'
c) 'What does he do for a living?' 'He's training to be **an army officer** / **a naval officer**.'
d) 'What does he look like?' 'He's **tall and slim** / **tall and well-built**.'
e) 'What does he do to stay healthy and fit?' 'He **goes to the gym** / **runs up mountains**.'
f) 'What kind of food does he eat?' 'He eats a **high-calorie** / **vegetarian** diet.'
g) 'Has he ever been unhealthy or unfit?' 'He used to be **really lazy** / **very unhealthy**.'

▲ Darren

2 You are going to tell your partner about the fittest/healthiest person you know.

- Ask yourself the questions in Exercise 1.
- Think about *what* to say and *how* to say it.
- Tell your partner about the fittest/healthiest person you know.

Reading

1 🌐 3.18 **Read three descriptions of people's first cars. Match each description (*a–c*) with one of the cars (*1–3*).**

My *first car*

a 'My first car was a Citroen 2CV. Someone gave it to me and it was very old. It used to break down almost every time I went out in it.

One day, it was raining heavily, and the windscreen wiper fell off. I couldn't see the road! I had to stop and wait for the rain to stop.

I used to have a love-hate relationship with that car – I loved it when it worked, but I hated it when it broke down.'

b 'It wasn't my car, it was my boyfriend's. It was a blue VW Beetle with a sunroof.

Every weekend we used to drive out of town with our tent in the back and drive until we felt like stopping.

It wasn't a big car, but I remember one weekend we went to Paris with four friends. There were six of us in this little car! I don't think we took any luggage, because there wasn't any room for suitcases. The engine was in the back, and there was only a tiny boot in the front. But we didn't use to worry about that sort of thing when we were younger.'

c 'Daddy gave me my first car for my 17th birthday. I didn't even have my driving licence. It was a little red Porsche with a blue steering wheel and blue seats. It was cute, but I didn't use it much because I used to prefer motorbikes. All my boyfriends had big motorbikes.

My daddy used to introduce me to all these nice guys – lawyers and businessmen – but I wasn't interested in them.

My poor daddy – I used to drive him crazy.'

2 **Answer the questions from memory. Then read and check your answers.**
- a) Which car was very old?
- b) Which car had blue seats?
- c) Which car broke down a lot?
- d) Which car had a tiny boot in the front?
- e) Which car was a 17th birthday present?
- f) Which car didn't have much room for luggage?

3 **What was the first car you drove? Or what was the first car you remember going in as a child? Describe it to your partner.**

Vocabulary

1 Find the names of six parts of a car in the descriptions on page 92.

windscreen wiper, …

2 Imagine you are going to buy a new car. Put the features in the box into the table below according to how important you think they are. Compare with a partner.

> air conditioning   easy to park   economical to run   environmentally friendly
> good sound system   large boot   leather seats   made in my country
> nice colour   powerful engine   satellite navigation system   sunroof

Important	Not important
easy to park	*air conditioning*

Grammar

used to + infinitive

My father **used to** be slim.
He **didn't use to** eat much.

Did he **use to** ride a bike?
Yes, he did.
No, he didn't.

1 Look at these extracts from the texts on page 92. Match each underlined verb structure with a description.

a) '*Every weekend <u>we used to drive</u> out of town …*'
b) '*… one weekend <u>we went</u> to Paris …*'
c) '*<u>I used to have</u> a love-hate relationship with that car …*'

1 a single action in the past
2 a repeated action in the past
3 a state in the past

Is it possible to use *used to* + infinitive to talk about a single action in the past?

2 Look at the sentences. Where possible, replace the past simple with *used to* or *didn't use to* + infinitive.

When I was a child …
a) <u>my parents had</u> a big old car. *my parents used to have a big old car.*
b) <u>my mother drove</u> me to school every day.
c) <u>I didn't like</u> going on long journeys. <u>I got</u> car sick.
d) one summer <u>we went</u> to France on a camping holiday.
e) <u>my father never washed</u> the car. <u>It always looked</u> dirty.
f) when I left home <u>my parents sold</u> the car and <u>bought</u> a smaller one.

Change the sentences so that they are true for you. Compare your sentences with a partner.

3 **Pairwork** **Student A:** page 119 **Student B:** page 124

4 **Grammar *Extra* 10, Part 2** page 144. Read the explanations and do the exercises.

Speaking: anecdote

1 🌐 3.19 **Listen to Patti talking about her dream car. Underline the correct information.**

a) 'What kind of car is it?' 'A **Chevrolet / Jaguar**.'
b) 'Is it a modern car, or is it an old model?' 'It's **old / new**.'
c) 'What colour is it?' 'It's **light blue / black**.'
d) 'What's it like inside?' 'It's **small / spacious**.'
e) 'What kind of seats has it got?' '**Red leather / Brown leather**.'
f) 'What kind of music do you listen to in your car?' '**Classical / Elvis**.'
g) 'Who would you like to take in your car?' '**My friends / George Clooney**.'
h) 'Where would you like to go?' '**Along the coast / Down 5th Avenue in New York**.'

2 You are going to tell your partner about your dream car.

- Ask yourself the questions in Exercise 1.
- Think about *what* to say and *how* to say it.
- Tell your partner about your dream car.

Useful phrases

1 **Read and match the conversations (*a–e*) with the pictures (*1–5*).**

a) A: Is he tired?
B: No, he's full of **beans / spinach / mushrooms.**
A: Oh no – he won't want to go to bed.

b) A: Have you met Pete's sister?
B: No, I haven't. Is she like Pete?
A: No, not at all. They're like chalk and **chicken / cheese / cherries.**

c) A: Hey, what do you think of the guy over there with the blue shirt on?
B: Um – he's OK, but he's not my cup of **soup / tea / hot chocolate.**
A: Good – he's mine.

d) A: No, I can't. It's too difficult.
B: No, it isn't. It's a piece of **toast / pizza / cake.** Come on.
A: No, no. Help! I'm going to fall over.

e) A: What was it like?
B: Awful – it was so crowded. We were packed in like **grapes / sardines / garlic.**
A: Oh dear. You won't go there again then, will you?

2 **Underline the correct alternative to complete the highlighted useful phrases.**

🔘 **3.20 Listen to the conversations and check your answers.**

Do you have any idioms like these in your language?

3 **Replace the underlined phrases with the useful phrases from the conversations.**
a) I think that learning English is <u>really easy</u>.
b) I hate places where you are <u>with lots of other people</u>.
c) My father and mother are <u>very different from one another</u>.
d) I'm always <u>very energetic</u> early in the morning.
e) Going clubbing is <u>not something I enjoy</u>.

🔘 **3.21 Listen, check and repeat the sentences.**

Are the sentences true or false for you? Compare with a partner.

Vocabulary *Extra*

Cars

1 Match the pictures with the parts of a car.

- [4] <u>bonn</u>et
- [ ] boot
- [ ] <u>bum</u>per
- [ ] gear stick
- [ ] <u>hand</u>brake
- [ ] <u>num</u>ber plate
- [ ] seat
- [ ] seat belt
- [ ] <u>stee</u>ring wheel
- [ ] <u>sun</u>roof
- [ ] tyre
- [ ] wheel
- [ ] <u>wind</u>screen
- [ ] <u>wind</u>screen <u>wip</u>ers

2 Work with a partner. Cover the words and look at the pictures. Ask and answer questions.

'What's this?'
'It's the gear stick.'

'What are these?'
'They're headlights.'

Focus on words used with driving

1 Match the two sentence halves to complete the definitions of the words and expressions in bold.

a) If you **give somebody a lift**,
b) If you **get stuck in a traffic jam**,
c) The **rush hour** is the period of the day
d) If you **run out of petrol**,
e) If you **overtake** somebody,
f) If your car **breaks down**,

1 when most people are going to or from work.
2 you take them somewhere in your car.
3 you speed up and go past them.
4 it stops working and you can't use it.
5 you can't drive because there is too much traffic.
6 you have no more petrol left and the car slows down and stops.

2 Complete the questions with the words in the box.

| down | hour | jams | lift | ~~overtaking~~ | petrol |

a) Do you drive fast and enjoy *overtaking* other cars?
b) Has your car ever broken _____ ?
c) When was the last time you ran out of _____ ?
d) Do you always go to work/school in the rush _____ ?
e) Are there a lot of traffic _____ in your city?
f) Have you ever given a _____ to a hitchhiker?

Ask and answer the questions with your partner.

11 Animals

Grammar Defining relative clauses. Unreal conditionals
Vocabulary Animals. Adjective + preposition. *that*
Useful phrases Polite requests

Reading & Speaking

1 How do you feel about animals? Do the questionnaire.

YOUR ATTITUDE TO animals

Tick the option that best describes your attitude to animals.

1 Animals are ...
a) as important as humans.
b) less important than humans.
c) more important than humans.

2 Animals ...
a) should be respected and protected.
b) are useful for humans.
c) are good friends for humans.

3 Hunting is ...
a) a popular activity in my country, but I don't like it.
b) a great sport.
c) very cruel.

4 Zoos are ...
a) important for protecting endangered species.
b) fun to visit.
c) depressing and unnatural.

5 Animal testing ...
a) is OK if there is no pain or suffering involved.
b) is essential for progress in the medical field.
c) is wrong. It should be illegal.

6 Sharks are ...
a) dangerous and scary.
b) exciting in films.
c) misunderstood.

7 Rabbits ...
a) cause accidents on the road.
b) are best in a red wine sauce.
c) are fluffy and nice.

8 Fur is ...
a) too expensive and not necessary.
b) fashionable and fabulous.
c) only for animals – not for humans.

2 Work in small groups. Discuss your opinions.

'I think zoos are fun to visit.'
'I disagree. I think they're depressing and unnatural.'

3 Which discussion was the most interesting? Tell the class.

'The discussion about number four was the most interesting. Javier and Cristina think zoos are fun to visit, but I think they're depressing and unnatural.'

Listening

1 Look at the animals and insects in the photos. Which ones do you like or dislike? Tell a partner.

◀ bat *'I hate bats.'*

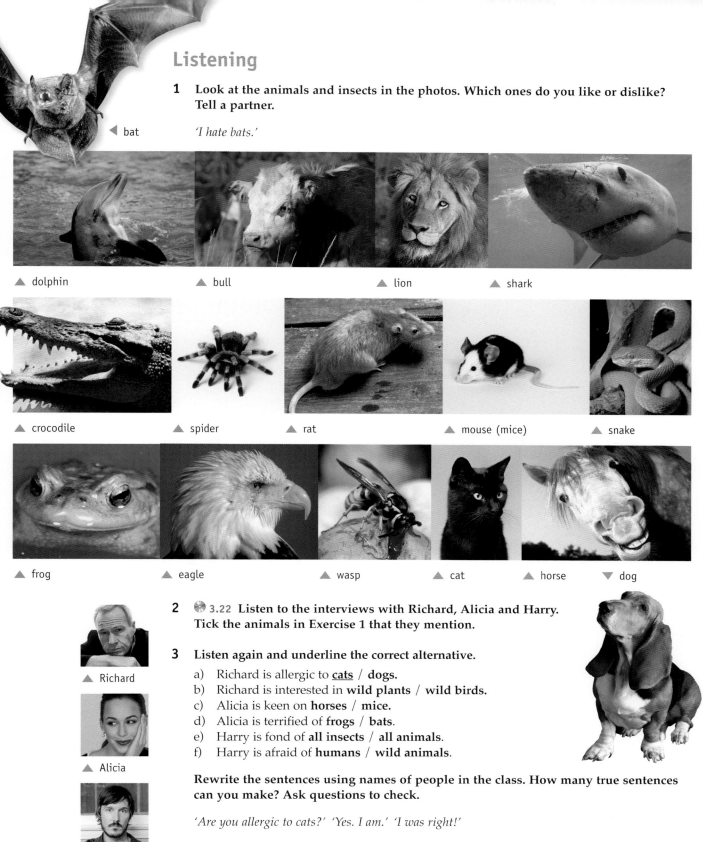

▲ dolphin   ▲ bull   ▲ lion   ▲ shark

▲ crocodile   ▲ spider   ▲ rat   ▲ mouse (mice)   ▲ snake

▲ frog   ▲ eagle   ▲ wasp   ▲ cat   ▲ horse   ▼ dog

2 🔘 **3.22** Listen to the interviews with Richard, Alicia and Harry. Tick the animals in Exercise 1 that they mention.

▲ Richard

3 Listen again and underline the correct alternative.

a) Richard is allergic to <u>cats</u> / **dogs**.
b) Richard is interested in **wild plants** / **wild birds**.
c) Alicia is keen on **horses** / **mice**.
d) Alicia is terrified of **frogs** / **bats**.
e) Harry is fond of **all insects** / **all animals**.
f) Harry is afraid of **humans** / **wild animals**.

▲ Alicia

Rewrite the sentences using names of people in the class. How many true sentences can you make? Ask questions to check.

'Are you allergic to cats?' 'Yes. I am.' 'I was right!'

▲ Harry

Vocabulary

1 Add the correct preposition. Then complete the sentences to make some true and some false statements about yourself.

a) I've never been keen *on football*.
b) I'm not very interested _____ .
c) My parents are fond _____ .
d) When I was a child I was afraid _____ .
e) I know several people who are allergic _____ .
f) I'm absolutely terrified _____ .

2 Read your partner's statements from Exercise 1 and guess which statements are true and which are false.

Vocabulary

1 **Test your knowledge of animals! Match the animals (*a–f*) with their defining characteristics (*1–6*).**

a) An elephant
b) A dolphin
c) A cheetah
d) A giraffe
e) An ant
f) A tortoise

1 is an animal that can last longer without water than a camel.
2 is an animal that can run at 100 kilometres per hour.
3 is an insect that can lift fifty times its own weight.
4 is an animal that can smell water fifteen kilometres away.
5 is an animal that can live to be two hundred years old.
6 is an animal that can recognise its own image in a mirror.

2 **Work in small groups. You have three minutes. Try to list an animal or an insect for each letter of the alphabet.**

A: ant   B: bird   C: cheetah   D: dog   E: …

Reading & Vocabulary

1 **Look at the photos. Which animal do you think goes best with each description (*a–c*)?**

a) An animal that knew when its owner was coming home.
b) An animal that loved classical music.
c) An animal that accidentally deleted some valuable files on a computer.

🔘 **3.23 Read the stories and check your ideas.**

▲ a Siamese cat

▲ a mynah bird

▲ a cow

Story 1

Mr and Mrs Roper live near London with their son, Robert, and a mynah bird called Sammy. Robert often goes away on business and he is sometimes away for weeks or even months. He hardly ever gets in touch with his parents to tell them when he is coming home. But he doesn't need to. Mr and Mrs Roper always know when their son is going to turn up, because Sammy starts calling 'Robbie' a few hours before Robert walks through the door.

Story 2

Ralph, a bank worker in San Francisco, owned a Siamese cat called Morris. One morning, Morris was unwell, and so Ralph decided to take him into work to keep an eye on him. While Ralph was speaking on the telephone, Morris got up, walked across the keyboard of his computer and accidentally keyed in a secret code that deleted files worth $100,000. As you can imagine, Ralph's employers were not amused.

Story 3

Pat and Tina were touring the north of England by car when they decided to pull up in a quiet place to have a picnic. While they were eating, they played some Mozart on a CD player. After a few minutes they looked up and realised that they were surrounded by cows who were listening to the music. When the Mozart was finished, they put on a pop CD. The cows immediately turned round and walked off.

2 **Read the stories again. Are these sentences true or false?**

a) Robert often <u>travels away from home</u> on business.
b) He always <u>contacts</u> his parents when he's coming home.
c) Mr and Mrs Roper never know when Robert is going to <u>arrive</u>.
d) Ralph took Morris to work to <u>look after</u> him.
e) Morris <u>typed</u> a secret code because he wanted to delete the files.
f) Pat and Tina decided to <u>stop the car</u> in a quiet place because they wanted to sleep.
g) The cows turned round and <u>left</u> when Pat and Tina put on a pop CD.

3 **Replace the underlined words and expressions in Exercise 2 with words and expressions from the stories.**

travels away from home = *goes away*

Which story do you like best? Do you know any other stories about animals? Tell a partner.

Grammar

Defining relative clauses

I know a woman. She's two metres tall.
I know a woman **who's/that's two metres tall.**

We live in a flat. It's too small for us.
We live in a flat **which is / that's too small for us.**

Use *who* for people.
Use *which* for things.
Use *that* for things and people.

1 Two sentences can combine to make one sentence using a relative pronoun. In each new sentence, cross out the relative pronoun which is *not* possible.

a) A vet is a person. He / She treats sick animals.

A vet is a person **that / which / who** treats sick animals.

b) A horse is an animal. It sleeps standing up.

A horse is an animal **that / which / who** sleeps standing up.

Complete the rules with *that, which* and *who.*

You use (1) _____ for people. You use (2) _____ for things.
You can use (3) _____ for people or things.

2 Use *that* to combine these sentences.

a) I've got a dog. It likes going for long walks. *I've got a dog that likes going for long walks.*

b) I've got a car. It isn't very easy to park.

c) I've got a sister. She works in a shop.

d) I've got an espresso machine. It makes great coffee.

e) I've got a friend. He lives in the USA.

f) I've got some shoes. They are too small for me.

Replace *that* with *which* or *who* in your sentences a–f. Which sentences are true for you?

3 Correct these ungrammatical sentences by crossing out the unnecessary word.

a) A person who ~~she~~ treats sick animals.
b) The only animal – apart from humans – which it gets sunburn.
c) A name for people who they are afraid of spiders.
d) A person who he studies birds.
e) The scientist who he developed the theory of evolution.
f) The largest animal that it has ever lived.

Match these words (*1–6*) with the definitions above.

1 arachnophobic *c*
2 an ornithologist
3 a vet
4 Charles Darwin
5 a pig
6 a blue whale

4 Pairwork **Student A:** page 120 **Student B:** page 125

5 Grammar *Extra* 11, Part 1 page 146. Read the explanations and do the exercises.

Pronunciation

1 🔵 3.24 **Listen and repeat the word pairs (a–e). What do you notice about the pronunciation of each pair?**

Words	Meanings
a) bare/bear	1 … Sir or Madam / a brown animal with long legs (eg Bambi)
b) dear/deer	2 a Christmas tree / hair that covers some animals
c) fir/fur	3 empty or undressed / a large animal with thick fur (eg a panda)
d) paw/poor	4 a cat has a long one / an imaginative story
e) tail/tale	5 a dog or cat's foot / the opposite of rich

2 **Match the words (a–e) with their meanings (1–5). In your language do you have words that sound the same but have different spellings and different meanings?**

Listening

1 🔵 3.25 **Listen to Tim, Gus and Maxine talking about their pets. Which questions does the interviewer ask?**

a) Can you describe your pet?
b) What does he/she eat?
c) Is he/she a good companion?
d) Who looks after him/her when you go away?
e) Do you and your pet look alike?
f) If you were an animal, what would you like to be?

▼ Tim, 24   ▼ Gus, 12   ▼ Maxine, 32

▲ Harriet, the pig   ▲ Hendrix, the spider   ▲ Page, the hamster

2 **Tick the characteristics that you think Tim, Gus and Maxine mentioned to describe their pets.**

a) He/She's a good companion. ✓
b) He/She listens to my problems.
c) He/She makes me laugh.
d) He/She frightens people away.
e) He/She keeps me fit because we go out for walks.
f) He/She looks cool.
g) He/She enjoys doing the same things as me.
h) He/She gives me unconditional love.

Listen to the interviews again and check your answers.

3 **Which of the characteristics in Exercise 2 would you look for in a pet? Which of these characteristics would you look for in a person? Discuss with a partner.**

Grammar

Unreal conditionals

If I was an animal,
I'd be a tiger.

He'd stop working
if he won the lottery.

Yasmina would like to be
a tiger.

1 Look at this question from the interview on page 100. Answer the questions.

if-clause	Main clause
if + past tense	*would* + infinitive
If you **were** an animal,	what **would** you **like** to be?

a) Is the question about a real situation or an imaginary situation?
b) Is the question about now or the past?
c) What tense is used in the *if*-clause?

Replace the word *animal* in the table above with the words in the box and/or your own ideas. Ask a partner the questions.

a car   a colour   a famous person   a fictional character   a month

2 Complete the *Imaginary situation* column with conditional sentences so that they are true for you. Compare your sentences with your partner.

Real situation	Imaginary situation
a) I'm not a man/woman.	→ *If I was a man/woman, I'd / I wouldn't _____ .*
b) I haven't got £1 million.	→ If _____ , I'd / I wouldn't _____ .
c) I don't speak English fluently.	→ If _____ , I'd / I wouldn't _____ .
d) I can't fly a plane.	→ If _____ , I'd / I wouldn't _____ .

3 Complete these 'moral dilemmas' with the correct verb form.

a) If you (find) _____ a wallet in the street with £20, would you give the wallet in to the police, but keep the cash?
b) If you saw your best friend's partner kissing someone else, (you tell) _____ your best friend?
c) If a shop assistant (give) _____ you too much change, would you keep the money?
d) If a friend left their bag at your house, (you look) _____ through it?

Work in small groups. Discuss your answers to each 'moral dilemma'. What other 'moral dilemmas' can you think of?

4 Grammar *Extra* 11, Part 2 page 146. Read the explanations and do the exercises.

Speaking: anecdote

1 ⊙ 3.26 Listen to Mandy talking about her friend's pet. Underline the correct information.

a) 'What kind of animal is it?' 'An **iguana** / **alligator**.'
b) 'Who is its owner?' '**Angus** / **Anton**.'
c) 'What's its name?' '**Indiana** / **Iggy**.'
d) 'How old is it?' 'About **five** / **fifteen**.'
e) 'What does it look like?' 'It's **green and almost a metre long** / **grey and very small**.'
f) 'Where does it sleep?' 'At the top of **a cupboard** / **the curtains**.'
g) 'What does it eat?' '**Meat** / **Vegetables**.'
h) 'How does it get exercise?' 'It **goes for walks in the park** / **runs around the garden**.'

2 You are going to tell your partner about your pet / a pet you know.

• Ask yourself the questions in Exercise 1.
• Think about *what* to say and *how* to say it.
• Tell your partner about the pet.

Useful phrases

1 🔊 **3.27 Read and listen to four telephone conversations. Who's going to look after Molly this weekend?**

a)

Sarah:	Hi, Mum!
Mum:	Hello, Sarah.
Sarah:	Could you look after Molly this weekend?
Mum:	Sorry, I can't. We're going to London this weekend.
Sarah:	OK, never mind.

b)

Sarah:	Hi, Aunty Vera.
Aunty V:	Hello, Sarah. What can I do for you?
Sarah:	I'm going away for the weekend. Would you mind looking after Molly for me?
Aunty V:	Oh, I'm afraid I can't. I'm, er, busy at the weekend.
Sarah:	OK, don't worry. See you soon.

c)

Rod:	Hi, Sarah. How are you?
Sarah:	Fine, thanks, but I've got a bit of a problem.
Rod:	Oh, what's the matter?
Sarah:	Nothing serious, but do you think you could look after Molly for the weekend?
Rod:	Molly? Oh, I'd really like to help, but I'm afraid I can't. I'm working at the weekend.
Sarah:	OK, no problem.

d)

Sarah:	Hello, Mrs Harvey. It's Sarah here.
Mrs H:	Hello, Sarah. How are you?
Sarah:	Fine, thank you. How are you?
Mrs H:	Oh, not too bad, dear.
Sarah:	Mrs Harvey, I'm going away at the weekend and I was wondering if you could look after Molly for me.
Mrs H:	Molly? Oh yes, that's no problem at all.
Sarah:	That's wonderful!
Mrs H:	Can I take her out of her cage?

2 Read the conversations again and complete the table.

Ask a favour		Accept/Refuse	Respond
a)	(1) *Could you look after Molly?*	Sorry, I can't.	Never mind.
b)	Would you mind looking after Molly?	(2) _____	OK, don't worry.
c)	(3) _____	(4) _____	OK, no problem.
d)	I was wondering if you could look after Molly.	(5) _____	(6) _____

🔊 **3.28 Listen and repeat the useful phrases.**

3 Notice the number of words in the useful phrases in Exercise 2. Complete this sentence with the correct alternative.

If you want to be formal or more polite, you usually use **more / fewer** words.

4 Work with a partner. Choose one of the situations below and write a conversation using some of the useful phrases.

- You want someone to write a job reference for you.
- You want someone to help you buy a new outfit for a friend's wedding.
- You want someone to lend you their car.

Practise your conversation.

Vocabulary *Extra*

Animals

1 Match the pictures and names of the baby animals with the adult animals.

- [5] *a kitten*: a cat
- [ ] _____ : a cow
- [ ] _____ : a dog
- [ ] _____ : a hen
- [ ] _____ : a horse
- [ ] _____ : a sheep

a puppy

a lamb

a calf

a foal

a kitten

a chick

2 Work with a partner. Cover the words and pictures. Ask and answer questions.

'What do you call a baby dog?' 'A puppy.'

Insects

1 Match the pictures with the common insects.

- [4] an ant
- [ ] a bee
- [ ] a <u>b</u>utterfly
- [ ] a <u>c</u>ockroach
- [ ] a fly
- [ ] a <u>m</u>osquito
- [ ] a <u>s</u>pider
- [ ] a wasp

2 Work with your partner. Cover the words and look at the pictures. Ask and answer questions.

'What's this?' 'It's a wasp.'

Focus on *that*

1 Complete the table with the examples in the box

> Look at that car. It's going too fast.   That's all right.   The woman that phoned me spoke French.
> ~~What's that strange noise?~~   Where are the photos that were on my desk?   Yes, that's right.

Some uses of *that*	Examples
a) *that* (+ noun) to refer to a person or thing NOT near you	'Who's that girl?' 'I don't know. I've never seen her before.' (1) *What's that strange noise?* (2) _____
b) *that* = relative pronoun	It's an insect that makes honey. (3) _____ (4) _____
c) Expressions with *that*	Hi. This is Jo. Is that Tanya? (5) 'You're Irish, aren't you?' '_____' (6) 'I forgot my homework.' '_____ . Bring it tomorrow.'

2 Write your own example sentences for each use of *that*.

12 Incredible

Grammar Past perfect. Passives. *will* and *might* for future possibility
Vocabulary Collocations with *do*, *get*, *go*, *have*, *make*, *take*. The weather
Useful phrases Exclaiming

Reading

1 Read two 'incredible but true' stories. In both stories a sentence is missing. Match sentences *a* and *b* with a story and then put the sentence in the appropriate position 1, 2, or 3.

a) At that time Amy didn't know that Ian had just started his journey from Sydney to London.

b) It was a reply from another Laura Buxton, who had found the balloon in her garden 225 kilometres away.

A *Two Lauras*

Laura Buxton was celebrating her grandparents' golden wedding anniversary, when she had an idea. **1** She decided to release a gold and white helium-filled balloon with her name and address and a note attached. In the note she asked the person who found the balloon to write back. Ten days later a letter arrived at her home. **2** Both Lauras were aged ten and both have three-year-old black Labradors, a guinea pig and a rabbit. **3** 'I chatted to Laura on the phone,' said the first Laura. 'I hope we can become best friends, because we have lots in common. We've made arrangements to meet up.'

B *Worlds apart*

Amy Dolby took her seat on the flight from London to Sydney, Australia. She was going to Australia to surprise her boyfriend, Ian Johnstone. **1** He wanted to propose to Amy on 1st July, because this was the fifth anniversary of their relationship. **2** They both stopped in Singapore to wait for connecting flights, but they didn't know that they were sitting a few metres away from one another. **3** When Ian arrived in Amy's hometown, she had been outside his door in Sydney all afternoon. When they found out what had happened, Ian proposed over the phone, and Amy accepted.

🔊 3.29 **Listen and check your answers.**

2 Are the following statements true or false?

a) Laura Buxton attached her name and address to a balloon. *True*
b) The two Lauras had never met before.
c) They had nothing in common.
d) Amy and Ian had been together for two years.
e) They met when they stopped in Singapore for connecting flights.
f) Ian asked Amy to marry him on the phone.

3 Pairwork **Student A:** page 120 **Student B:** page 125

4 Work in small groups. Discuss the questions.

- Have you ever read or heard about 'incredible but true' stories like the stories in Exercise 1?
- Do you know any people (couples, friends, colleagues) who have met in a strange way?
- Have any strange coincidences ever happened to you?

Grammar

Past perfect

I
You
He
She   'd (had) worked
It
We
They

Had you **worked?**
Yes, I **had.**
No, I **hadn't.**

1 Work with a partner. Look at this sentence from one of the stories on page 104 and discuss the questions.

When Ian <u>arrived</u> in Amy's hometown, she <u>had been</u> outside his door in Sydney all afternoon.

a) Which verb is in the past simple? Which is in the past perfect?
b) Which tense shows clearly that one past event happened before the other past event?
c) How do you form these two past tenses? Complete the table.

	Affirmative	Negative	Question
Past simple	*He arrived*	(1) _____	(2) _____ ?
Past perfect	*She had been*	(3) _____	(4) _____ ?

2 In each sentence pair underline the action that happened first.

a) 1   I had breakfast when <u>I got to work</u> this morning.
    2   <u>I'd had breakfast</u> when I got to work this morning.

b) 1   When I got home yesterday, my mum made dinner.
    2   When I got home yesterday, my mum had made dinner.

c) 1   When I started learning English, I'd been to England several times.
    2   When I started learning English, I went to England several times.

d) 1   This lesson started when I arrived.
    2   This lesson had started when I arrived.

You can use *already* in a past perfect sentence to make it clearer which action happened first. Rewrite the past perfect sentences above with *already*.

a) 2   I'd already had breakfast when I got to work this morning.

Are any of the sentences true for you?

3 Think about times that you have felt some of the emotions below. Remember what had happened to make you feel that way.

When was the last time you	felt / were	completely relaxed / a bit depressed / embarrassed really frightened / very angry ill / sad / really tired / worried	**?**	What had happened? What had you done?

Tell your partner.

'The last time I felt really tired was on Saturday. I'd been out till 3.00 a.m. ...'

4   Grammar *Extra* 12, Part 1   page 148. Read the explanations and do the exercises.

Vocabulary

1 Underline the collocations with *have*, *make* and *take* in the stories on page 104. Then complete these statements with collocations from the box.

> ~~have a go~~   have a laugh   make a promise   make money   take photos   take risks

a) Everybody should *have a go* at doing something dangerous once in their life.
b) If you don't _____ , you won't succeed in life.
c) If you can't _____ with your partner, you're in the wrong relationship.
d) The press shouldn't _____ of famous people without their permission.
e) The only reason to get a job is to _____ .
f) You should never _____ if you can't keep it.

2 Work with your partner. Decide if you agree or disagree with the statements.

Reading

1 You are going to read an article about a special hotel in Sweden. Match the figures in column *A* with the probable meanings in column *B*.

A	B
40,000	= The year the first hotel was built.
1990	= The temperature inside the hotel.
64	= The number of tons of ice and snow used to build the hotel.
14,000	= The temperature outside the hotel.
-30	= The number of rooms in the hotel.
-5	= The number of hotel guests last year.

Read the article and check your answers.

THE COOLEST HOTEL
IN THE WORLD

Can you imagine a hotel that is entirely made of ice? Well, it exists in Sweden, but only in winter. In spring, the hotel melts away and disappears into the river.

5 The Ice Hotel is situated on the shores of the Torne River in the old village of Jukkasjarvi, Sweden.

Every winter, work starts on building a new Ice Hotel, involving 40,000 tons of ice and snow. 10,000 tons of ice is taken from the Torne River, and 30,000

10 tons of snow is provided by Mother Nature.

The first Ice Hotel was built in 1990. It started as a single room – now it has 64 rooms, as well as an ice chapel, an art gallery, a cinema, a theatre and an Absolut Ice Bar. Last winter, more than 14,000

15 guests spent the night at the Ice Hotel.

Outside, the temperature is -30°C, but inside the hotel, the temperature is always around -5°C. All the furniture is made of ice, including the beds, but nobody gets cold. The beds are covered

20 with reindeer skins and guests are given warm clothes and special arctic sleeping bags.

In the Absolut Ice Bar, the drinks are served in glasses made of ice, so there is no need for ice cubes!

25 Every year the interior of the hotel is designed by different artists from all over the world. It is described by visitors as 'absolutely stunning', 'one of the most beautiful places I've ever seen' and 'unique'.

2 Work with a partner. Answer the questions about the Ice Hotel.

a) Where is it situated?
b) What is it built of?
c) What is the furniture made of?
d) What are the beds covered with?
e) Who is the interior designed by?
f) How is it described by visitors?

What's the best or worst hotel you've ever stayed in? Tell your partner.

Grammar

Passives

English **is spoken** here.
Rome **wasn't built** in a day.

Were these toys **made**
in China?
Yes, they **were**.
No, they **weren't**.

1 Look at the table and decide if the statements *a–c* are true or false.

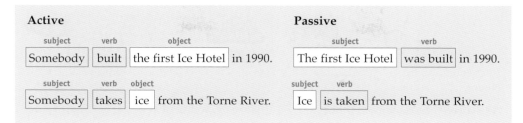

Active		
subject	verb	object
Somebody	built	the first Ice Hotel in 1990.

	subject	verb	
Somebody	takes	ice	from the Torne River.

Passive		
subject	verb	
The first Ice Hotel	was built	in 1990.

subject	verb	
Ice	is taken	from the Torne River.

a) The object of an active sentence becomes the subject of a passive sentence.
b) You make the passive with the correct form of *be* (*is, was*, etc.) + a past participle (*made, used*, etc.).
c) You can use passive verb structures to talk about actions when it doesn't matter (or you don't know) who performed them.

2 Complete the questions and answers.

a) '*Was* your house built before 1980?'   'Yes, it *was*.'   'No, it *wasn't*.'
b) '*Were* your shoes designed in Italy?'   'Yes, they _____ .'   'No, they _____ .'
c) '*Is* your salary paid by cheque?'   'Yes, _____ .'   'No, _____ .'
d) '_____ you invited to any parties last week?'   '_____ .'   '_____ .'
e) '_____ your name spelt the same in English?'   '_____ .'   '_____ .'
f) '_____ your mobile phone made in Japan?'   '_____ .'   '_____ .'

🔘 **3.30** Listen, check and repeat.

3 Work with a partner. Ask and answer the questions in Exercise 2.

4 Grammar *Extra* **12, Part 2** page 148. Read the explanations and do the exercises.

Speaking: anecdote

1 🔘 **3.31** Listen to Curro talking about the most incredible building he's ever seen. Underline the correct information.

a) 'What is the most incredible building you've ever seen?' 'The **Colosseum** / **Alhambra**.'
b) 'Where is it?' 'In **the South of Spain** / **Rome**.'
c) 'When did you first see this building?' '**When I was eighteen** / **Two years ago**.'
d) 'When was it built?' '**In the 13th or 14th century** / **Five years ago**.'
e) 'Can you describe it?' '**The style is Moorish** / **It's a modern building**.'
f) 'What is so incredible about it?' 'The **location** / **interior design**.'
g) 'How many times have you been there?' '**Only once** / **Four times**.'

2 You are going to tell your partner about the most incredible building you've ever seen.

- Ask yourself the questions in Exercise 1.
- Think about *what* to say and *how* to say it.
- Tell your partner about the most incredible building you've ever seen.

Vocabulary & Listening

1 Complete the table with the appropriate words.

Noun	(1) *sun*	cloud	(3) _____	fog	(5) _____	snow	(6) _____
Adjective / Phrase	It's sunny. It's fine / dry. It's warm / hot.	It's (2) _____ . It's dull.	It's rainy / wet. It's raining.	It's (4) _____ .	It's windy. It's cold / freezing.	It's snowing.	It's stormy.

2 Read the winter weather forecast for the North Pole. Underline the most likely information.

> **The North Pole in winter**
>
> Today will start off extremely (1) **wet / cold** with temperatures of (2) **minus 13 / minus 30** degrees Celsius. It will be very (3) **warm / windy** in the afternoon, and it will probably (4) **rain / snow** later on. It will be (5) **dark / sunny** all day. Tomorrow will be the same, and the next day, and the day after. Summer might be a bit (6) **warmer / colder** , but not much.

🌐 3.32 Listen and check your answers.

3 Invent a weather forecast for autumn, winter, spring or summer for your own country by replacing the highlighted words in Exercise 2. Ask a partner to read your weather forecast and guess the season.

Grammar

will and might for future possibility

It'll definitely be dry.
I think it'll be sunny.
It **might** be cloudy.
I don't think it'll rain.
It definitely **won't** freeze.

(*won't* = will not)

1 Complete these predictions about the weather with the word in brackets.

a) The south definitely have better weather than the north. (will)
   The south will definitely have better weather than the north.

b) Tomorrow probably be warmer than today. (will)

c) I think we have a lot of snow next winter. (will)

d) It rain later today. (might)

e) I don't think there be any storms tomorrow. (will)

f) It probably be so sunny tomorrow. (won't)

g) It definitely freeze tomorrow. (won't)

will happen
✓✓✓✓✓
✓✓✓
✓
might happen
✗
✗✗✗
✗✗✗✗✗
won't happen

Rewrite the sentences so they are true for where you live. Compare with your partner.

2 Work with your partner. Use words and phrases in the box to complete the predictions (*a–f*) about people in the class.

> definitely   I don't think   I think   might   probably   will   won't

a) _____ retire by the age of sixty.
   Ricardo will probably retire by the age of sixty.

b) _____ live and work in a foreign country.
   I don't think Rosa will live and work in a foreign country.

c) _____ set up and run a company.

d) _____ travel round the world.

e) _____ write a famous song.

f) _____ have five or more children.

Read out your predictions and see if people agree or disagree with you.

Reading & Speaking

1 **Work with a partner. Read the instructions, consult**
   ***The Oracle* and find out about your future!**

The Oracle

You'll need some dice!

Instructions

- Choose a question (*A–F*) you want to ask.
- Take it in turns to roll the dice with the question in your mind.
- Find the letter corresponding to your question and the number you threw on the dice. Find your answer where they meet. For example: you asked question D (*How many children will I have?*) and you threw 4, so *The Oracle* says 'One of each.'

Questions

A: What will the love of my life look like?
B: Will I be famous one day?
C: Will I travel the world?
D: How many children will I have?
E: Where will I be most happy?
F: What will I look like in ten years' time?

	1	2	3	4	5	6
A	Not as you expect.	Gorgeous.	Not classically good-looking but you'll never look at anybody else.	Very fit.	He/She will have wonderful eyes.	He/She'll look like you.
B	No, you won't.	No, but you'll meet someone famous.	You'll be well-known in your profession.	You'll be in the news for doing something crazy.	You'll have your fifteen minutes of fame.	Yes, but you'll have to work very hard.
C	Yes, for pleasure.	Yes, for your job.	No, but you'll travel in your own country.	No, but you'll meet people from all over the world.	You'll have wonderful holidays abroad.	You'll travel when you're older.
D	More than you expect.	The same as your parents.	Your career will be more important.	One of each.	You'll have a big family.	Enough.
E	At home in bed.	In the mountains.	Abroad.	Near the sea.	Everywhere.	In a big city.
F	Completely different.	Like your mother.	Fabulous.	Younger than you are.	No different.	Like your father.

How likely/unlikely do you think the predictions from *The Oracle* are?

2 **Think about the topics in the box below and use the sentence beginnings to write**
   about your life in the future. Discuss your ideas with your partner.

> family   children   relationships   health and fitness   house   job   travel
> possessions   money   free time   hair   English

> I'll definitely … / I definitely won't …   I'll probably… / I probably won't …
> I hope I'll … / I hope I won't …   I think I'll … / I don't think I'll …

Useful phrases

1 🔵 **3.33 Listen to the conversation between Agnes and Betty and underline the topics in the box that they talk about.**

> politics   clothes   cooking   celebrities   houses   children   travel   weddings

2 **Complete the conversation with *very* or *absolutely*.**

A: Oh, look at that dress.

B: It's (1) *very* pretty, isn't it?

A: It's (2) *absolutely* gorgeous!

B: It's Armani. £7,500.

A: What? That's (3) _____ expensive.

B: I know. It's (4) _____ ridiculous! ... Oh, is that George Clooney?

A: Yes. Oh, dear. He looks (5) _____ tired, doesn't he?

B: Tired? He looks (6) _____ exhausted!

A: And look at his suit. It's not (7) _____ nice.

B: It's (8) _____ awful! What's happened to him?

A: I don't know. ... Oh, that house is lovely.

B: It's (9) _____ big, isn't it?

A: It's (10) _____ enormous! Who does it belong to?

B: Er ... Cristiano Ronaldo.

A: Who's he?

B: I've no idea. ... Ahh. Look at the little girl. She's (11) _____ cute.

A: She's (12) _____ adorable! Who are her parents?

B: Angelina Jolie and Brad Pitt.

A: That's (13) _____ strange. She doesn't look anything like them.

B: I know! It's (14) _____ incredible!

Listen again and check your answers.

3 🔵 **3.34 Listen and repeat the useful phrases. Notice and practise the intonation.**

a) 'It's very pretty.' 'It's absolutely gorgeous!'
b) 'That's very expensive.' 'It's absolutely ridiculous!'
c) 'He looks very tired.' 'He looks absolutely exhausted!'
d) 'It's not very nice.' 'It's absolutely awful!'
e) 'It's very big.' 'It's absolutely enormous!'
f) 'She's very cute.' 'She's absolutely adorable!'
g) 'That's very strange.' 'It's absolutely incredible!'

4 **Work with a partner. Complete the table with the appropriate adjectives from the box.**

> delicious   funny   good   ~~impossible~~

With *very*	difficult	(2) _____	(3) _____	tasty
With *absolutely*	(1) *impossible*	hilarious	brilliant	(4) _____

5 **Imagine Agnes and Betty are looking at a different page in their magazines. Continue their conversation using the adjectives in Exercises 3 and 4 or your own ideas. Practise the conversation.**

Vocabulary *Extra*

Weather

1 Match the pictures with the words.

	Noun	Adjective
9	breeze	*breezy*
☐	cloud	____
☐	fog	____
☐	____	hot
☐	humidity	____
☐	____	icy
☐	____	misty
☐	rain	____
☐	____	showery
☐	____	stormy
☐	sun	____
☐	____	windy

2 Complete the *Noun* and *Adjective* columns.

3 Look at the different ways of saying how hot or cold it is. Write a temperature in °C to show what each term means to you.

boiling = over 30°C

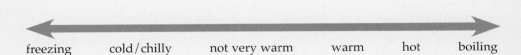

freezing   cold/chilly   not very warm   warm   hot   boiling

Compare your ideas with a partner.

Focus on *do, get, go, have, make, take*

1 Complete the collocation tables with the verbs in the box.

> do   ~~get~~   go   have   make   take

a) *get*	better changed dressed lost married	b) ____	a go a good time a laugh a rest lunch	c) ____	a bus a photo an exam responsibility risks
d) ____	a decision a living a promise mistakes money	e) ____	a course research some homework the housework the shopping	f) ____	for a drink for a walk home mad skiing

2 Look in your dictionary. Find another collocation for each verb.

Review D

▶ Grammar *Extra* pages 144–149

Grammar

1 Complete the sentences with the *will* future.

a) Jim (help) *will help* you with your work.
b) The doctor (not have) _____ time to see you today.
c) We (send) _____ you a postcard from New York.
d) (Sara be) _____ here again tomorrow?
e) They (not eat) _____ at that restaurant again.
f) (you see) _____ Liz later?

2 Underline the correct conjunctions.

a) **If** / **When** he likes the company, he'll take the job.
b) **If** / **When** they finish dinner, they'll go home.
c) You'll see our house in front of you **as soon as** / **if** you turn the corner.
d) **If** / **When** you go to bed, please put the cat outside.
e) **As soon as** / **If** it rains today, I'll stay inside.
f) Don't worry – I'll phone you **as soon as** / **if** I get home.

3 Where possible, replace the past simple with *used to* / *didn't use to* + infinitive.

When I was a child …
a) I lived in a flat. *I used to live in a flat.*
b) I broke my arm.
c) I didn't have a bicycle.
d) I won a dance competition.
e) my family didn't watch TV.
f) I didn't like classical music.

Write down three things you used to do. Make one of them false. Can your partner guess which one is false?

4 Use *who* or *which* to combine the sentences.

a) She has a cat. It never stops eating.
    She has a cat which never stops eating.
b) I have a friend. She lives in Australia.
c) I have a phone. It takes good photos.
d) Where are the eggs? They were in the fridge.
e) Those are the people. They bought my old house.
f) She has a boyfriend. He's a doctor.

5 Complete the conversation with the correct form of the verbs.

A: What (1 you do) *would you do* if you (2 win) _____ £10 million?
B: I think I (3 buy) _____ a new car and a new house. What about you?
A: If I (4 win) _____ £10 million, I (5 get) _____ a car too, but I (6 not buy) _____ a new house. I like our house now.
B: (7 you give) _____ any money to me?
A: Maybe. Why?
B: Because if I (8 have) _____ any money I (9 give) _____ you half of it.
A: Ahh. You're so nice.

6 Read the story and number the events (*a–f*) in order (1–6).

Yesterday Mike had a bad day. He woke up late, and his wife had already gone to work. He got dressed and rushed to the station, but when he got to the station, the train had left and he had missed it. He had an important meeting at 10.00. But when he got to work, the meeting had already started. His boss was furious!

a) Mike arrived at the station.
b) Mike's wife went to work. *1*
c) The meeting started.
d) The train left the station.
e) Mike woke up.
f) Mike arrived at work.

7 Write questions in the past passive.

a) your car / make / in Spain ?
    Was your car made in Spain?
b) your house / build / in the 20th century ?
c) your shoes / make / in Brazil ?
d) your jacket / design / by Armani ?
e) watch / make / in Japan ?
f) your computer / manufacture / in China ?

Answer the questions. Compare with your partner.

8 Spot the mistake! Cross out the incorrect sentence.

1 a) Did you use to visit the zoo?
   b) Did you used to visit the zoo?

2 a) A teacher is a person who works in a school.
   b) A teacher is a person which works in a school.

3 a) If you would have a pet, what would it be?
   b) If you had a pet, what would it be?

4 a) When I got home I had made lunch.
   b) When I got home I made lunch.

5 a) This watch is make of gold.
   b) This watch is made of gold.

6 a) It might rain tomorrow.
   b) It might to rain tomorrow.

Vocabulary

1 Complete the sentences with the words and expressions in the box.

> a brisk walk   a good network   ~~a healthy life~~
> extended family   fit   in a hurry

a) For *a healthy life* I try to eat well and exercise often.
b) I have a big _____ .
c) I always go for _____ after lunch.
d) I should slow down. I'm always _____ .
e) It's important to have _____ of friends.
f) I do martial arts to keep _____ .

Tick the statements that are true for you. Compare with a partner.

2 Put the words in the box in three groups.

> ~~beans~~   chicken   garlic   lettuce   nuts   onion
> orange   peach   prawns   sausage   soup
> tea   tomato   trout

Fruit and vegetables	Meat and fish	Other
		beans

3 Complete the words in the recipe.

Healthy roast potatoes
1 *Peel* and wash the potatoes. B__ __l them for ten minutes.
2 Ch__p some garlic and mix it with some olive oil.
3 P__t the olive oil and garlic in the bottom of a dish.
4 Sl__c__ the potatoes and put them in the olive oil in the dish.
5 B__k__ them in the oven for an hour and a half.

4 Underline the correct preposition.

a) I'm very fond **on** / **of** chocolate.
b) I'm terrified **on** / **of** snakes.
c) I'm not very keen **on** / **of** tennis.
d) I'm not afraid **of** / **by** spiders, but I don't like them.
e) I'm allergic **of** / **to** strawberries.
f) I'm very interested **in** / **of** old French films.

Tick the statements that are true for you. Compare with your partner.

5 Find sixteen animals in the box. Look → and ↓.

E	R	A	V	C	A	T	I	P	D
A	S	H	A	R	K	H	N	E	O
G	W	L	I	O	N	F	R	O	G
L	E	B	M	C	I	A	T	W	Z
E	X	R	D	O	L	P	H	I	N
H	W	A	Q	D	X	B	A	T	M
O	A	T	L	I	F	U	I	Y	O
R	S	J	F	L	P	L	D	E	U
S	P	I	D	E	R	L	U	N	S
E	O	G	Y	V	S	N	A	K	E

6 Complete the questions with *take, have* or *make*.

a) Would you prefer to *make* money or have a job you love?
b) Would you like to _____ a go at bungee jumping?
c) Do you _____ risks, or are you careful?
d) Do you ever _____ promises that you couldn't keep?
e) Do you like to _____ a laugh, or are you a serious person?
f) Do you _____ great photographs?

Answer the questions. Compare with your partner.

7 Use the words in the box to complete five phrases beginning with *It's* and four phrases beginning with *I like.*

> ~~clouds~~   ~~rainy~~   snow   snowing   storms
> sunny   the sun   wet   windy

a) It's *rainy*, _____ , _____ , _____ , _____
b) I like *clouds*, _____ , _____ , _____

Pronunciation

1 Look at some words from Units 10–12. Say the words and add them to the table.

> ~~afraid~~   ~~animal~~   arrive   dangerous   enjoy
> ~~fitness~~   gardening   healthy   holiday   lettuce
> promise   rainy   relax   sardine   terrified

A: ☐☐	B: ☐☐	C: ☐☐☐
fitness	*afraid*	*animal*

2 Underline the stressed syllable.

🌐 3.35 Listen, check and repeat.

Reading & Listening

1 🌐 **3.36 Read the article and match the animals (*a–e*) to the incredible journeys they make.**

a) Albatross — 3,500 kilometres
b) Humpback whale — 40,000 kilometres
c) Monarch butterfly — 3,000 kilometres
d) Green turtle — 8,000 kilometres
e) Wildebeest — 2,000 kilometres

THE TOP FIVE MOST
incredible animal journeys

Albatrosses spend 85% of their lives travelling. They can even sleep while they're flying. Most albatrosses fly around the world at least once a year and some do it several times. And what's even more incredible is that the 40,000-kilometre journey can take them as little as forty-six days.

Humpback whales are experienced long-distance travellers. They spend the summer in the Arctic, where they eat a ton of food every day. As soon as winter comes, they swim 8,000 kilometres to warmer waters in the Pacific Ocean near the Equator to give birth. They don't eat during the winter. There are now around 40,000 humpback whales in our oceans, but there used to be around 120,000.

Every autumn thousands of **Monarch butterflies** start their journey in the east of the United States and fly west for the warm air of Mexico. Some can fly as far as 3,500 kilometres. They have to fly fast to finish their journey before winter. When spring comes, they leave Mexico and travel back east, where they lay their eggs and die.

Female **green turtles** return to their birthplace every two or three years to start a family. They swim 2,000 kilometres from their home in Brazilian waters to Ascension Island in the Atlantic Ocean. They lay between 100 and 200 eggs on the beach and cover them before returning to the water and swimming home.

Serengeti wildebeest spend more than half of their lives travelling. Every May, around one and a half million wildebeest travel approximately 3,000 kilometres around Tanzania and Kenya looking for food and water. They return when the rain comes, in November, and give birth.

2 **Read the text again and find which animal …**

a) spends the most time travelling in a year.
b) travels in large numbers looking for water.
c) dies after it lays its eggs.
d) spends the summer in a cold place and the winter in a warm place.
e) returns to its birthplace to lay eggs.

3 🌐 **3.37 Listen to Dom talking to Lou about a long journey. Are these statements true or false?**

a) Lou went on holiday with Dom. *False.*
b) Koh Tao means 'Turtle Island'.
c) Their journey started in the evening.
d) They slept well on their journey.
e) They enjoyed the coffee at the station.
f) They waited for four hours for the bus to arrive.
g) It rained all the time.

4 **Listen again and match the narrative linker with the event.**

a) At first — 1 we arrived at Koh Tao.
b) After an hour — 2 we felt excited.
c) The next morning — 3 it started raining.
d) Four hours later — 4 the bus arrived.
e) Then — 5 at three o'clock, the train stopped.
f) Eventually — 6 we started feeling quite tired.

Writing & Speaking

1 **Complete the text about a journey. Use the words in the box.**

At first	Eventually	four days	suddenly
Then	The next day	~~Two years ago~~	

(1) *Two years ago* we decided to drive from São Paulo to Recife, in the north-east of Brazil. We set off early in the morning of 26th December. (2) _____ we made good progress. We spent the night in a small, friendly hotel. (3) _____ we passed Rio de Janeiro on our journey north, but some roads had been damaged by rain, which slowed us down. After (4) _____ , we arrived in Porto Seguro, where we met up with some friends for New Year. (5) _____ our problems started. We were driving to Salvador when, (6) _____ , our car broke down. We couldn't go anywhere for three more days while the car was being fixed. After that we went on, but the engine problems continued. (7) _____ we decided to turn back. We were only 280 kilometres away from Recife!

2 **Put the words in the correct order to make questions.**

a) journey / start / you / did / your / Where ?
   Where did you start your journey?
b) you / did / go / Where ?
c) there / you / How / get / did ?
d) did / Where / at / night / stay / you ?
e) have / you / Did / problems / any ?
f) enjoy / you / your / Did / journey ?
g) journey / the / How / long / take / did ?
h) you / Would / again / it / do ?

Which questions were answered by the text?

3 **Think about the longest journey you've ever been on.**

- Think about how you would answer the questions in Exercise 2.
- Tell your partner about your journey.
- Use some of the expressions in Exercise 1.

4 **Write an account of the longest journey you've ever been on. Use some of the phrases from Exercise 1 and answer some of the questions from Exercise 2.**

▶ 🔊 **3.38 Song:** *I Have A Dream*

Pairwork: Student A

Unit 1 UK quiz

You are going to ask Student B some general knowledge questions about the UK.

- Complete the questions with *What, Which, Who, Where* or *How.*
- Ask Student B the questions and give the three possible answers (*a, b, c*). (The correct answers are highlighted.)
- Compare your scores.

1 *What* **is the capital city of Wales?**
   a) Edinburgh b) Cardiff c) Belfast

2 **_____ does the British Prime Minister live?**
   a) Buckingham Palace
   b) The Tower of London
   c) 10 Downing Street

3 **_____ is the nickname of the clock tower on the Houses of Parliament?**
   a) Big Bill b) Big Ben c) Big Bob

4 **_____ is Queen Elizabeth's daughter?**
   a) Princess Ann b) Princess Margaret
   c) Princess Diana

5 **_____ pop star is not British?**
   a) Robbie Williams b) George Michael
   c) Madonna

6 **_____ many players are there in a cricket team?**
   a) Five b) Eleven c) Fifteen

Unit 2 Eight cities

You have eight maps of different countries (*a–h*).

- Four cities are marked on maps *a–d*. Describe to Student B exactly where these cities are.
- Student B will describe the locations of the other four cities (*e–h*). Mark them on your maps.
- Compare your maps with Student B.

▲ Japan ▲ France ▲ South Korea ▲ Iceland

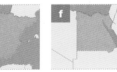 

▲ Spain ▲ Egypt ▲ Australia ▲ Czech Republic

Unit 3 What were you doing yesterday?

Find out if you were doing the same things at the same times as Student B yesterday.

- Complete the sentences in the *Me* column describing what you were doing yesterday at those times.
- Ask Student B questions beginning: *What were …?* and complete the *Student B* column.
  Student A: What were you doing at 6.00 a.m?
  Student B: I was sleeping.
- Were you doing the same thing or different things?

Me	Student B	✓ = We were doing the same thing ✗ = We were doing different things
a) At 6.00 a.m. I was _____	*He / She was* _____	_____
b) At 7.30 a.m. I was _____	_____	_____
c) At 10.00 a.m. I was _____	_____	_____
d) At 1.00 p.m. I was _____	_____	_____
e) At 6.00 p.m. I was _____	_____	_____
f) At 11.00 p.m. I was _____	_____	_____

Unit 4 What's happening in your life?

How much do you know about what's happening in Student B's life at the moment?

- Write sentences in the affirmative or negative according to what you think.
- Ask Student B questions to check if you were right or wrong.

Student A: Are you trying to give up smoking?   Student B: Yes, I am.   Student A: I was right!

Student B's name: _____	✓ = I was right! ✗ = I was wrong!
a) try to give up smoking *He/She is trying to give up smoking.*	✓
b) learn to type _____	_____
c) write a book _____	_____
d) look for a new place to live _____	_____
e) apply for jobs _____	_____
f) learn to dance _____	_____
g) _____	_____

Unit 5 Trivia quiz

You and Student B each have six trivia questions. You have the correct answers to Student B's questions in the box below. Student B has the correct answers to your questions.

- Look at the trivia questions in the table and guess the answers.
- Complete the *My guess* column with your ideas.
- Ask Student B the questions and complete the *Correct answer* column.
- Compare your guesses with the correct answers. How good or bad were your guesses?

Trivia questions	My guess	Correct answer
a) How fast can a dolphin swim?	_____	_____
b) How much money did JK Rowling (author of *Harry Potter*) earn in 2005?	_____	_____
c) How many words does a woman speak in a normal day?	_____	_____
d) What percentage of the body's energy does the brain use?	_____	_____
e) What is the longest distance ever travelled in a wheelchair?	_____	_____
f) What is the highest rugby score ever recorded?	_____	_____

Answers to Student B's questions   105 km/h $93,820,000   2,175   2%   4,203 km   9–0

Unit 6 Experiences

What experiences has Student B had?

- Write Student B's name in the space below.
- Write statements (*a–g*) that you think are true.
- Write questions to check your statements.
- Ask Student B the questions.

_____ (Student B's name) ...	Questions	✓ = I'm right! ✗ = I'm wrong!
a) break his/her leg *Ana has (never) broken her leg.*	*Have you ever broken your leg?* _____	_____
b) sing karaoke	_____	_____
c) ride a horse	_____	_____
d) go fishing	_____	_____
e) drink whisky	_____	_____
f) buy a painting	_____	_____
g) _____	_____	_____

Unit 7 Your perfect week

Imagine that next week is going to be your perfect week.

- Fill in your diary page below with two appointments each day. Use your imagination!
- Include three activities that you would like to do with Student B.
- Ask Student B if he or she is free to join you at those times.
- Discuss other possible times and note the final arrangements.

Student A: Would you like to go shopping on Monday afternoon?
Student B: No, thanks. I'm having a cup of tea with David Beckham.
Student A: How about Thursday afternoon?
Student B: Oh, yes. I'd love to.

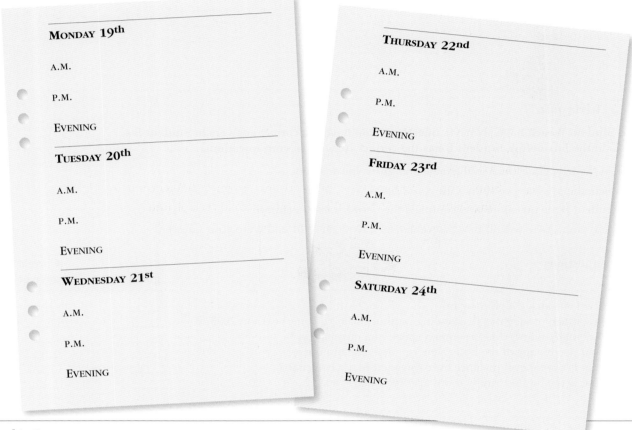

MONDAY 19th

A.M.

P.M.

EVENING

TUESDAY 20th

A.M.

P.M.

EVENING

WEDNESDAY 21st

A.M.

P.M.

EVENING

THURSDAY 22nd

A.M.

P.M.

EVENING

FRIDAY 23rd

A.M.

P.M.

EVENING

SATURDAY 24th

A.M.

P.M.

EVENING

Unit 8 School obligations

You are going to talk about things you had to do and things you didn't have to do when you were at school.

- Complete the sentences in the *Me* column with *I had to* or *I didn't have to*.
- Ask Student B questions beginning *Did you have to …* and complete the Student B column.

Student A: Did you have to get up before 7.00 a.m.?   *Student B: Yes, I did.*

- Compare your experiences. Were they the same or different?

Me	Student B	✓ = The same ✗ = Different
a) _____ get up before 7.00 a.m.	He/She _____	_____
b) _____ walk to school.	_____	_____
c) _____ learn English.	_____	_____
d) _____ wear a school uniform.	_____	_____
e) _____ turn off my mobile phone in class.	_____	_____
f) _____ do homework every night.	_____	_____

Unit 9 Spot the differences!

- Look at pictures *1* and *2*. Student B has the same faces, but there are two small differences in each face.
- Describe the two faces to Student B and find the two differences in each picture.

Student A: In the first picture it's a man's face. He has a beard. He has straight hair …
Student B: In my picture he has curly hair.

- Look at pictures *3* and *4*. Student B has the same faces, but there are two small differences in each face.
- Listen to Student B describing the two faces and find the two differences in each picture.

Student B: In the third picture it's a woman's face. She has dark hair. She has blue eyes …
Student A: In my picture she has brown eyes.

Unit 10 Ten years ago

- Think about your life ten years ago.
- Write six sentences – five true and one false – describing ways in which your life was different then. Choose from the topics below or use your own ideas.

| car | clothes | favourite actors | friends | going out | hair styles | hobbies | holidays |
| music | school | sport | TV programmes |

I used to have a red Ferrari.   I used to wear Armani suits.   I used to …

- Read all your sentences. Student B guesses which sentence is false.
- Compare your lives then and now. How similar were your lives ten years ago?

Unit 11 Animal definitions

You are going to read out three definitions of some common English expressions. The definitions with crosses are false, and the one with a tick is true. Student B has to guess which definition (*1, 2* or *3*) is the correct one.

- Complete one false definition for each expression. Use your imagination!
- Read out your three definitions and see if Student B can guess which one is correct.
- Then listen to Student B's expressions and guess which of his/her definitions is correct.

a) A '**fat cat**' is ...
   1 somebody who is high up in the world of business. ✓
   2 somebody who needs to go on a diet. ✗
   3 somebody who _____ . ✗

b) A person who's '**chicken**' is ...
   1 somebody who _____ . ✗
   2 somebody who isn't brave. ✓
   3 somebody who talks a lot. ✗

c) A '**white elephant**' is ...
   1 a gift that is very unusual and valuable. ✗
   2 a gift that you don't want because you don't know what to do with it. ✓
   3 a gift that is _____ . ✗

d) A '**ratty**' person is ...
   1 somebody who is easily annoyed. ✓
   2 somebody who doesn't dress very well. ✗
   3 somebody who _____ . ✗

e) A person who '**bugs**' you is ...
   1 somebody who imitates you. ✗
   2 somebody who _____ . ✗
   3 somebody who annoys you. ✓

Unit 12 Emily and Peter

You are going to complete a story about Emily and Peter. You have parts of the story. Student B has other parts.

- Dictate your parts of the story to Student B.
- Listen and write down Student B's parts of the story.
- Compare your completed texts. They should be identical.

TEXT
before marriage

A clairvoyant had once told Emily Brown that she would meet her husband when she was 21.

She was _____

One day, she tapped the text message, 'Do you want to talk?' into her mobile. She then invented a number and sent the message.

She didn't know _____

He phoned Emily, and they chatted for about an hour. They found that they had lots in common and made arrangements to meet.

They _____

Pairwork: Student B

Unit 1 UK quiz

You are going to ask Student A some general knowledge questions about the UK.

- Complete the questions with *What, Which, Who, Where* or *How*.
- Ask Student A the questions and give the three possible answers (*a, b, c*). (The correct answers are highlighted.)
- Compare your scores.

1 *What* is the population of the UK?
   a) 40 million   b) 60 million
   c) 100 million

2 _____ is John Lennon airport?
   a) Liverpool   b) Manchester   c) Belfast

3 _____ is the nickname of the UK flag?
   a) The Union Jack   b) The Union Jill
   c) The Union John

4 _____ was Robin Hood's enemy?
   a) The Sheriff of Tottenham
   b) The Sheriff of Birmingham
   c) The Sheriff of Nottingham

5 _____ political party did Margaret Thatcher lead?
   a) The Labour Party   b) The Conservative Party
   c) The Liberal Democrat Party

6 _____ many pence are there in a pound?
   a) Ten   b) Fifty   c) One hundred

Unit 2 Eight cities

You have eight maps of different countries (*a–h*).

- Four cities are marked on maps (*e–h*). Describe to Student A exactly where these cities are.
- Student A will describe the locations of the other four cities (*a–d*). Mark them on your maps.
- Compare your maps with Student A.

▲ Japan

▲ France

▲ South Korea

▲ Iceland

Barcelona •
▲ Spain

Cairo •
▲ Egypt

Melbourne •
▲ Australia

Prague •
▲ Czech Republic

Unit 3 What were you doing yesterday?

Find out if you were doing the same things at the same times as Student A yesterday.

- Complete the sentences in the *Me* column describing what you were doing yesterday at those times.
- Ask Student A questions beginning: *What were …?* and complete the *Student A* column.

   Student B: What were you doing at 6.00 a.m?
   Student A: I was sleeping.

- Were you doing the same thing or different things?

Me	Student A	✓ = We were doing the same thing ✗ = We were doing different things
a) At 6.00 a.m. I was _____	He / She was _____	_____
b) At 7.30 a.m. I was _____	_____	_____
c) At 10.00 a.m. I was _____	_____	_____
d) At 1.00 p.m. I was _____	_____	_____
e) At 6.00 p.m. I was _____	_____	_____
f) At 11.00 p.m. I was _____	_____	_____

Unit 4 What's happening in your life?

How much do you know about what's happening in Student A's life at the moment?

- Write sentences in the affirmative or negative according to what you think.
- Ask Student A questions to check if you were right or wrong.

  Student B: Are you trying to do more exercise?   *Student A: Yes, I am.*   *Student B: I was right!*

Student A's name: _____	✓ = I was right! ✗ = I was wrong!
a) try to do more exercise *He/She is trying to do more exercise.*	✓
b) learn to drive _____	_____
c) plan a trip abroad _____	_____
d) read a good book _____	_____
e) look for a new job _____	_____
f) learn to play the guitar _____	_____
g) _____	_____

Unit 5 Trivia quiz

You and Student A each have six trivia questions. You have the correct answers to Student A's questions in the box below. Student A has the correct answers to your questions.

- Look at the trivia questions in the table and guess the answers.
- Complete the *My guess* column with your ideas.
- Ask Student A the questions and complete the *Correct answer* column.
- Compare your guesses with the correct answers. How good or bad were your guesses?

Trivia questions	My guess	Correct answer
a) How fast can a cheetah run?	_____	_____
b) How much money did Dan Brown (author of *The Da Vinci Code*) earn in 2005?	_____	_____
c) How many words does a man speak in a normal day?	_____	_____
d) What percentage of the body's weight is the brain?	_____	_____
e) What is the longest distance ever travelled on a windsurfer?	_____	_____
f) What is the highest World Cup football score ever recorded?	_____	_____

Answers to Student A's questions   30 km/h $80,137,000   7,120   20%   40,075.16 km   194–0

Unit 6 Experiences

What experiences has Student A had?

- Write Student A's name in the space below.
- Write statements (*a–g*) that you think are true.
- Write questions to check your statements.
- Ask Student A the questions to find out if you are right or wrong.

_____ (Student A's name) ...	Questions	✓ = I'm right! ✗ = I'm wrong!
a) go to the USA *Jan has (never) been to the USA.*	*Have you ever been to the USA?*	_____
b) give a speech	_____	_____
c) break the speed limit	_____	_____
d) cut somebody's hair	_____	_____
e) cry at the cinema	_____	_____
f) forget his/her mother's birthday	_____	_____
g) _____	_____	_____

Unit 7 Your perfect week

Imagine that next week is going to be your perfect week.

- Fill in your diary page below with two appointments each day. Use your imagination!
- Include three activities that you would like to do with Student A.
- Ask Student A if he or she is free to join you at those times.
- Discuss other possible times and note the final arrangements.

Student B: Would you like to go to the beach on Tuesday afternoon?
Student A: No, thanks, I'm going shopping with Paris Hilton.
Student B: How about Wednesday afternoon?
Student A: Oh, yes. I'd love to.

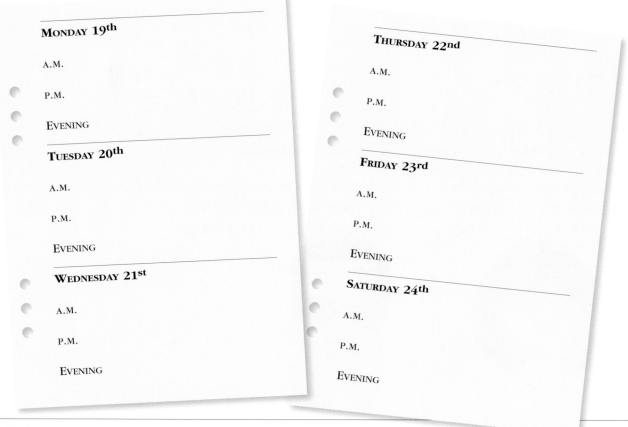

MONDAY 19th

A.M.

P.M.

EVENING

TUESDAY 20th

A.M.

P.M.

EVENING

WEDNESDAY 21st

A.M.

P.M.

EVENING

THURSDAY 22nd

A.M.

P.M.

EVENING

FRIDAY 23rd

A.M.

P.M.

EVENING

SATURDAY 24th

A.M.

P.M.

EVENING

Unit 8 School obligations

You are going to talk about things you had to do and things you didn't have to do when you were at school.

- Complete the sentences in the *Me* column with *I had to* or *I didn't have to*.
- Ask Student A questions beginning *Did you have to …* and complete the Student A column.

Student B: Did you have to go to school by bus?   Student A: Yes, I did.

- Compare your experiences. Were they the same or different?

Me	Student A	✓ = The same ✗ = Different
a) _____ go to school by bus.	He/She _____	_____
b) _____ play team sports.	_____	_____
c) _____ sit at the same desk every day.	_____	_____
d) _____ have lunch at school.	_____	_____
e) _____ take exams every year.	_____	_____
f) _____ go to bed before 10.00 p.m.	_____	_____

Unit 9 Spot the differences!

- Look at pictures *1* and *2*. Student A has the same faces, but there are two small differences in each face.

- Listen to Student A describing the two faces and find the two differences in each picture.

Student A: In the first picture it's a man's face. He has a beard. He has straight hair …
Student B: In my picture he has curly hair.

- Look at pictures *3* and *4*. Student A has the same faces, but there are two small differences in each face.

- Describe the two faces to Student A and find the two differences in each picture.

Student B: In the third picture it's a woman's face. She has dark hair. She has blue eyes …
Student A: In my picture she has brown eyes.

Unit 10 Ten years ago

- Think about your life ten years ago.

- Write six sentences – five true and one false – describing ways in which your life was different then. Choose from the topics below or use your own ideas.

car   clothes   favourite actors   friends   going out   hair styles   hobbies   holidays
music   school   sport   TV programmes

I used to like Michelle Pfeiffer.   I used to go out with my friends every Friday night.   I used to …

- Read all your sentences. Student A guesses which sentence is false.

- Compare your lives then and now. How similar were your lives ten years ago?

Unit 11 Animal definitions

**You are going to read out three definitions of some common English expressions.
The definitions with crosses are false, and the one with a tick is true. Student A has to
guess which definition (*1, 2 or 3*) is the correct one.**

- Complete one false definition for each expression. Use your imagination!
- Listen to Student A's expressions and guess which of his/her definitions is correct.
- Then read out your three definitions and see if Student A can guess which one is correct.

a) A '**catty**' person is …

   1 somebody who is independent and a little unfriendly. ✗

   2 somebody who says cruel things about other people. ✔

   3 somebody who _____ . ✗

b) A '**fishy**' story is …

   1 a story that has a funny ending. ✗

   2 a story that _____ . ✗

   3 a story that isn't completely honest. ✔

c) A film that's considered to be a '**turkey**' is …

   1 a film that doesn't have a famous star in it. ✗

   2 a film that _____ . ✗

   3 a film that isn't successful. ✔

d) A '**book worm**' is …

   1 somebody who _____ . ✗

   2 somebody who reads a lot. ✔

   3 somebody who doesn't like reading. ✗

e) A '**mousy**' person is …

   1 somebody who lives in a small apartment. ✗

   2 somebody who is quiet and prefers not to be noticed. ✔

   3 somebody who _____ . ✗

Unit 12 Emily and Peter

**You are going to complete a story about Emily and Peter. You have parts of the story.
Student A has other parts.**

- Listen and write down Student A's parts of the story.
- Dictate your parts of the story to Student A.
- Compare your completed texts. They should be identical.

TEXT
before marriage

A clairvoyant had _____

She was now nearly 22 and hadn't met the love of her life yet.

One day _____

She didn't know that the number belonged to her future husband. Peter Baldwin was at work 140 miles away when he got the message.

He phoned Emily, _____

They got married six months later.

Grammar *Extra*

Unit 1 **Questions. Tense review**

Questions

Word order

The usual word order for questions is:

Question word	(Auxiliary) verb	Subject	
—	Is	she	happy?
—	Have	they	left?
What	does	'niece'	mean?
Where	are	you	going?
When	did	he	graduate?

Yes/No **questions and short answers**

In *Yes / No* questions with *be* you put *am / are / is / was / were* before the subject.
'**Is** she tired?' 'Yes, she is.'
'**Were** they late?' 'No, they weren't.'

In *Yes / No* questions with the present simple and the past simple you put *do / does / did* before the subject.
'**Do** you live here?' 'Yes, I do.'
'**Did** Jim and his two sisters go to university?' 'No, they didn't.'

In *Yes / No* questions with other verb structures you put the auxiliary verb before the subject.
'**Have** you been to Oslo?' 'Yes, I have.'
'**Can** she drive?' 'No, she can't.'

Wh **questions**

Questions with *What, Where, How many*, etc. have the same word order as *Yes / No* questions.
You put a question word at the beginning of the question.
Why is she tired? **Where** do you live? **How many** times have you been to Oslo?

Tense review

Tense	Uses	Affirmative	Negative	Question
Present simple	Facts / habits / routines	He **works**.	He **doesn't work**.	**Does** he **work**?
Past simple	Completed action at a specific past time	She **worked** yesterday.	She **didn't work** yesterday.	**Did** she **work** yesterday?
Present continuous	Activities in progress now	They**'re working** now.	They **aren't working** now.	**Are** they **working** now?
Future (*be*) *going to*	Future plans and intentions	We**'re going to work** at home tomorrow.	We **aren't going to work** at home tomorrow.	**Are** we **going to work** at home tomorrow?
Present perfect	Completed action in 'time up to now'.	It**'s worked** recently.	It **hasn't worked** recently.	**Has** it **worked** recently?

Unit 1 Exercises

1 Write *Yes/No* questions with *you*.

Somebody wants to know if you …
a) like jazz
   Do you like jazz?
b) can swim
c) went skiing last winter
d) are wearing jeans today
e) have been to Egypt
f) are going to drive home after the lesson

2 Write short answers to the questions in Exercise 1.

a) Yes, I do. / No, I don't.

Tick the short answer that is true for you.

3 Think of a person you know well. Use the information in Exercise 1 and write *Yes/No* questions and short answers with *he* or *she*.

a) Does he like jazz?
   Yes, he does. / No, he doesn't.

Tick the short answer that is true (if you know it).

4 Insert the subject *you* in the correct position to make questions.

a) How far do live from the school?
   How far do you live from the school?
b) When did last go to the theatre?
c) What are going to do this evening?
d) How many cups of coffee have had today?
e) What kind of pen are using at the moment?
f) Where did buy your shoes?

Ask your partner the questions.

5 Complete the questions with *you* and then match the questions and the answers.

a) What / do? *What do you do?*   1   In 2005.
b) Who / work for?   2   On foot.
c) Which department / work in?   3   I'm a computer programmer.
d) How / get to work?   4   Because I love computer games.
e) When / start working there?   5   In the games department.
f) Why / like working there?   6   £63,000 a year.
g) How much / earn?   7   Microsoft.

Write your own answers to the questions.

6 Name the tense for each sentence.

a) We're studying Shakespeare in our English class. *Present continuous.*
b) My parents named me after my uncle.
c) I've recently learnt to drive.
d) My friends are going to organise a party for me tomorrow.
e) I like getting up early in the morning.

Put each sentence into the negative.

a) We aren't studying Shakespeare in our English class.

Tick the sentences (affirmative or negative) that are true for you.

a) We're studying Shakespeare in our English class. ✓

Unit 2 **Nouns and quantity expressions**

Countable nouns

Most nouns in English are countable. They have a singular and a plural form.

Regular forms		
Singular	**Plural**	**Spelling**
a place	two places	Add **s**.
a church	three churches	Add **es** after *ch, sh, s, x*.
a city	ten cities	Add **ies** after a consonant + *y*.
a leaf	ten thousand leaves	Add **ves** after vowel + *f*

Irregular forms	
Singular	**Plural**
a person	two people
a child	two children
a man	two men
a woman	two women
a foot	two feet
a tooth	two teeth

⚠ *a* **or** *an*?
With singular nouns you use *a* before a consonant sound: *a town*, *a university*.
You use *an* before a vowel sound: *an airport*, *an office*.

⚠ **Plural nouns**
Some nouns are always plural and don't have a singular form. You can't use *a / an* or put a number in front of them.
I have some pink jeans. (NOT ~~I have a pink jeans.~~)
Common plural nouns: *clothes, glasses, jeans, knickers, pants, pyjamas, scissors, shorts, sunglasses, tights, trousers.*

Uncountable nouns

Some nouns in English are uncountable. They only have a singular form. You can't use *a/an* or put a number in front of them.
We had bad weather. (NOT ~~We had a bad weather.~~)

Common uncountable nouns: *advice, architecture, food, furniture, homework, information, knowledge, love, money, music, news, traffic, transport, weather, work.*

Quantity expressions

These are ways you can talk about quantity if you can't or don't want to use an exact number.

With countable nouns: *(only) a few / (far) too many / How many …?*
Only a few people saw what happened.
How many emails do you get every day?

With uncountable nouns: *(only) a little / (far) too much / How much …?*
There's a little wine left but no beer.
How much homework do you get?

With countable and uncountable nouns: *a lot of / lots of / not … enough*
She has a lot of problems.
He didn't give me enough information.

too + much / many (+ noun) = excessive or more than necessary.
I have too much work and not enough time.

Unit 2 **Exercises**

1 **Write the plural forms for the following countable nouns.**

a) a name *names*   c) a menu   e) a family   g) a person   i) a day   k) a camera
b) a place   d) a bus   f) a wife   h) a foot   j) a mouse l) a watch

2 **Put the nouns in the box into the table.**

| ~~advice~~ ~~child~~ city   homework   information   money |
| news   office   problem   tooth   weather   woman |

Countable nouns	Uncountable nouns
child	*advice*

Add three more nouns to each column.

3 **Complete the sentences with *a/an* or *some*.**

a) I have *some* money in my pocket.
b) I have _____ gold ring on my finger.
c) I have _____ black jeans at home.
d) I have _____ scissors in my bag.

e) I have _____ homework to do this evening.
f) I have _____ laptop I use for work.
g) I have _____ great music on my MP3 player.
h) I have _____ sunglasses in my car.

Tick the sentences that are true for you.

4 **Underline the correct form of *be*.**

a) What **is / are** the weather like today?
b) What **was / were** the traffic like this morning?
c) What **is / are** the people like in your street?
d) What **is / are** the furniture like in your living room?
e) What **was / were** the English teachers like at your secondary school?
f) What **was / were** the food like at the last restaurant you went to?

Ask your partner the questions.

5 **Complete the sentences with *be + a lot of*.**

In my city …
a) there *are a lot of* parks.
b) there _____ good nightlife.

c) there _____ good restaurants.
d) there _____ traffic.

e) there _____ pollution.
f) there _____ bookshops.

Make the sentences negative. Use *not be + much/many*.

a) *There aren't many parks.*

Which sentences are true for your city?

6 **Look at Paul. What do you think is wrong with his lifestyle? Write sentences with *too much/many* and *not enough*.**

a) drink / beer
   He drinks too much beer.
b) eat / pizzas
c) eat / fruit and vegetables
d) smoke / cigarettes
e) do / exercise
f) watch / television
g) get / fresh air

Unit 3 Past simple. Past continuous

Part 1: Past simple

Affirmative	Negative	Question	Short answer Yes	Short answer No
I/You/He/She/It/We/They **worked**.	I/You/He/She/It/We/They **didn't** (**did not**) work.	Did I/you/he/she/it/we/they work?	Yes, I/you/he/she/it/we/they **did**.	No, I/you/he/she/it/we/they **didn't**.

Spelling: regular verbs

Add *ed/d* after most verbs: work – work**ed**, demonstrate – demonstrate**d**

Delete *y* and add *ied* for verbs that end in a consonant + *y*: study – stud**ied**; try – tr**ied**

Add a consonant + *ed* for verbs that end in one vowel + one consonant: stop – stop**ped**; plan – plan**ned**

The ten most frequently used irregular verbs are:

1   say – said
2   get – got
3   go – went
4   know – knew
5   think – thought
6   see – saw
7   make – made
8   come – came
9   take – took
10   give – gave

See a fuller list of irregular verbs on page 159.

You can use the past simple as the main tense to talk about past events and past situations. It's commonly used to tell stories.

⚠ There is only *one* past form for every verb except *be*.

Affirmative	Negative	Question	Short answer Yes	Short answer No
I/He/She/It **was** tired.	I/He/She/It **wasn't** (**was not**) tired.	**Was** I/he/she/it tired?	Yes, I/he/she/it **was**.	No, I/he/she/it **wasn't**.
You/We/They **were** tired.	You/We/They **weren't** (**were not**) tired.	**Were** you/we/they tired?	Yes, you/we/they **were**.	No, you/we/they **weren't**.

Part 2: Past continuous

Affirmative	Negative	Question	Short answer Yes	Short answer No
I/He/She/It **was working**.	I/He/She/It **wasn't** (**was not**) working.	**Was** I/he/she/it tired?	Yes, I/he/she/it **was**.	No, I/he/she/it **wasn't**.
You/We/They **were working**.	You/We/They **weren't** (**were not**) working.	**Were** you/we/they tired?	Yes, you/we/they **were**.	No, you/we/they **weren't**.

Spelling: *ing*-forms

Delete *e* and add *ing* for verbs that end in *e*: have – hav**ing**; make – mak**ing**

Add a consonant + *ing* for verbs that end in one vowel + one consonant: run – run**ning**; stop – stop**ping**

You can use the past continuous to describe a 'longer' activity that was in progress when other past events happened. You usually use it in contrast with the past simple.

*I saw her when I **was driving** home.*

*They **were playing** tennis when it started raining.*

Unit 3 Exercises

Part 1

1 Write the past simple forms for these verb sets.

a) work *worked* / go / call / help
b) take / make / wake / bake
c) try / play / study / copy
d) stop / plan / chat / walk

In each set, which verb is the odd one out? Why?

a) 'go – went' is the odd one out because it's irregular.

2 Write the past simple forms of these irregular verbs.

a) teach *taught*
b) sit
c) say
d) know

e) speak
f) make
g) begin
h) ring

i) fall
j) learn
k) catch
l) fly

m) sink
n) throw
o) swim
p) read

q) understand
r) bring
s) run
t) sleep

u) find
v) wear
w) buy
x) come

y) meet
z) think

3 Use the prompts in brackets to write negative sentences about the past.

a) My father taught me how to swim. (how to drive)
   My father didn't teach me how to drive.
b) I went to a state school. (private school)
c) My parents gave me money for my birthday. (a present)
d) I had fish for dinner last night. (meat)
e) I studied French at school. (English)
f) I played tennis when I was young. (basketball)

Tick the sentences that are true for you.

Part 2

1 Write the *ing*-form of these verbs.

a) come *coming*
b) eat

c) hit
d) leave

e) play
f) put

g) smoke
h) study

i) swim
j) wake

k) win
l) work

2 Complete the questions and short answers about these times yesterday.

a) **8.00 a.m.** *'Were* you having breakfast?' 'Yes, I *was.*' 'No, I *wasn't.*'
b) **8.30 a.m.** *'Were* you driving to work?' 'Yes, I _____ .' 'No, I _____ .'
c) **10.00 a.m.** '_____ your mother working?' 'Yes, she _____ .' 'No, she _____ .'
d) **4.00 p.m.** '_____ you walking around town?' 'Yes, I _____ .' 'No, I _____ .'
e) **8.00 p.m.** '_____ your parents watching TV?' 'Yes, they _____ .' 'No, they _____ .'

Ask your partner the questions.

3 Complete the sentences with the past simple or the past continuous.

a) We (move) *moved* house several times when I was a child.
b) My parents met when they (study) _____ at university.
c) When I finished school, I (start) _____ work in a bank.
d) When I looked out of the window this morning, it (rain) _____ .
e) When I got to work, I (switch on) _____ my computer.
f) When the teacher came into the classroom, I (talk) _____ to my friend on the phone.

Tick the sentences that are true for you.

Unit 4 Verb patterns. Present simple and present continuous

Part 1: Verb patterns – verbs with two objects

Some common verbs can have two objects. Two different word orders are possible, but the meaning is the same. The word order **verb + person + thing** is more common, especially with object pronouns (*me, you, him,* etc.).

	verb	+	(indirect object) person	+	(direct object) thing	=		verb	+	(direct object) thing	+	to/for	+	(indirect object) person
I	bought		him		a present.	=	I	bought		a present		for		him.
He	lent		her		some money.	=	He	lent		some money		to		her.

Common verbs with the pattern **verb + thing + *to* + person**: *give, lend, offer, pass, read, send, show, teach, tell.*
Common verbs with the pattern **verb + thing + *for* + person**: *buy, find, get, make.*

⚠ You can't use the word order **verb + person + thing** with certain verbs: eg *describe, explain, say* or *suggest.*
He explained the situation to me. (NOT ~~He explained me the situation~~.)
She said hello to us. (NOT ~~She said us hello~~.)

Part 2: Present simple and present continuous

Present simple

Affirmative	Negative	Question	Short answer *Yes*	Short answer *No*
I/You/We/They **work**.	I/You/We/They **don't** (**do not**) **work**.	**Do** I/you/we/they **work**?	Yes, I/you/we/they **do**.	No, I/you/we/they **don't**.
He/She/It **works**.	He/She/It **doesn't** (**does not**) **work**.	**Does** he/she/it **work**?	Yes, he/she/it **does**.	No, he/she/it **doesn't**.

Spelling: 3rd person singular

Add *s* after most verbs: live – live**s**; play – play**s**; work – work**s**
Add *es* after *ch, sh, s, x*: watch – watch**es**; finish – finish**es**
Delete *y* and add *ies* after a consonant + *y*: study – stud**ies**
Irregular forms: do – **does**; go – **goes**; have – **has**

You can use the present simple to talk about:
*   things that are always true. *He looks like his father.   Ice forms at 0 degrees.*
*   things that happen regularly or all the time. *He plays tennis on Friday.   She never gets up before 9.00 a.m.*

Present continuous

Affirmative	Negative	Question	Short answer *Yes*	Short answer *No*
I'm (**am**) working.	I'm not (**am not**) working.	**Am** I working?	Yes, I **am**.	No, I'm not.
You/We/They're (**are**) working.	You/We/They **aren't** (**are not**) working.	**Are** you/we/they working?	Yes, you/we/they **are**.	No, you/we/they **aren't**.
He/She/It's (**is**) working.	He/She/It **isn't** (**is not**) working.	**Is** he/she/it working?	Yes, he/she/it **is**.	No, he/she/it **isn't**.

Spelling: *ing*-forms

Delete *e* and add *ing* for verbs that end in *e*: have – hav**ing**; make – mak**ing**
Add a consonant + *ing* for verbs that end in one vowel + one consonant: run – run**ning**; stop – stop**ping**

You can use the present continuous to talk about:
*   activities that are in progress at the moment of speaking. *'What are you doing?' 'I'm writing an email.'*
*   activities that are in progress around the moment of speaking. *Cars are getting cheaper, but house prices are going up.*

Unit 4 **Exercises**

Part 1

1 Complete the sentences about last Christmas.

a) Anna: some socks ➔ Grandad
    Anna gave Grandad some socks.
b) John: an MP3 player ➔ Tony
c) Dick: some chocolates ➔ Molly

d) Sue: a cookery book ➔ Carla
e) Becky: a CD ➔ Eric
f) Jimmy: some earrings ➔ Sally

What presents did you give people last year?

I gave my mum a foot spa.

2 Underline the appropriate prepositions.

a) Could you send the money **for** / **to** me?
b) She explained the rules **for** / **to** them.
c) My dad bought this **for** / **to** me for my birthday.
d) I've told that joke **for** / **to** everybody!
e) He described the house **for** / **to** her.

f) We showed our holiday photos **for** / **to** him.
g) Ian is getting some ice creams **for** / **to** us.
h) They didn't say goodbye **for** / **to** us.
i) I don't want to make breakfast **for** / **to** him!
j) Can you lend your bike **for** / **to** Sue?

3 Re-read the sentences in Exercise 2. Where possible, change the word order and rewrite the sentences without the prepositions.

a) Could you send me the money?   *b) (Not possible to change.)*

Part 2

1 Write these verbs in the present simple 3rd person singular.

a) be *is*
b) cry
c) do
d) go
e) have
f) hear
g) pay
h) push
i) say
j) study
k) take
l) touch

2 Write the *ing*-form of these verbs.

a) become
b) choose
c) cut
d) fly
e) live
f) meet
g) shine
h) shut
i) sit
j) start
k) stay
l) wear

3 Write a question in the present simple and a question in the present continuous for each prompt.

a) you / wear / perfume?
    Do you wear perfume?
    Are you wearing perfume?
b) you / use / an electronic dictionary?
c) you / plan / your holidays?
d) your parents / work?
e) your teacher / wear / glasses?
f) What / you / do?

Answer the questions. Think about the difference in meaning for each question.

4 Complete the questions with *you* in the most appropriate tense: present simple or present continuous.

a) Where / come from?
    Where do you come from?
b) How many languages / speak?
c) What / wear today?
d) Why / learn English?
e) What time / usually go to bed?
f) What colour pen / use to do this exercise?

Answer the questions.

Unit 5 Comparative and superlative adjectives. Phrasal verbs

Part 1: Comparative and superlative adjectives

	Adjective	Comparative	Superlative
Short adjectives: add *er/est* Adjectives ending in a consonant or *e*	new nice	new**er** nic**er**	new**est** the nic**est**
Adjectives ending in a single vowel + a single consonant	fit	fit**ter**	the fit**test**
Adjectives ending in *y*	healthy	health**ier**	the health**iest**
Irregular adjectives	good bad far	better worse further	the best the worst the furthest
Long adjectives: add *more / the most*	exciting	**more** exciting	**the most** exciting

You use comparative adjectives to compare people/things with other people/things.
*Fernando Alonso is **older than** Lewis Hamilton.*

You can use *a bit* or *much* to modify comparisons.
*Wembley Stadium is **a bit bigger than** the Stade de France.*
*Cristiano Ronaldo is **much better-looking than** Wayne Rooney.*

You use *not as* + adjective + *as* to make negative comparisons.
*Golf is **not as dangerous as** motor racing.*

You use superlative adjectives to compare people/things with all the other people/things in their group.
*Mohamed Ali was **the greatest** sportsman of all time.*
*Football is **the most popular** sport in the world.*

Part 2: Phrasal verbs

The term 'phrasal verb' usually refers to all multi-word verbs, consisting of a verb + particle(s). Phrasal verbs can be divided into three basic types.

1   Verb + particle (INTRANSITIVE)
Some phrasal verbs are intransitive and don't take a direct object.
***Sit down** and enjoy it.*
*When are you going to **grow up**?*

2   Verb + object + particle (TRANSITIVE – SEPARABLE)
The biggest group of phrasal verbs is transitive. These verbs take a direct object.
With separable verbs, when the direct object is a noun, you can put it before or after the particle.
***Take off** your shoes.* OR ***Take** your shoes **off**.*
When the direct object is a pronoun, you have to put it between the verb and the particle.
***Switch** it **off**, please.* (NOT ~~Switch off it.~~)

3   Verb + particle + object (TRANSITIVE – NOT SEPARABLE)
With this type of phrasal verb you always put the direct object – noun or pronoun – after the particle.
*She **looks after** her grandmother.*
*I **ran after** the bus, but it didn't stop.*

Unit 5 Exercises

Part 1

1 Complete the table with the adjectives in the box. There are three adjectives in each section.

> ~~bad~~ ~~famous~~ far good ~~happy~~ interesting ~~kind~~ lazy lucky nice ~~sad~~
> strong successful thin wet

a)	Add *er*/*r*	*kind – kinder than*
b)	Double letter + *er*	*sad – sadder than*
c)	Delete *y*, add *ier*	*happy – happier than*

d)	Irregular	*bad – **worse** than*
e)	*more* + adjective	*famous – **more famous** than*

2 Write sentences comparing the places. Use *a bit* or *much* and the comparative form of the adjective.

a) France / big / Spain
    France is a bit bigger than Spain.
b) India / hot / the UK
c) The River Nile / long / the Amazon
d) Tokyo / expensive / Bangkok
e) Rome / far north / Barcelona
f) Manila / crowded / Helsinki

Rewrite the sentences using *not as … as* so they have the same meaning.

a) *Spain isn't as big as France.*

3 Use *a bit* / *much* / *not as … as* to write true sentences comparing the following. Use the adjectives in the box or your own ideas.

> complicated confident difficult energetic expensive
> healthy large modern old sophisticated

a) your mum / your dad
    My mum is older than my dad.
b) English / your language
c) you ten years ago / you now
d) your first mobile phone / the mobile phone you have now
e) the house you were born in / the house you live in now
f) your town ten years ago / your town now

Compare your sentences with a partner

Part 2

1 Rewrite these sentences so that they have the same meaning.

a) Can you turn off the light, please?
    Can you turn the light off, please?
b) She threw my letter away.
c) I'd like to try on this dress, please.
d) Pick all the papers up before you leave!
e) Write down your name, please.
f) I gave back his pen.

2 Put the words in brackets in the correct order to complete each sentence. Consult your dictionary if necessary.

a) I'm very similar to my mother – I *take after her*. (after / take / her)
b) I have good relations with my neighbours – I _____ . (get / well / them / with / on)
c) I keep my neighbours' pet when they go on holiday – I _____ . (look / it / after)
d) I lived with my grandparents when I was a child – they _____ . (up / brought / me)
e) My children always leave their things on the floor – they don't _____ . (away / them / put)
f) I invent excuses when I'm late – I _____ . (make / up / them)
g) I stopped going to the gym – I _____ . (up / it / gave)
h) When I see a new phrasal verb I consult my dictionary – I _____ . (it / look / up)

Are any of the sentences true for you?

Unit 6 Permission and obligation (present). Present perfect simple

Part 1: *can* for permission; *have to* for obligation

Affirmative	Negative	Question	Short answer *Yes*	Short answer *No*
I/You/He, *etc.* **can work.**	I/You/He *etc.* **can't (cannot) work.**	**Can** I/you/he, *etc.* **work?**	Yes, I/you/he, *etc.* **can.**	No, I/you/he, *etc.* **can't.**

You can use *can* and *can't* to talk about permission.
- *can* means something is permitted: it's OK. *In the UK, you **can** leave school when you are sixteen.*
- *can't* means something isn't permitted: it isn't OK. *You **can't** vote until you are eighteen.*

Affirmative	Negative	Question	Short answer *Yes*	Short answer *No*
I/You/We/They **have to work.**	I/You/We/They **don't have to work.**	**Do** I/you/we/they **have to work?**	Yes, I/you/we/ they **do.**	No, I/you/we/ they **don't.**
He/She/It **has to work.**	He/She/It **doesn't have to work.**	**Does** he/she/it **have to work?**	Yes, he/she/it **does.**	No, he/she/it **doesn't.**

You use *have to / don't have to* to talk about necessity or obligation.
- *have to* means something is necessary or it's obligatory. *In the UK, you **have to** drive on the left.*
- *don't have to* means something isn't necessary or it isn't obligatory. *You **don't have to** wear a helmet on a bicycle.*

Part 2: Present perfect simple

Affirmative	Negative	Question	Short answer *Yes*	Short answer *No*
I/You/We/They**'ve (have) worked.**	I/You/We/They **haven't (have not) worked.**	**Have** I/you/we/ they **worked?**	Yes, I/you/we/ they **have.**	No, I/you/we/ they **haven't.**
He/She/It**'s (has) worked.**	He/She/It **hasn't (has not) worked.**	**Has** he/she/it **worked?**	Yes, he/she/it **has.**	No, he/she/it **hasn't.**

See the list of irregular verbs on page 159.

You can use the present perfect to talk about completed actions in time 'up to now'. You don't focus on *when*.

Time 'up to now'

*I've done a lot of silly things **in my life**.*

Common time expressions which describe time 'up to now': *today, this week, recently, never, over the years.*
With these time expressions you usually use the present perfect.
*My brother **has never been** to a pop concert.   I **haven't seen** any good films **recently**.*

⚠ *been* is the past participle of *be*, but you can also use it as a past participle of *go*. Compare:
- *He's been to Rome.* = He went and came back.
- *He's gone to Rome.* = He went and is in Rome now.

'Finished' time

*I did a lot of silly things **when I was at university**.*

Common time expressions which describe 'finished' time: *yesterday, last month, in 1990, a few minutes ago.*
With these time expressions you use the past simple.
*She **called** you **a few minutes ago**.   I **didn't go** to the mountains **last summer**.*

Unit 6 Exercises

Part 1

1 Work with a partner. Test your knowledge of life in Britain. Underline the correct modals in these sentences.

a) You **have to** / <u>can</u> leave school when you're sixteen.
b) You **don't have to** / **can't** wear a helmet on a bicycle.
c) You **have to** / **can** vote when you're eighteen.
d) You **don't have to** / **can't** get married until you're sixteen.
e) You **have to** / **can** buy alcohol when you're eighteen.
f) You **have to** / **can** drive on the left.
g) You **have to** / **can** drive a car when you're seventeen.
h) You **don't have to** / **can't** carry an ID card.

Tick the sentences that are true for your country.

2 Write similar sentences about the things you *can, can't, have to* or *don't have* to do in your country.

Part 2

1 Complete the tables with the correct past participles for these irregular verbs.

Infinitive	Past simple	Past participle
be	was / were	(1) *been*
do	did	(2) _____
take	took	(3) _____
drink	drank	(4) _____
break	broke	(5) _____
see	saw	(6) _____
eat	ate	(7) _____

Infinitive	Past simple	Past participle
write	wrote	(8) _____
forget	forgot	(9) _____
ride	rode	(10) _____
become	became	(11) _____
stand	stood	(12) _____
give	gave	(13) _____
go	went	(14) *gone* / (15) _____

2 Write the sentences in the negative.

a) I've been on television.
   I haven't been on television.
b) I've sung karaoke.
c) I've driven a sports car.
d) I've met a famous person.
e) I've climbed a mountain.
f) I've phoned a TV programme.

Tick the sentences that are true for you.

3 Write present perfect questions with *you* for the sentences in Exercise 2.

a) *Have you been on television?*

Ask your partner the questions.

4 Underline the correct tense.

a) I<u>'ve never been</u> / **never went** to Australia.
b) I **haven't done** / **didn't do** my homework last night.
c) My parents **haven't phoned** / **didn't phone** me recently.
d) I've **never eaten** / **didn't eat** sushi.
e) I've **been** / **went** skiing last winter.
f) I've **had** / **had** a PlayStation when I was a child.

Tick the sentences that are true for you.

Unit 7 Dynamic and stative meanings. Future forms

Part 1: Dynamic and stative meanings

Dynamic meanings: 'actions'

Most verbs have dynamic meanings. They describe actions: something 'happens'. You can use them with simple forms to talk about habits or routines, or continuous forms to talk about activities in progress.

I **recycle** all paper, plastic and bottles.   We**'re destroying** the planet.   The phone **is ringing**.

Stative meanings: 'states'

Some verbs connected with knowledge, emotion or possession have stative meanings. They describe states: nothing 'happens'. You cannot use them with continuous forms.
I **want** a fairer system.   I **don't feel** strongly about politics.

Common verbs with stative meanings:
*   feelings: *hate, like, love, prefer, want.*
*   thoughts: *believe, feel, know, think, understand.*
*   possession: *belong, have, own.*
*   senses: *feel, hear, see, smell, sound, taste.*
*   appearance: *appear, look (like), seem.*

⚠ Some verbs can have both dynamic and stative meanings:
Rosie is having a great time at university. (*have* = dynamic meaning)
Brian has a beautiful house. (*have* = stative meaning)

Part 2: Future forms: *(be) going to* and present continuous

Affirmative	Negative	Question	Short answer *Yes*	Short answer *No*
I'm (am) going to work.	I'm not (am not) going to work.	**Am** I going to work?	Yes, I **am**.	No, I'm not.
You/We/They**'re** (are) going to work.	You/We/They**'re not** (are not) going to work.	**Are** you/we/they going to work?	Yes, you/we/they **are**.	No, you/we/they **aren't**.
He/She/It**'s** (is) going to work.	He/She/It **isn't** (is not) going to work.	**Is** he/she/it going to work?	Yes, he/she/it **is**.	No, he/she/it **isn't**.

You can use *(be) going to* to talk about your future intentions. You have made a decision about a future event and you are talking about that decision.

One of these days I'm going to get fit.   *He's going to tell me all about his holidays.*

You can use the present continuous to talk about future arrangements. You have arranged a future event and you are talking about that arrangement.

Are you doing anything on Thursday?   *We're meeting the President this afternoon at 2.00 p.m.*

For present continuous verb forms see page 132.

Unit 7 Exercises

Part 1

1 Look at the picture of Toby in his bedroom. Complete the sentences with the present continuous or the present simple.

a) Toby (have) *is having* a rest.
b) He (think) _____ about his girlfriend.
c) He (listen) _____ to music.
d) He (have) _____ a motorbike.
e) He (love) _____ chocolate.

f) He (think) _____ Liverpool is the best football team.
g) He (look) _____ like his father.
h) He (know) _____ a lot of people.
i) He (plan) _____ a holiday.
j) He (seem) _____ happy.

2 Use the same dynamic or stative meanings of the verbs in Exercise 1 and write example sentences that are true for you.

a) *I'm having a coffee.*

Part 2

1 Complete these New Year resolutions with *going to* + a verb in the box.

| change   get   give up   ~~join~~   not eat   not watch   spend   start |

a) the Green Party
   I'm going to join the Green Party.
b) yoga classes

c) a better job
d) so much fast food
e) my hairstyle

f) so much TV
g) smoking
h) less time on the computer

Which resolutions would be good for you?

2 Look at Jane's diary. Complete the conversation.

Rick: Would you like to meet for a coffee tomorrow morning?
Jane: I can't. (1) *I'm going to the dentist.*
Rick: What about later in the morning?
Jane: Sorry, but (2) _____ .
Rick: OK. Are you free for lunch?
Jane: I'd love to, but (3) _____ .
Rick: And the afternoon?
Jane: (4) _____ with Tim, and then at 4.30 (5) _____ .
Rick: Dinner?
Jane: Look, I'm really sorry but from 7.30 to 9.30 (6) _____ .
Rick: OK, OK. Another time … By the way, who's Tim?

Write sentences describing any arrangements you have made for the next few days.

26th MAY

9.20: Dentist

11.00: Meet Mum in town

1.00: Lunch with Vicky

3.00: Tennis with Tim

4.30: Collect the children from school

7.30-9.30: Drink with Tim

Unit 8 Permission and obligation (present and past). Advice

Part 1: *can/could* for permission; *have to / had to* for obligation

Affirmative	Negative	Question	Short answer *Yes*	Short answer *No*
I/You/He, *etc.* could work.	I/You/He, *etc.* couldn't (could not) work.	Could I/you/he, *etc.* work?	Yes, I/you/he, *etc.* could.	No, I/you/he, *etc.* couldn't.

Affirmative	Negative	Question	Short answer *Yes*	Short answer *No*
I/You/He, *etc.* had to work.	I/You/He, *etc.* didn't have to work.	Did I/you/he, *etc.* have to work?	Yes, I/you/he, *etc.* did.	No, I/you/he, *etc.* didn't.

Permission: *can/could; can't/couldn't*			Obligation: *have to / don't have to; had to / didn't have to*	
	Permitted	Not permitted	Necessary	Not necessary
Present	You **can do** it.	You **can't do** it.	You **have to do** it.	You **don't have to do** it.
Past	You **could do** it.	You **couldn't do** it.	You **had to do** it.	You **didn't have to do** it.

You can use *can/could* to talk about permission. *could* is the past form of *can*.
When I was fourteen I **could** *stay out as long as I wanted.*
Swiss women **couldn't** *vote in elections until 1971.*

You use *have to / had to* to talk about necessity or obligation. *had to* is the past form of *have to*.
I **had to** *wear a uniform at school.*
In the 1960s you **didn't have to** *wear a helmet on a motorbike.*

Part 2: *must* and *should* for advice

Affirmative	Negative	Question	Short answer *Yes*	Short answer *No*
I/You/He, *etc.* must work.	I/You/He, *etc.* mustn't (must not) work.	Must I/you/he, *etc.* work?	Yes, I/you/he, *etc.* must.	No, I/you/he, *etc.* mustn't.
I/You/He, *etc.* should work.	I/You/He, *etc.* shouldn't (should not) work.	Should I/you/he, *etc.* work?	Yes, I/you/he, *etc.* should.	No, I/you/he, *etc.* shouldn't.

You can use *must* and *should* to give advice. *must* is stronger than *should*.
You **must** *lose weight (or you'll die)!*
You **should** *lose weight (because you'll feel much healthier).*

Unit 8 Exercises

Part 1

1 Write the following sentences in the negative.

When I was fourteen ...

a) I had to make my bed every morning.
   I didn't have to make my bed every morning.
b) I could wear whatever I wanted.
   I couldn't wear whatever I wanted.
c) I had to keep my bedroom clean and tidy.
d) I had to help my parents in the house.
e) I had to travel everywhere by bicycle.
f) I could invite friends home at the weekend.
g) I could stay out after 10.00 p.m.
h) I could play my music as loud as I wanted.

Tick the affirmative or negative sentences that are true for you..

2 Write questions with *you* for the sentences in Exercise 1.

a) *Did you have to make your bed every morning?*

Work with a partner. Ask and answer the questions.

Part 2

1 Complete the sentences. Use an appropriate form of *should* or *must*.

a) You *mustn't* touch that. It's very hot!
b) It's only a cough, but you _____ take this medicine four times a day.
c) Mum, you _____ kiss me in front of my friends. It's embarrassing.
d) Tell David he _____ tidy his room immediately!
e) I think young people _____ show more respect to their elders.
f) You _____ go out with John. He's not good enough for you.
g) This is a security announcement. All passengers _____ keep their bags with them at all times!

2 Who said it? Match sentences (*a–g*) with a person in the box.

| a best friend | a doctor | a parent | a parent |
| an old man | a teenage boy | an airport announcer |

a) *a parent*

Unit 9 *for* and *since*. Present perfect simple and continuous

for and *since*

for + 'a period of time' and *since* + 'a point in time' are two ways of saying the same thing.
You use *for* when you give the **length** of the time: *for a few days / for three years / for ages.*
You use *since* when you give the **beginning** of the time: *since Monday / since I left school / since 1997.*

Present perfect simple and continuous

Affirmative	Negative	Question	Short answer *Yes*	Short answer *No*
I/You/We/They've (have) worked.	I/You/We/They **haven't** (**have not**) worked.	**Have** I/you/we/they worked?	Yes, I/you/we/they **have**.	No, I/you/we/they **haven't**.
He/She/It's (has) worked.	He/She/It hasn't (has not) worked.	**Has** he/she/it worked?	Yes, he/she/it **has**.	No, he/she/it **hasn't**.

See the list of irregular verbs on page 159.

Affirmative	Negative	Question	Short answer *Yes*	Short answer *No*
I/You/We/They've (have) been working.	I/You/We/They **haven't** (**have not**) **been working**.	**Have** I/you/we/they **been working**?	Yes, I/you/we/they **have**.	No, I/you/we/they **haven't**.
He/She/It's (has) been working.	He/She/It **hasn't** (**has not**) **been working**.	**Has** he/she/it **been working**?	Yes, he/she/it **has**.	No, he/she/it **hasn't**.

You usually use the present perfect continuous to describe the duration of a continuous or repeated action from a point in the past up to now.

*We've **been studying** Greek for ten years.*
*She's **been going** to the same hairdresser since the 1990s.*

⚠ **Stative meanings**
You <u>don't</u> use the present perfect continuous for verbs with stative meanings. Use the simple form.
*She's **known** Tom since they were at school.* (NOT ~~She's been knowing~~ …)
*They've **had** the same computer since 2003.* (NOT ~~They've been having~~ …)

See the list of common verbs with stative meanings on page 138.

Note: You can also use the simple form to indicate unchanging, 'permanent' situations.
Compare:
*I've **been living** here since the summer.*
*I've **lived** here all my life.*

Unit 9 **Exercises**

1 **Complete the sentences with *for* or *since*.**

a) I've had these football boots *for* fifteen years.
b) I've had this hairstyle _____ ages.
c) I've had this pen _____ my last birthday.
d) I've had this bag _____ a long time.
e) I've had the same sandals _____ last summer.
f) I've had the same ring tone on my mobile _____ I bought it.
g) I've had my driving license _____ I was eighteen.
h) I've had a passport _____ five or six years

Rewrite the sentences so they are true for you.

2 **Write the *ing*-form and the past participle for each of these verbs.**

a) steal *stealing, stolen*   h) get
b) grow   i) tell
c) sell   j) cost
d) drive   k) hear
e) send   l) lose
f) pay   m) build
g) feel   n) lend

3 **Look at the information. Use the underlined verb to write a sentence in the present perfect simple or continuous.**

a) We <u>are</u> married. We got married in 2007.
   We've been married since 2007.
b) I'<u>m reading</u> the newspaper. I started reading half an hour ago.
   I've been reading the newspaper for half an hour.
c) He <u>likes</u> jazz. He got interested in jazz when he was at university.
d) She'<u>s learning</u> to swim. She started lessons in September.
e) She <u>works</u> in a shop. She got the job last May.
f) They <u>live</u> together. They moved in together last summer.
g) I <u>play</u> the guitar. I started playing when I was eight.
h) We <u>have</u> a motorbike. We bought it three years ago.

Use the same underlined verbs to write present perfect sentences about yourself.

4 **Write questions using *How long* ... Use the continuous form where possible.**

a) know / best friend?
   How long have you known your best friend?
b) wear / the same sunglasses?
c) go / to the same dentist?
d) listen to / the same kind of music?
e) be / in the same job?
f) drive / the same car?
g) live / in the same house?
h) do your shopping / in the same supermarket?

Write answers to the questions.

Unit 10 *will* (future). Future time clauses. *used to*

Part 1: *will* (future). Future time clauses

Affirmative	Negative	Question	Short answer *Yes*	Short answer *No*
I/You/He, *etc.* 'll (will) work.	I/You/He, *etc.* won't (will not) work.	Will I/you/he, *etc.* work?	Yes, I/you/he, *etc.* will.	No, I/you/he, *etc.* won't.

will is a modal verb. You can use *will* to talk about the future when there is no present plan, intention or arrangement.

Compare:
What are you doing / going to do this weekend? (= I think you have plans, intentions or arrangements.)
What will you do this weekend? (= I don't think you know.)

Future time clauses

When you are talking about the future, you use a future form in the main clause but you use a present tense in the subordinate clauses after *when, if, as soon as, before, after,* etc.
Two different sentence formations are possible.

Conjunction	Subordinate clause	Main clause
When If	he gets home, it rains tomorrow,	he's going to have a bath. we'll play at the weekend.

Main clause	Conjunction	Subordinate clause
He's going to have a bath We'll play at the weekend	when if	he gets home. it rains tomorrow.

Part 2: *used to*

Affirmative	Negative	Question	Short answer *Yes*	Short answer *No*
I/You/He, *etc.* used to work.	I/You/He, *etc.* didn't use to work.	Did I/you/he, *etc.* use to work?	Yes, I/you/he, *etc.* did.	No, I/you/he, *etc.* didn't.

You can use *used to* + infinitive to talk about past habits (repeated actions in the past) or past states. It describes things that were true in the past, but are probably not true now.

*I **used to** go to school by bus.*
*I **didn't use to** enjoy English lessons.*
*What sort of car **did** you **use to** have?*

⚠ It isn't possible to use *used to* + infinitive to talk about a single action in the past.
You use the past simple.
*One weekend we **went** to Paris.* (NOT ~~One weekend we used to go to Paris.~~)

Unit 10 Exercises

Part 1

1 Underline the most appropriate future form.

a) 'I've forgotten my dictionary.' 'Don't worry: <u>**I'll lend**</u> / **I won't lend** you mine.'
b) If you don't hurry up, **you'll be** / **you won't be** in time for your train.
c) This is a great present. **Dom will love** / **Dom won't love** it!
d) I think **Anna will get** / **Anna won't get** the job. She's the best person for it.
e) We've got a problem with the car. **We'll arrive** / **We won't arrive** before 11.00 p.m.
f) **They'll play** / **They won't play** outside if the weather is bad.

2 Write the correct form for the verb in brackets.

a) As soon as the lesson (finish) *finishes*, Sue's going to buy a lottery ticket.
b) Terry will get married when he (meet) _____ the right woman.
c) As soon as Rob (get home) _____ this evening, he's going to do his homework.
d) If it (rain) _____ tomorrow, Jenny will probably come to class by car.
e) If Dana (go) _____ abroad this summer, she'll probably go to England.
f) Tom will probably get a well-paid job when he (leave) _____ university.

Work with a partner. Replace the names with names of people in the class. How many true statements can you make?

Part 2

1 Complete the conversation with the affirmative, negative and question forms of *used to*.

A: What (1 your dad do) *did your dad use to do* before he left his job?
B: He (2 be) _____ a corporate lawyer. He worked in London for a big company.
A: (3 he enjoy) _____ his job?
B: Well, he (4 say) _____ he found it a bit boring. And he (5 not like) _____ travelling to London every day. You know, he (6 leave) _____ the house at 6.00 every morning and he (7 not arrive) _____ home before 7.30 p.m. I remember he (8 get) _____ very tired.
A: (9 your dad earn) _____ a lot of money?
B: Oh, I suppose he did. We (10 have) _____ really nice holidays in the USA and we often (11 eat out) _____ in expensive restaurants. Money was never a problem.
A: So what happened?
B: I don't know exactly. He always (12 tell) _____ me he wanted to 'smell the flowers'. So last year he left the company and bought a small organic farm.
A: What's life on the farm like?
B: It's OK – a bit boring perhaps, but Dad's really happy.

What job did you use to want to do when you were a child? Discuss with a partner.

2 Look at the following statements. Where possible, replace the past simple verb forms with *used to* or *didn't use to*.

a) I was born in a hospital.
b) As a child, I ~~lived~~ *used to live* in a small village.
c) I shared a bedroom with my brother/sister.
d) I had a pet mouse called Jerry.
e) I watched Cartoon Network on TV every day.
f) My parents gave me lots of pocket money.
g) We went to Disneyland once as a special treat.
h) I didn't enjoy English lessons at school.

3 How many of the statements in Exercise 2 were true for you as a child? Rewrite the sentences so that they are all true for you. Compare your sentences with your partner.

Unit 11 Defining relative clauses. Unreal conditionals

Part 1: Defining relative clauses

A relative clause can define or identify the thing or person introduced in the main clause.
It comes immediately after the person or thing it is describing.
*A cheetah is an <u>animal</u> **that can run at 100 kilometres an hour**.*
*The <u>woman</u> **who does my hair** is called Muriel.*

The relative pronoun (*that, which, who*) becomes the subject of the verb in the relative clause.
You use *that* (or *which*) for things and *who* (or *that*) for people.

           subject   verb
People | who | come | *from Manchester are called Mancunians.*

               subject   verb
A butcher's is a shop | that | sells | *meat.*

Part 2: Unreal conditionals

You can use a conditional sentence to talk about a present (or future) situation that is imaginary
or not probable. These sentences are usually called 'unreal conditionals'.
They have two clauses: an *if*-clause and a main clause.

if-clause

To show that a present (or future) situation is imaginary, you use a past tense.

Real situation	Imaginary situation
I **am** not an animal. →	If I **was/were** an animal, …
I **live** in an apartment. →	If I **lived** in an igloo, …

Note: *If I/he/she/it **were*** is more formal than *If I/he/she/it **was***. You always use *were* in the fixed
expression *If I **were** you …*

Main clause

You usually use *would* + infinitive in the main clause.

I/You/He, *etc.* **'d** (**would**) **work.**	I/You/He, *etc.* **wouldn't** (**would not**) **work.**	**Would** I/you/ he, *etc.* **work?**	Yes, I/you/he, *etc.* **would.**	No, I/you/he, *etc.* **wouldn't.**

if-clause	Main clause
If I had $1 million,	I**'d travel** round the world.
If I could live anywhere,	I**'d choose** somewhere hot.

Unit 11 Exercises

Part 1

1 Complete these quotations by inserting *who* or *that* in the correct position. In each case, the relative clause describes the underlined word.

a) 'A camel is a <u>horse</u> *that* has been designed by a committee.' (Alec Issigonis – designer of the Mini)

b) 'Everybody knows how to raise children – except the <u>people</u> have them.' (P.J. O'Rourke – US humorist)

c) 'How can you govern a <u>country</u> has 246 varieties of cheese?' (Charles de Gaulle – French president)

d) 'Go on, get out! Last words are for <u>fools</u> haven't said enough.' (Karl Marx, on his death bed)

e) 'Life is <u>something</u> happens when you can't get to sleep.' (Fran Lebowitz – US humorist)

f) 'A bank is a <u>place</u> will lend you money if you can prove you don't need it.' (Bob Hope – US humorist)

g) '<u>Women</u> want to be equal with men don't have ambition.' (Timothy Leary – US philosopher)

h) '<u>People</u> get nostalgic about childhood were obviously never children.' (Bill Watterson – US humorist)

Which quotation do you like best? Discuss with a partner.

2 Write sentences that define the underlined words. Use the information in brackets.

a) Most of the <u>people</u> speak perfect English. (They work with me.)
   Most of the people who work with me speak perfect English.

b) <u>People</u> make me angry. (They complain all the time.)

c) I've met lots of <u>people</u>. (They have the same name as me.)

d) We should ban <u>cars</u>. (They use too much petrol.)

e) I think <u>dictionaries</u> are useless. (They don't give good examples.)

f) <u>The family</u> have a dog and a cat. (They live next door.)

Are any of these sentences true for you?

Part 2

1 Complete the sentences with the correct verb forms to describe imaginary situations.

a) If I (can) *could* sing, I (join) *'d join* a rock band.

b) If I (win) _____ the lottery, I (give) _____ half the money to charity.

c) If I (be) _____ more organised, I (not be) _____ late for everything.

d) If I (have) _____ more time, I (read) _____ more.

e) If I (not work) _____ so hard, I (not be) _____ so tired.

f) If I (lose) _____ my job, I (have to) _____ sell my car.

Which sentences are true for you? Compare with a partner.

2 Complete at least five of these sentences in an appropriate way.

a) If I met Brad Pitt …

b) If I could order any food I wanted …

c) If I saw a lion …

d) If I had a Ferrari …

e) If I didn't have to work …

f) If I could speak English perfectly …

g) If there were twenty-five hours in the day …

h) If money was no problem …

i) If I could fly …

j) If today was the last day of my life …

Compare your sentences with your partner.

Unit 12 Past perfect. Passives

Part 1: Past perfect

Affirmative	Negative	Question	Short answer *Yes*	Short answer *No*
I/You/He, *etc.* 'd (had) worked.	I/You/He, *etc.* hadn't (had not) worked.	Had I/you/he, *etc.* worked?	Yes, I/you/he, *etc.* had.	No, I/you/he, *etc.* hadn't.

See the list of irregular verbs on page 159.

You use the past perfect when you are talking about the past and you want to refer to an earlier past time. The past perfect clearly shows that one past event happened earlier than other past events.

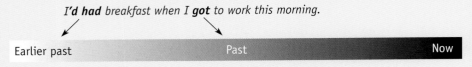

I'd had breakfast when I got to work this morning.

Earlier past — Past — Now

Part 2: Passives

In passive sentences, the object of the active verb becomes the subject of the passive verb.

Active

subject verb object
Somebody built the first Ice Hotel in 1990.

Passive

subject verb
The first Ice Hotel was built in 1990.

You can use passive verbs to talk about actions when it doesn't matter (or you don't know) who performed them.
My shoes were designed in Italy.
All the furniture is made of ice.

Affirmative	Negative	Question	Short answer *Yes*	Short answer *No*
They're made in China.	They aren't made in China.	Are they made in China?	Yes, they are.	No, they aren't.
It was built here.	It wasn't built here.	Was it built here?	Yes, it was.	No, it wasn't.

Unit 12 Exercises

Part 1

1 Read this story about reincarnation. Choose the correct tense – past simple or past perfect – for the verbs (*1–12*).

Jenny Cockell was sure that she (1) **lived / had lived** before. She often dreamt about Mary Sutton, a young Irish woman who (2) **died / had died** more than twenty years before Jenny was born. Jenny thought that her dreams (3) **were / had been** real memories and that she (4) **was / had been** Mary in a previous life.

In her dreams she saw the house in Ireland where Mary and her family (5) **lived / had lived**. As her visions continued and became more detailed, Jenny (6) **realised / had realised** that Mary (7) **died / had died** in 1930 and that her children could still be alive. She decided to travel to Ireland and find out.

In Ireland, Jenny quickly found the house that she (8) **saw / had seen** in her dreams. Then, after a few more investigations she managed to contact Mary Sutton's eldest son, Sonny. It was an emotional day when Jenny (9) **met / had met** the son who she (10) **didn't see / hadn't seen** for fifty years. 'I talked to him about our family life together. I (11) **reminded / had reminded** him of the day when he had caught a rabbit. There were lots of other memories, and they convinced him that I (12) **was / had been** his mother in a previous life.'

Jenny Cockell has written the story of her extraordinary past life experiences in a book entitled *Yesterday's Children*.

2 Did Sonny think that Jenny was his mother? What do you think?

Part 2

1 Write passive sentences with the verbs in brackets.

a) This school (open) _____ in the 1990s.
 This school was opened in the 1990s.
b) My car (park) _____ outside my house every day.
c) My house (clean) _____ once a week.
d) Our classroom (paint) _____ recently.
e) My name (pronounce) _____ differently in English.
f) My watch (make) _____ in Switzerland.

Tick the sentences that are true for you.

2 Write questions to ask your partner with the sentences in Exercise 1.

a) *Was this school opened in the 1990s?*

Ask your partner the questions.

3 Complete the information about Burj al Arab. Choose the correct passive structures for the verbs in brackets.

The world's tallest hotel (1 call) *is called* Burj al Arab or 'Tower of the Arabs'. It (2 build) _____ on an artificial island and (3 connect) _____ to the mainland at Jumeirah, Dubai by a private bridge. Building work (4 start) _____ in 1994 and (5 complete) _____ three years later. The hotel (6 design) _____ to look like the sail of an Arab sailing ship. Burj al Arab (7 consider) _____ to be the world's only seven-star hotel and has become an iconic structure symbolising modern Dubai.

Recordings

Unit 1

 1.01

(M = Marie; B = Benjamin)

M: Hi, I'm Marie.

B: Hi Marie. My name's Benjamin, but nobody calls me Benjamin. Well, my parents do, but my friends call me Ben.

M: Ben – that's nice.

B: Thanks. Actually, my old friends call me Tree.

M: Tree? Why?

B: Well, as you can see, I'm very tall.

M: Oh, ha ha. … My friends call me lots of different names.

B: Really?

M: Yes. My mum's French and my dad's English, so I've got English and French friends, and they call me different things.

B: What do your French friends call you?

M: They use my full name – Anne-Marie.

B: And your English friends?

M: They just call me Marie. Some of them call me Marie Antoinette.

B: Marie Antoinette! Oh dear.

M: Well, it could be worse. My brother calls me Baby, because I'm the youngest in the family.

B: That's not so bad – my sisters call me Big Ben.

M: Ha ha. Oh no!

1.06

Dan Carter is my best friend. We met when we were five years old, because our parents were friends and we went to the same school. He lives in Brussels now – he's a teacher at the International School there. So I only see him in the summer when he comes home to visit his family. Of course, we stay in touch by email and phone. He's important to me because he knows me so well. When I'm feeling down or when I need to talk to somebody, I can always call him. Recently, I had girlfriend problems and he was great. I'd say his best quality is that he's a really good listener. He just lets you talk and he listens. But he isn't perfect! He's always late for everything and he never says sorry. Never! One day last summer, we arranged to meet at seven o'clock to play football, and he arrived at half past nine! It was nearly dark! Oh well, nobody's perfect, are they? Last time I saw him was on my birthday, and we had a great time. We always have a great time.

Unit 2

1.11

Paulo

(I = Interviewer; P = Paulo)

I: Do you like your city?

P Oh yes, I feel lucky to be living in a city that's so big and exciting.

I: What's the architecture like?

P: A mixture of old and new. There are too many high-rise buildings in some parts of the city. But there are plenty of cheap restaurants and interesting cafés and bars. And the nightlife is great. We also have the most famous beach in the world – Copacabana Beach.

I: Ah. What's the weather like?

P: It's great most of the time. The only time I don't like Rio much is in the summer: it's too hot and humid.

Armelle

(I = Interviewer; A = Armelle)

I: Where do you live?

A: Well, I live in a small village with my parents. My grandparents live here too, and my aunts and uncles. In fact, I think I'm related to about fifty per cent of the people in my village.

I: What's your village like?

A: It's very pretty. The countryside is beautiful, and the air is lovely and clean. But at night it's too quiet. I find it so dull and boring here – there aren't any discos or cinemas.

I: What are the people like?

A: Oh, they're kind and really friendly, but there aren't many young people. I want to go and live in the city. Soon.

Luigi

(I = Interviewer; L = Luigi)

I: What do you think of your city?

L: It is a very special place. It's such a romantic city.

I: What's the city centre like?

L: The buildings are beautiful, and we have San Marco, one of the most famous churches in the world. The Piazza San Marco is wonderful, and during carnival in February Venice is the best place in the world to be.

I: Do you like living here?

L: No, I really hate living here. It's horrible. There are too many tourists everywhere. It gets very noisy and crowded.

I: Oh dear. What are the shops like?

L: Well, because of the tourists the shops are too expensive, and the canals are so dirty and polluted. My city is too small for all these people. Why don't they leave us in peace?

1.13

The best place I've ever visited is Buenos Aires, the capital of Argentina. It's a crazy city, but I really love it.

The first time I went there was on my summer holiday. It was the year before I went to university. So I was young and excited, and it was my first time in South America.

I flew there on my own, but I went to stay with friends. Of course I visited all the tourist places – the Colon Theatre, the Plaza de Mayo, La Boca, and my friends took me to watch a tango show. That was great. I even took some tango lessons, but I'm not very good.

I also went out dancing a lot – Buenos Aires nightlife is fantastic. The streets are crowded at three o'clock in the morning with people going to restaurants and discos. The discos are open until six or seven o'clock in the morning – in fact, Buenos Aires never sleeps!

Now I go back to Buenos Aires as often as possible. I've been there three times, and last year I went there for New Year.

What I particularly like about Buenos Aires is the people. Argentinian people are very special. They're loud and energetic and really good fun. I love them.

Unit 3

1.16

(E = Edna; F = Fred)

E: We first met fifty years ago.

F: I joined the army and I went to Blackpool in the north of England for my training. On the first day I went to the canteen, and this little lady was serving lunch.

E: Yes, I was. I liked him so I gave him extra chips.

F: Anyway we started talking. Then, one night, there was a party.

E: I said to Fred, 'I'll be your girl tonight,' and that was it.

F: Yes, we went out together for three wonderful months.

E: We did.

F: Then we both moved to different places. At first we wrote to each other. We wrote twice a week.

E: Yes, but then we stopped. I don't know why. But we lost touch with each other. Then we got married to other people. I had two children, and Fred had a daughter, didn't you?

F: That's right. I was married for forty-eight years, and then my wife died.

E: And I got divorced after thirty years of marriage.

F: So we were both single again.

E: And one day, my grandson took me to Blackpool for the day. I visited all the old places and I thought about Fred. I wanted to find him.

F: She didn't even know whether I was alive.

E: No, I didn't. So I wrote a letter to the editor of the local newspaper.

F: I have a cousin in Blackpool. She doesn't usually buy the newspaper. But on that day she did. She bought the paper and she saw the letter. And she realised that Edna was looking for me.

E: He rang me up. I nearly had a heart

attack. I said, 'Is that my Fred?' I was so happy.

F: We met soon after that. We realised we were still in love and we moved in together a few months later.

E: We got married last summer. I didn't want to lose him again!

🔊 1.19

(I = Introducer; BB = Bobby Brown; R = Rosie; D = Dave)

I: It's time for our popular competition, *Get Personal*, with your host, Bobby Brown.

BB: Good evening and welcome to this week's *Get Personal*. Let's meet our first couple, Rosie and Dave. As you know, Rosie and Dave are in separate studios – Rosie can't hear Dave, and Dave has no idea what Rosie is saying. But they can both hear me. OK, are you ready to play *Get Personal*?

R&D: Yes, Bobby.

BB: Right, we'll start with you, Rosie. We want you to remember exactly what was going on when you first met Dave. OK?

R: OK, Bobby.

BB: Now Rosie, how did you first meet Dave?

R: Well, I was working as a nurse, and Dave was my patient. He came into the hospital for an operation.

BB: OK, Rosie. I want you to think about the moment when you first met. What time of day was it?

R: Um, I was working nights that week. So early evening.

BB: Uh huh. And what was the weather like?

R: Oh dear, I think it was raining. Yes, it was raining when I arrived at work.

BB: What were you both wearing when you saw one another for the first time?

R: Now that's easy. I was wearing my nurse's uniform, and he was wearing pyjamas. Blue pyjamas. Or were they green? No, blue.

BB: Finally, who spoke first and what did he or she say?

R: Dave spoke first. In fact he shouted at me. He said, 'Nurse, I'm going to be sick.'

BB: Oh well, that's *very* romantic! Thank you, Rosie.

🔊 1.20

(BB = Bobby Brown; R = Rosie; D = Dave)

BB: Now, Dave, it's your turn. Where and how did you first meet?

D: Well, I went into hospital for an operation, and Rosie was working there as a nurse.

BB: What time of day was it?

D: Oh, I don't know. Lunchtime? No, hang on, it was later than that. Early evening.

BB: What was the weather like?

D: Oh dear. It was summer, so I suppose the sun was shining.

BB: What were you both wearing when you saw one another for the first time?

D: Rosie was wearing her nurse's uniform and she was also wearing lovely perfume. I was wearing my favourite blue pyjamas.

BB: Finally, Dave, who spoke first and what did he or she say?

D: Rosie spoke first. She said, 'How are you feeling?' And I think I said, 'I feel terrible.'

🔊 1.24

(T = Tim; A = Anna)

T: Excuse me. Do you know what time we arrive in London?

A: Yes, I think we get there at about 2.30.

T: Thanks. I see you're reading *Pride and Prejudice*. Are you enjoying it?

A: Yes, I am.

T: I didn't like the film much.

A: Oh, I did. I thought it was great. I really like Keira Knightley.

T: Oh, so do I. I think she's really good in *Pirates of the Caribbean*.

A: Me too. I love that film. Johnny Depp's brilliant.

T: I know. I'm going to see his new film tomorrow night.

A: Really? So am I. Where are you going to see it?

T: Piccadilly Circus.

A: Me too!

T: Oh, that's great. I don't know what time it starts.

A: No, neither do I. But my husband has the tickets, so he knows.

T: Oh. That's good.

🔊 1.25

a) 'I didn't like the film much.' 'Neither did I.' 'Me neither.' 'Oh, I did.'

b) 'I really like Keira Knightley.' 'So do I.' 'Me too.' 'Oh, I don't.'

c) 'I think she's really good.' 'So do I.' 'Me too.' 'Oh, I don't.'

d) 'I'm going to see Johnny Depp's new film.' 'So am I.' 'Me too.' 'Oh, I'm not.'

e) 'I don't know what time it starts.' 'Neither do I.' 'Me neither.' 'Oh, I do.'

Review A

🔊 1.28

(C = Carol; J = Jessica)

C: OK, so who's that in this photo, Jessica?

J: Oh, that's my friend, Mark.

C: Friend? Really?

J: OK, boyfriend!

C: Hmm. Where did you meet him?

J: At university in London – about five years ago.

C: Oh, right.

J: Yeah. I didn't actually like him at first. And I already had a boyfriend. But one day a group of us spent the day together at the beach. We went swimming and chatted and I discovered that Mark was a very interesting person and he really liked travelling.

C: You like travelling too, don't you?

J: Yes, I love it. Anyway, we talked all evening, and after that we became really good friends. But after university he went back to his home in the USA – he's American – and I stayed here.

C: Oh no!

J: Then Mark and I started emailing and phoning each other a lot because we wanted to go scuba diving in Egypt with friends.

C: Ah. In the Red Sea?

J: That's right. Anyway, I saw Mark in Egypt with all our friends. It was a lot of fun. Then, last summer I went to the USA to visit him. I asked him to come back to England with me, and he did.

C: Really? That's brilliant.

J: Yes, we're good together. In fact we're planning a trip to the Bahamas at the moment ... Hey, life is good!

Unit 4

🔊 1.32

The last present I bought was for my sister. It was her birthday. In fact, it was her thirtieth birthday. Thirty isn't very old, but she was quite upset. She liked being in her twenties and she thought thirty was really old. Anyway, I didn't know what to get her, so I went on the internet to find something. I didn't have any ideas, but I wanted something special. Eventually, I found a really good present. I thought it was unusual, and just perfect for her – it was a foot spa. My sister's a teacher and she stands up all day, so a foot spa is great for relaxing in the evening. It was expensive – about £50 – but she's my sister, and thirty is a special birthday. I bought a lovely card and wrote a funny message in it – I put, 'Now you're thirty you're too old to die young!' Ha ha. On her birthday, I gave her the present, but unfortunately she didn't like it – at all. She said that a foot spa is a good present for a grandmother, not for a young woman. I was really surprised – I'd love a foot spa. And then, when she read the card, she cried! What a disaster.

🔊 1.33

(I = Interviewer, C = Conor, J = Jim)

I: Right, OK. Question one. Do you mind going round the shops?

C: Not really. But after about an hour I want to go home

J: Actually, I can't stand going round the shops. My girlfriend knows this, so she usually chooses to go without me.

I: Right, OK. Um let's see. Question two. What kind of shops do you enjoy going into?

C: Book shops. I spend a lot of time reading book reviews so I always have a list of books I'd like to buy.

J: I enjoy looking at electronic equipment but I can't afford to buy it. It's usually far too expensive.

I: Right. OK. Question three. Are there any kinds of shops you hate going into?

C: I hate supermarkets. I usually forget to buy the things I went there for, so

I avoid going into them. Fortunately, I can do most of my food shopping online.

J: I refuse to go into shoe shops with my girlfriend. She tries on ten pairs and then decides to buy the first pair.

I: Right. OK. Last question. Question four. Do you enjoy buying clothes for yourself?

C: Not really. I only go into a clothes shop when I need to buy a new shirt or something. For me, shopping is a necessity, not a pleasure.

J: I love having new clothes, but I never manage to find time to go shopping.

🌐 1.34

Keiko is wearing a black silk waistcoat, a white cotton shirt, black woollen trousers and black leather boots.

Robert is wearing a plain green linen top, a red cotton skirt, a light green silk scarf around his head, gold earrings, a gold necklace, and yellow leather sandals.

🌐 1.35

a) a striped, woollen hat
b) patterned silk ties
c) a pinstriped jacket
d) a checked shirt

Unit 5

🌐 2.01

When I was at secondary school, we did sport every Wednesday afternoon. Two hours, from 1.30 to 3.30. Wednesdays were my worst day of the week. I hated doing sport at school. In summer we did swimming and tennis, and in winter we did hockey. I really, really hated hockey. It was always cold when we played hockey, but we wore shorts! Horrible, grey shorts. My legs were very thin and they were so cold that they turned blue. I was always happy when it was raining or snowing – then we stayed inside and did Scottish dancing. I loved that.

At my school we had a sports field and tennis courts and a swimming pool. I love swimming, but the swimming pool wasn't heated so it was freezing.

I didn't like my sports teacher, and she didn't like me. Her name was Miss Rockham. We called her Rocky. She looked like a boxer, and she had a very loud voice. She loved hockey. In fact, I think she played for the national hockey team.

Of course, I didn't play for the school hockey team, but I loved dancing so much that I joined a dance club after school. My best sporting moment was when my dance club won a competition for disco dancing. Rocky didn't think that dancing was a real sport, but I disagree. Dancing kept me fit, and I didn't have to wear grey shorts.

🌐 2.02

David Beckham is the oldest. He was born in 1975. Thierry Henry's next. He was born in 1977. After that, it's Fernando Alonso – born in July 1981. Then, Roger Federer, a few days later, in August, 1981. Cristiano Ronaldo was born in 1985 and Rafael Nadal is the youngest. He was born in 1986.

🌐 2.03

(MD: marketing director; AE: advertising executive)

MD: OK, what are we looking for exactly?

AE: We're looking for the new face of 'Iso-tonic', the new energy drink.

MD: Yes, I know ... but what kind of face are we looking for?

AE: Ah, well, we need a sports celebrity. Probably a man. Someone good-looking and healthy.

MD: Good. Do we have any ideas?

AE: Yes, we're thinking of David Beckham or Thierry Henry.

MD: Hmm, Beckham is more famous than Henry …

AE: Hmm. But he isn't as interesting.

MD: Are they the same age?

AE: Um, I think Beckham is a bit older than Henry.

MD: Hmm. I think we need a younger man.

AE: How about Fernando Alonso?

MD: Who's he?

AE: He's a Formula One champion – he's young, successful …

MD: But Formula One is too dangerous. We want this man to be the face of 'Iso-tonic' for a few years. How about tennis? Federer, Nadal …?

AE: Hmm. Nadal isn't as successful as Federer.

MD: No, but Nadal's much younger than Federer, so he could be more successful in future.

AE: Hmm.

MD: OK, who's your favourite sports star?

AE: Oh, Cristiano Ronaldo. I think he's the best-looking, most interesting, most successful sportsman in the world.

MD: Well, let's use him then. Perfect. I want you to get in touch with him immediately.

🌐 2.04

a) At 5,894 metres, Mount Kilimanjaro is much higher than Mount Fuji, which is 3,776 metres.

b) Surprisingly, London isn't as wet as Rome. The annual average in London is 594 millimetres, whereas in Rome the annual average is 749 millimetres.

c) The US army is much smaller than the North Korean Army. There are 524,900 American soldiers compared to over one million North Koreans.

d) Heathrow Airport in London is a bit busier than Los Angeles International Airport. In one year, Heathrow serves 51,368,000 passengers, and Los Angeles serves 51,030,000.

e) Ireland isn't as big as Cuba. Ireland is 83,030 square kilometres, but Cuba is 114,530.

f) Big Ben is a bit taller than the Statue of Liberty. Big Ben is 96 metres tall, and the Statue of Liberty is 93 metres tall.

🌐 2.05

a) It's as light as a feather.
b) He's as free as a bird.
c) They're as good as gold.
d) She's as pretty as a picture.
e) It's as solid as a rock.
f) It's as old as the hills.

🌐 2.06

Three quarters.
Nought point two five.
Nought point three three.
One and a half.
An eighth.
A quarter.
One point five.
Nought point one two five.
A third.
Nought point seven five.

🌐 2.07

a) two hundred and forty-nine kilometres an hour
b) forty-two point one nine five kilometres
c) eight point two percent
d) six million, one hundred and eighty-eight thousand
e) Thirty-two nil

🌐 2.08

(P = Presenter; A = Avril)

P: We all know the expression 'laughter is the best medicine'. But a recent study shows that adults don't laugh enough. The study shows that young children laugh up to four hundred times a day, while adults only laugh seventeen times a day. According to medical research, fifteen to twenty minutes of laughter a day really does keep the doctor away. Well now you can join one of the laughter clubs to get your regular twenty minutes of laughter. It sounds funny, and it even looks a little funny, but this is a laughter club. Avril is the teacher here. Avril, how did the laughter clubs start?

A: They started in India eleven years ago. Dr Kataria started a club in Mumbai, and now there are hundreds of laughter clubs all over the world. In India, people are very serious about the benefits of laughter.

P: And what are the benefits of laughter?

A: When you laugh, you release happy chemicals – endorphins. This can reduce the effects of stress and you feel more relaxed. Laughter boosts the immune system and relaxes the mind. Also, laughing is good for the heart and good for the lungs.

P: What happens in laughter club? What exactly do you do?

A: We just laugh.

P: Do you listen to funny stories?

A: Oh no. We don't need anything to make us laugh. We do exercises, and when you start laughing, you can't stop.

P: What kind of exercises?

A: Well, we start the class with a laughing exercise called ho ho ha ha ha. After that, we do different kinds of laughing. There's 'social laughter' … silent laughter … and the loud, explosive laugh … which exercises the lungs.

🔊 2.09

a)

(L = Luke; S = Sally)

L: OK, are you ready?
S: Yes.
L: Right. Stand up on the board.
S: OK. Ohhhhh!
L: Ha ha ha!
S: Don't be horrible.
L: Oh, sorry. OK, try again. Good! Great. Hold on. Don't let go.
S: Ohhhhh! It's too difficult. I can't do it.
L: Don't be silly. Of course you can do it. Be patient. Come on, try again.
S: I look stupid.
L: Don't worry! Everyone looks stupid the first time. Now, stand up on the board. That's it. Be careful. Good. Well done. Now, don't go too fast, Sally. Sally! Come back!
S: Wheeee!

b)

(F = Father; J = Jimmy)

F: OK, Jimmy, kick the ball to me.
J: Daddy, Daddy, look at me.
F: Oh, that's very good, Jimmy. Now, this time, don't throw the ball – kick it.
J: Kick?
F: Yes, with your foot. Look, like this.
J: Like this?
F: No, no, don't pick it up – that's it. Now kick it. No, don't touch the ball with your hand. Use your foot. Yes, that's it. Ouch!
J: You OK, Daddy?
F: Aagh!

c)

(M = Mother; R = Rebecca)

M: Right, watch me. Throw the ball in the air. Watch the ball, and hit it. OK? Now you try. Throw the ball in the air and hit the – oh, OK, try again. This time, don't look at me – look at the ball. Throw the ball in the air. Watch the ball and, … oh dear.
R: I hate this stupid game. I want to go horse-riding. You're horrible.
M: Don't be rude, Rebecca. Pick up your racket and try again.

Unit 6

🔊 2.10

Mark, a company director
I think I wanted to be a soldier – I liked the uniform, and lots of boys want to be soldiers when they're young, don't they? Later on I thought of being an engineer, but I didn't do any work at school so I couldn't go to university. In the end I started working with my father and now I'm the director of my own company, so I'm quite pleased with the way things turned out.

Lucy, a surgeon
I've always wanted to be a surgeon, right from when I was a small child. It's my vocation. When I was at school, my best friend wanted to be a ballet dancer, but even then I knew what I wanted to do. There's never been a doctor in our family but my father's a butcher, so I suppose it's similar!

Frank, a teacher
When I was five, I wanted to be a farmer or a vet because I loved animals. Later, I wanted to be a pilot, but my eyes weren't good enough. When I was at university I wanted to be a snowboarder, but I wasn't good enough to be a professional. After university I had no idea what I wanted to do so I became a teacher, and I love it.

Mia, a model
My dream was to be an archaeologist. My family went on holiday to Egypt, and I loved the Pyramids so much that I became really interested in ancient history. But when I was sixteen I had the chance to earn a lot of money as a model, so I stopped studying, and I've been working as a model for five years now. I want to start studying again when I'm thirty.

🔊 2.12

a) said, read, fed, been
b) known, bought, flown, grown
c) rung, sung, brought, hung
d) drank, taught, thought, fought

🔊 2.13

(P = Presenter; I = Interviewer; Mr R = Mr Reynold)

P: And this week, in our regular report from England, we visited a department store with a difference …
I: Mr Reynold, can you tell us what is so special about your department store?
Mr R: Well, Reynold's is a large department store and you can find everything you want for the home here. Oh, and it stays open late on Thursdays and Saturdays.
I: Yes, that's right, but isn't there something special about the staff – you know – has anybody retired recently?
Mr R: Ah, oh, I see. No. Nobody has retired recently, and we never force anybody to retire here.
I: How old is your oldest employee?
Mr R: Well, that's Arthur. Arthur is our cleaner, and he's 87.
I: 87! And he cleans the store every day?
Mr R: Well, not alone, no. He works with two other cleaners. They're not so old – Mabel's 70 and Ivy's 75 – no 76. That's right, she's just had her birthday.
I: And they don't want to retire?
Mr R: No, I think they enjoy the work, and it keeps them young. Also, we pay a decent salary, and they get four weeks' paid holiday a year.

I: So how many workers do you have who are over retirement age?
Mr R: Well, we employ a staff of 105 and half of those are over 65. The young ones work in the office – we've got computers now you know.
I: Really? Has the store changed much over the years?
Mr R: No, not really. I started working here in 1948 and I've only had two secretaries in all that time. Edith, my first secretary, resigned when she was 72.
I: Oh, why did she leave Reynold's so young?
Mr R: Well, she was getting married to someone who lived in another town.
I: Jeez! That's amazing … Do you think you will ever retire, Mr Reynold?
Mr R: Oh yes. I'm nearly 86! My son's going to take over the business next year. He's only 64.

🔊 2.14

My friend Hannah has the best job in the world – she's a personal trainer. She has about ten clients, and she writes an exercise programme for each person. She doesn't work for anybody – she's self-employed.

She starts work very early every day because some of her clients like to do exercise before they go to work. I think she starts her first client at seven o'clock in the morning.

I think it's a great job, because Hannah loves sport and so she gets money for doing what she loves. She earns a reasonably good salary. I think she charges £35 an hour, so her salary depends on the number of hours she works. She loves her job because she helps people to get fit and healthy.

I'd love to do her job, because she doesn't have to work in an office all day and she doesn't have to go to the gym in her free time either. She's her own boss so she can go on holiday when she wants, and she always looks fantastic in a swimming costume.

🔊 2.15

(C = Chair; L = Layla; M = Mike; J = Jack; E = Elsie)

C: Good afternoon everybody. Welcome to Quit Smoking. I'm John and I'm an ex-smoker. Can you tell the group who you are, and what you do.
L: Hello. My name's Layla. I work for a big company and we produce high quality audio equipment. I'm responsible for sales and promotion.
M: Good morning. My name's Mike. I've just left university and at present I'm unemployed. I'm looking for a job in publishing.
J: Hi. I'm Jack and I work as a bodyguard. I'm self-employed and I'm based in London, but my job involves a lot of foreign travel. I have to take important clients safely from one place to another.
E: My name's Elsie. I'm a photographer

and I work for a music magazine. We're based in Brighton. I run the photography department and I'm in charge of taking photographs of rock stars and bands, so I travel a lot, especially to the United States.

C: Thank you. Right, let's get this meeting started. Coffee is at …

Review B

🔘 **2.19**

(T = Tom; P = Patsy)

T: Patsy and I are very different …
P: Yes, very different. In fact we're complete opposites. Tom's water and I'm air. He's a Scorpio and I'm an Aquarius.
T: Mm, I don't really believe in all that …
P: And Tom's much older than me. I think that also makes a difference.
T: I don't see what difference …
P: The clothes he wears make him look older, too.
T: That's true. On the other hand, Patsy dresses like a teenager.
P: No, I don't. But I do enjoy finding fashionable clothes at good prices. I always buy him really good clothes but, he never wears them.
T: We've been married for twenty-two years …
P: Is it that long?
T: … and sometimes we can't understand why we've stayed together …
P: Yes. He likes watching sport on TV, whereas I like getting out there and playing it. I can't stand watching it on TV.
T: She loves shopping, but I prefer sitting in my garden with a newspaper.
P: So, why are we together? Simple – I love him. He's a good husband and a good father to our children. And he's one of the funniest people I've ever met.
T: I think I'm the luckiest person I know.

Unit 7

🔘 **2.21**

Jo, 26
I work for an organisation called Eco Holidays, and we're demonstrating against mass tourism. I'm not against tourism but I believe in responsible tourism. We're against big hotels and package holidays. With Eco Holidays you can really experience the local culture. We organise accommodation with local families. Would you like some information about our holidays?

Jake, 14
I'm having fun with my friends. It's my first demonstration. I don't feel strongly about politics, but I'm worried about global warming. I don't really care about people – they can look after themselves. I'm in favour of protecting wild animals – I want to help polar bears and penguins. If the ice caps melt, where will they live?

Debbie, 37
I'm here because we're destroying the planet. I'm protesting against multinational companies. They're polluting our rivers and oceans and they're causing global warming. I'm in favour of small family-run companies. I'm against food imports. I support local farmers and I buy food from farmers' markets, not supermarkets.

Ronny, 27
I'm riding my bicycle today because I'm against big cars in the city. I'm not anti-cars – in fact, I have a car – but I just think more people should use public transport. Leave your car at home – ride a bicycle!

🔘 **2.23**

(H = Helen; C = Carole)

H: I've decided I'm going to change my life.
C: Yeah, me too. I want a bigger house, a bigger salary and a better boyfriend.
H: No, I'm serious. I'm going to do something important.
C: What do you mean?
H: I want to help people less fortunate than me – I'm going to go abroad and work with children.
C: Oh. Well, that's um … Where are you going?
H: Ghana.
C: Ghana? What about the animals?
H: No, I'm not going to work with animals – I want to help people.
C: No, I mean the dangerous animals – crocodiles, lions, snakes, …
H: Oh, I see. I'm not just going there alone. I've joined an organisation, and they're going to arrange everything for me. I'm going to work in an orphanage.
C: Good for you. How much are they going to pay you?
H: Nothing. I'm a volunteer. In fact, I'm going to pay them £25 a week.
C: You're going to pay *them*. I see. When are you going?
H: Soon – next month.
C: Wow. How exciting. I'd love to visit South America.
H: Africa. Ghana's in Africa.
C: Oh is it? There are a lot of dangerous animals in Africa.
H: I told you, I'm not …

🔘 **2.24**

(M = Mum; H = Helen)

M: Who's picking you up at the airport?
H: I've told you, Mum.
M: I know, but I'm worried. Ghana's a long way from here.
H: OK. Let's go through it again. I'm arriving in Accra at ten o'clock in the morning, and the volunteers' coordinator is meeting me. That's Bob White. He's taking me to my accommodation.
M: And you're staying with a family.
H: Yes, I'm staying with a Ghanaian family.
M: Don't you want to stay in a hotel?
H: No, I want to have an authentic experience, so I'm staying with the Odoi family.

M: You must write down their name and address for me.
H: Yes, don't worry. Then, I'm starting work on Monday.
M: And where exactly are you working?
H: In a small town near Accra.
M: How are you getting there?
H: By bus. Mrs Odoi's going to make sure I get the right bus.
M: When are you coming back?
H: On 15th September. Just in time for your birthday.

Unit 8

🔘 **2.28**

I wasn't very academic at school, but I loved art. Yes, art was my favourite subject because I was good at it. We had a wonderful teacher – she was called Miss Lewis, and I remember the first day she arrived at school. She didn't look like a teacher. She had long black hair, and she wore bright colours. She was quite young – thirty, thirty-one, something like that, and we all fell in love with her – boys and girls! She wasn't just beautiful – she was a really good teacher too. Her lessons were interesting and varied. We only had three hours of art each week on Wednesday afternoons. Miss Lewis loved photography and she taught us how to develop our own photographs. I really enjoyed that, and for a while I wanted to be a professional photographer. In the end I realised that it was difficult to make a living as a photographer so I went to university and studied engineering. But I still love taking photos and recently I won a competition – Miss Lewis would be proud of me!

🔘 **2.30**

a) 'Did Gordon have to obey his dad without questions?' 'Yes, he did.' 'No, he didn't.'
b) 'Did Gordon have to go to church on Sundays?' 'Yes, he did.' 'No, he didn't.'
c) 'Could Gordon bring his girlfriends home?' 'Yes, he could.' 'No, he couldn't.'
d) 'Did Tony have to do his homework every night?' 'Yes, he did.' 'No, he didn't.'
e) 'Could Scott come home at any time?' 'Yes, he could.' 'No, he couldn't.'
f) 'Does Scott have to hide things from his dad?' 'Yes, he does.' 'No, he doesn't.'

🔘 **2.31**

(S = Scott; G = Gordon)

S: Fasten your seatbelt, grandad.
G: But I'm sitting in the back.
S: Yes, and you have to fasten your seatbelt in the back now.
G: Oh dear. All these rules and regulations. In my day, we didn't have to wear seatbelts at all.
S: And it was much more dangerous.
G: But we didn't drive so fast. And there weren't so many cars on the road. In my day, we couldn't drive fast because there weren't any motorways.

G: Hmm, very funny. Actually, I had a beautiful motorbike – a Triumph – and I didn't have to wear a helmet. Not like nowadays.

S: Do you really think life was better in your day, grandad?

G: Well, life was less complicated. For example, we didn't have all these credit cards in my day. We had to use cash to buy things

S: But not everything was better, grandad. You had to do military service – I wouldn't like that.

G: I was proud to do military service. In my day, a man had to be a man. Not like these days – men and women look exactly the same to me. In my day, you couldn't have long hair, or wear earrings or carry a handbag like some men do nowadays.

S: Ha ha. But some things were more difficult in your day, grandad – like travelling.

G: That's right, we couldn't travel by air like you do today – it was too expensive. But we travelled by train and bus. I remember the first time I went to France.

🔊 2.32

(L = Liz; M = Martin; J = John; A = Anne)

L: This is my mum, and this is my dad.

M: Hello, Mrs Farley … Mr Farley.

J: Nice to meet you, Martin. Please call us John and Anne.

A: Come in. Take a seat.

J: That's a very smart suit. Have you come straight from work?

M: Oh, no, I usually wear jeans at work!

J: Oh … what do you do?

M: Ah, er, I'm a um sort of, interior design consultant.

L: He works in a furniture shop.

A: Oh, that's nice. Um, Liz tells us you were in France recently.

M: Yes, that's right, I went to Paris last month.

A: Lovely. Did you like it?

M: Well, it's a beautiful city, but the people were very rude.

A: Oh. Did you know John's mother's from Paris?

M: Oh dear, no, I didn't. I'm sorry. I didn't mean … um …

J: Don't worry, my mother's very rude too. … Now Martin, would you like a beer?

M: Oh, yes, please. Um, is that a photo of Liz when she was younger?

J: Yes, she was ten here. Would you like to see some more photos?

L: Oh, Dad!

M: Oh, yes, please, er … John.

A: OK, John, you get the photo albums out, and I'll chat to Martin. So Martin, what are you going to do in the future?

M: Well, in my free time I'm studying at the college …

🔊 2.34

(J = Jean; E = Elaine)

J: How are your children?

E: Oh Jenny's very well. She's a dentist now.

J: Oh very good.

E: Yes, it's a good job, but I don't think she should work.

J: Oh, why?

E: Well, her son's only three. I think mothers should stay at home and look after the children.

J: Oh yes, I agree. I think children need their mothers at home.

E: Absolutely. My daughter thinks fathers should stay at home and look after the children.

J: Oh no, I don't agree with that. It's a woman's job.

E: Exactly. Now, what about your son? Is he married yet?

J: No, but he's living with his girlfriend.

E: Oh dear. I don't think couples should live together before they get married.

J: Oh, I'm not so sure. I don't think my son's ready to get married.

E: No, he's like my Simon. He's thirty-six and he's still living at home.

J: Really? I think young people should leave home when they're eighteen.

E: Well, it depends. Simon can't afford to leave home.

J: Well, when we were young, …

Unit 9

🔊 3.02

1 I'd love to meet your friends – let's make a date now. We could try that new restaurant in town.

2 No, no, don't do it like that. Do it like this. Go on, do it again, and, oh, then get me a cup of tea.

3 No problem – I'm sure I can win. I know I'm faster than the others.

4 I'm working here to get some experience, but I'm going to start up my own company soon.

5 Yeah, whatever – I really don't mind. I'll be happy if we go out. I'll be happy if we stay in. Let's do whatever you want to do.

6 Look, are you sure you're OK? Because I can stay longer if you want. Anyway, you know where I am if you need me. Take care.

🔊 3.03

Your description of a dog is your own personality.
Your description of a cat is your partner's personality.
Your description of a rat is your enemy's personality.
Your description of coffee is how you see love.
Your description of an ocean is your own life.

🔊 3.04

(P = Presenter; K = Kath; R = Roy; C = Cindy; H = Hans)

P: Welcome to *The Holiday Programme*. We start off with a report from Thailand. In this report, we spoke to tourists on the beach in Ao Nang in the south of Thailand. We asked them what they were doing in Thailand.
First, we spoke to Kath and Roy.

K: We're on our honeymoon and we're staying in the Rayavadee hotel. It's wonderful. They put rose petals in our bath.

R: Next week we want to go to the north. I want to go trekking in the jungle, and Kath wants to do a cookery course. We both love Thai food, so I think it's a great idea.

P: Then we spoke to Cindy.

C: I'm on holiday and I'm doing a scuba diving course. I like swimming in the sea so I spend most of my day on the beach, and then in the evening I go shopping. I have a shop back home in Sydney so I'm always looking for things to take back there.

P: Finally, we spoke to Hans.

H: I'm living here at the moment. I come from Germany but I've rented a house here for six months because I'm writing a novel. I think Thailand is a perfect place to live – it's cheap, hot and inspiring. My girlfriend isn't very happy about it though – I have a dog in Germany, and she had to stay at home and look after it!

🔊 3.05

(P = Presenter; B = Becky; J = Jeff)

P: In our second report from Thailand, we met two people who came here on holiday and never went home. Becky, how long have you been here in Thailand?

B: I arrived here in 2004. I only came here for a holiday but I liked it so much I stayed.

P: What have you been doing here since 2004?

B: I've been running a bar on the beach. It was difficult at first, because I opened my bar two months before the tsunami in December 2004. Our bar was OK, but tourists stayed away for a long time after that, and I almost had to close the bar. But I've had a lot of support from my husband, and now the bar is going very well.

P: Did you get married here?

B: Yes, my husband's Thai, and we've been married for two years now.

P: Do you go back to the UK often?

B: I haven't been to the UK for a few years.

P: What do you miss about home?

B: Certainly not the weather, or the food. I guess I miss my family and friends, but they love coming here.

P: Jeff, how long have you been here?

J: For about six months.

P: What have you been doing here since you arrived?

J: I've been working in a dive centre.

P: Have you learnt the language?

J: Thai? Ha ha. No, it's really difficult. I've been having lessons for a few months, but I'm not a very good student.

P: What do you like most about living in Thailand?

J: Apart from the obvious things like the weather, the food and the laid-back lifestyle, I like the fact that it's close to other interesting places. I've been to Laos, Cambodia, Bali and Malaysia. But I always like coming back to Thailand. I'm not going home for a long time.

Review C

🔘 3.11

(I = Interviewer; K = Kyle; N = Naomi)

I: Tell me, Kyle, how did your family decide to go green?

K: It was Dad's idea, really. When we were young, Dad had an important job with an oil company. He was very ambitious, and we didn't see him a lot, because he was always flying around the world. But when he was forty-three, he lost his job. After he lost his job, he changed completely. He started working as a gardener, met new friends and that's how he became interested in green issues.

I: Very different from his old life?

K: Yeah. He actually became a bit of a rebel. So when he asked us about going green, I wasn't surprised.

I: How did you feel about the changes you had to make, Naomi?

K: I was very happy. Last year Dad and I took part in a demonstration about climate change in London. It was fun, and I had a great day, but when I went back home I felt I needed to do more. These are serious problems. We all have to make changes to our lives now!

I: What about you, Kyle?

K: Mostly it's OK. I don't mind walking and cycling. I agree with recycling bottles and paper and all that, but I get tired of eating potatoes, salad and apples. Sometimes I just want to eat a hamburger, turn all the lights on in every room in the house, and have a big bath. And I'd really like to get a motorbike when I'm older.

I: What about your friends, what do they think?

N: They're all very worried about climate change. At my school I've started an environmental group. We're trying to persuade people to change their lives. My friends think I'm very bossy, but all this is too important! We must do something before it's too late. We mustn't close our eyes to this problem.

K: My friends think my dad is crazy, but he's actually much happier now – more relaxed and easygoing. They generally think we're doing a good thing. I think everybody is responsible for climate change and should do everything they can to stop it. I hope the changes my family is making can help, but I'm not sure.

Unit 10

🔘 3.13

(R = Receptionist; W = Woman)

R: New Life Centre. Can I help you?

W: Yes. Could you give me some information about your centre?

R: Certainly. When would you like to come?

W: Actually, it's not for me. It's for my husband. It's a surprise for his birthday.

R: Ah, lucky man!

W: Yes … Could you tell me something about the programme?

R: Sure. As soon as he arrives here he'll take a fitness test.

W: Right. Umm, he isn't very fit.

R: Well, we start every day at 7.30 a.m. He'll do a yoga class before breakfast.

W: Ha ha. He usually has a cigarette before breakfast!

R: Oh dear. If he has a cigarette here, he'll be in big trouble. It's a strictly no smoking area.

W: Well, it's a good idea for him to give up smoking. He says he'll give up as soon as he feels more relaxed.

R: Oh well, this is the ideal place to relax. After the morning walk, he'll have a sauna and jacuzzi.

W: Oh, he'll enjoy that. But what's this walk?

R: They go for a brisk walk in the morning from 8.30 to 12.30. That's four hours.

W: Four hours! He hates walking. He only walks from the front door to his car.

R: Oh, don't worry. When they get to the top of the mountain, they have a twenty-minute break before they come down again.

W: And what about the afternoon? Will he relax?

R: No, not really. He'll go to the gym in the afternoon. But he'll have time to relax in the evening.

W: Oh my goodness. I don't think he'll thank me for this.

R: Believe me, when he finishes the week he'll feel like a new man.

W: If he finishes the week!

🔘 3.14

a) 'Will he take a fitness test?' 'Yes, he will.' 'No, he won't.'

b) 'Will he do yoga?' 'Yes, he will.' 'No, he won't.'

c) 'Will he have a cigarette?' 'Yes, he will.' 'No, he won't.'

d) 'Will he have a sauna and a jacuzzi?' 'Yes, he will.' 'No, he won't.'

e) 'Will he go for a four-hour walk?' 'Yes, he will.' 'No, he won't.'

f) 'Will he have time to relax in the afternoon?' 'Yes, he will.' 'No, he won't.'

🔘 3.17

The fittest person I know is my cousin, Darren. He's twenty-six and he's training to be an army officer. Darren's tall and well-built and he looks fantastic in his uniform. He's also very strong, and he has amazing stamina. For his training, he has to do really difficult exercises. For example, he has to

run up mountains carrying about forty kilos of equipment on his back. That's almost like carrying a person! He has to eat a really high-calorie diet, but he's always loved his food so that's not too difficult for him. He says he's enjoying the training, but it's hard to believe because he used to be so lazy. When he was a student, he never got up before midday, and he never did any housework. Now, he gets up at 5.30 in the morning, and he has to iron his uniform every day!

🔘 3.19

My dream car is an old car. I love cars from the fifties or sixties, and my favourite is a Chevrolet. A really big, old Chevrolet. It has to be black – definitely black – with a silver bumper and big flashy headlights. Inside, it's really spacious with plenty of room to stretch your legs. The seats are soft and made of leather. Red leather. No, brown leather. Brown is more sophisticated. Oh, and there's a beautiful old radio with Elvis playing really loud. I love Elvis.

I'd like to take all my friends out in my car. I can imagine wearing glamorous evening clothes and going to a fancy restaurant in New York. As we drive down Fifth Avenue, everybody turns to look at our fabulous car …

Unit 11

🔘 3.22

(I = Interviewer; R = Richard; A = Alicia; H = Harry)

Richard

I: So Richard, which animals do you like or dislike?

R: I like dogs and I hate cats.

I: Oh, why?

R: Because I'm allergic to cats.

I: Oh I see.

R: But I'm interested in wild birds. In fact I'm writing a book on South American eagles. I find the Black-chested Buzzard Eagle particularly fascinating.

I: Gosh. Um, are there any animals you're afraid of?

R: Yes, bulls. I once went camping in southern Spain. When I put the tent up, there weren't any animals in the field, but when I woke up, I could see this shadow outside the tent – a big shadow. And I could hear heavy breathing.

I: Oh my goodness. A bull?

R: No, actually it was a cow. A very big cow. But I thought it was a bull.

Alicia

I: Which animals do you like or dislike. Alicia?

A: Well, I like most animals but I'm particularly keen on horses. I think they're wonderful, beautiful animals. I don't like mice, obviously. And I really can't stand frogs. Urggh, they're horrible.

I: Are you afraid of frogs?

A: Afraid? I'm terrified of them.
I: Are there any other animals you're afraid of?
A: Well, most wild animals. I don't think I'd like to meet a lion or a crocodile in the street. I enjoy watching documentaries about them, but I wouldn't have one as a pet.

Harry
I: And Harry, which animals do you like or dislike?
H: I'm fond of all animals.
I: Have you ever had any experience of wild animals?
H: Yes. I used to work in a zoo.
I: Oh, lovely.
H: You wouldn't think it was lovely if you were an animal. How would you like to live in a cage?
I: Oh no, that would be, um … Are there any animals you're afraid of?
H: No, I'm afraid of humans.
I: Well, thank you for your help. Bye.

3.25
Tim
(I = Interviewer; T = Tim)
I: Can you describe your pet?
T: She's very fat and not very pretty. But she's got a lovely curly tail.
I: Is she a good companion?
T: Yes, absolutely. I always tell her my problems, and she listens.
I: Do you and your pet look alike?
T: I hope not.
I: If you were an animal, what would you like to be?
T: A dolphin. I love the sea, and dolphins are intelligent and funny – like me!

Gus
(I = Interviewer; G = Gus)
I: Can you describe your pet?
G: He's black and has eight hairy legs.
I: Is he a good companion?
G: Yeah. He's like a friend. But other people are afraid of him. He frightens people away.
I: Do you and your pet look alike?
G: I'm not that hairy – but I think he looks cool, like me.
I: If you were an animal, what would you like to be?
G: A lion, because they're big and tough and they rule.

Maxine
(I = Interviewer; M = Maxine)
I: Can you describe your pet?
M: She's very fluffy and very loveable. My boyfriend doesn't like her because she bit him – she doesn't like men.
I: Is she a good companion?
M: Yes, she's good company for me when my boyfriend goes away on business. And she enjoys doing the same things as me – she loves to sleep all day and party all night long.
I: Do you and your pet look alike?
M: I think that she's better looking than me – who could resist those brown eyes?
I: If you were an animal what would you like to be?
M: I *am* an animal. Miaow.

3.26
I know somebody who's got an iguana as a pet. It's a man I work with called Angus. The iguana is called Iggy and it's probably about five years old – that's how long I've known Angus and he got it soon after we met. It was a birthday present from his wife. It's almost a metre long from the tip of its nose to the end of its tail and it's a lovely green colour. Like all reptiles, iguanas never stop growing, so Iggy will get bigger and bigger. It's quite shy and nervous, which is exactly the opposite of Angus who's very outgoing and confident. It's definitely better looking than Angus though. Iggy doesn't sleep in a cage. At the moment, it lives at the top of the curtains in Angus' living room. When it was young, it ate crickets, but now it's adult it doesn't need so much protein – in fact it's completely vegetarian. Angus takes it for walks in the park on a lead. It's funny – when it's frightened, it runs up Angus's body and sits on his head.

Unit 12

3.30
a) 'Was your house built before 1980?' 'Yes, it was.' 'No, it wasn't.'
b) 'Were your shoes designed in Italy?' 'Yes, they were.' 'No, they weren't.'
c) 'Is your salary paid by cheque?' 'Yes, it is.' 'No, it isn't.'
d) 'Were you invited to any parties last week?' 'Yes, I was.' 'No, I wasn't.'
e) 'Is your name spelt the same in English?' 'Yes, it is.' 'No, it isn't.'
f) 'Was your mobile phone made in Japan?' 'Yes, it was.' 'No, it wasn't.'

3.31
The most incredible building I've ever seen is the Alhambra. It's a beautiful palace in Granada in the south of Spain. The first time I saw the Alhambra Palace was when I was eighteen – I went to visit my brother who was studying at university in Granada. I think it was built in the thirteenth or fourteenth century for the Moorish kings. Alhambra is an Arabic name – it means 'red', probably because of the colour of the walls. It's an enormous building, I don't know who the architect was, but the style is Moorish, or Islamic. I love the gardens – water is very important. You can hear water running wherever you go. But it isn't only the building that's so great. I think the location is the most incredible thing about it. It's built on a hill overlooking Granada with the Sierra Nevada mountains in the background. I've been there four times, and each time I think it is more beautiful. In my opinion, it is definitely one of the seven wonders of the modern world.

Review D

3.37
(D = Dom; L = Lou)
D: That's incredible! I'm just reading about albatrosses, Lou. Did you know that they fly around the world at least once a year? That's 40,000 kilometres!
L: Wow! That's a long way. What's the longest journey you've been on, Dom?
D: Not as far as an albatross. I think it was in Thailand.
L: Oh, yeah?
D: Emma and I were living in Bangkok and we decided to go to Koh Tao for our holidays.
L: Koh Tao?
D: Yeah. It means 'Turtle Island' in Thai. It's near Koh Samui.
L: Ah, I see.
D: Anyway, we had to take a night train from Bangkok to Chumphorn in the south of Thailand and then a boat from there to Koh Tao.
L: How exciting!
D: So, we were taken to the train station in Bangkok and then we waited there for two hours. We left the station at around 7.30 p.m.
L: Oh, right.
D: Yeah. At first we felt really excited, but after about an hour we started feeling quite tired. It was noisy and hot. I think I got to sleep at around 11.30 p.m.
L: Oh, that's not so bad.
D: Mm. The next morning, at three o'clock, the train stopped, and we were told to get off. It was the middle of the night, so it was still dark. We had to wait in a small station for a bus to take us to the boat.
L: How did you feel?
D: Really tired! And hungry and thirsty, but the only place we could get a drink was from an old lady who served terrible coffee.
L: Oh, poor you.
D: Then the mosquitoes started biting us – and they were hungry, too! Well, they bit me but they didn't really bite Emma.
L: Oh, dear!
D: Four hours later the bus arrived, and we were taken to the boat. Then it started raining as the boat moved out into the open sea.
L: Oh, how annoying!
D: Suddenly, as quickly as it had started, the rain stopped, and the sun came out.
L: Aha! A happy ending!
D: Yes, it was. Eventually we arrived at Koh Tao, seventeen hours after our journey had begun.
L: Ahh. Were you tired?
D: Absolutely exhausted, but really happy.

Phonetic symbols & Spelling

Single vowels

/ɪ/	ship	/ʃɪp/	(build, business, England, gym, lettuce, spinach, women)
/iː/	need	/niːd/	(bean, he, key, niece, people, sardine)
/ʊ/	put	/pʊt/	(could, foot, woman)
/uː/	pool	/puːl/	(flew, fruit, lose, rule, shoe, through, two)
/e/	egg	/eg/	(breakfast, friend, many, said)
/ə/	mother	/ˈmʌðə/	(arrive, colour, husband, lemon, nervous, police)
/ɜː/	verb	/vɜːb/	(learn, curly, skirt, word)
/ɔː/	saw	/sɔː/	(abroad, caught, four, horse, talk, thought, towards, water)
/æ/	back	/bæk/	—
/ʌ/	bus	/bʌs/	(blood, does, enough, onion)
/ɑː/	arm	/ɑːm/	(aunt, heart, laugh, past)
/ɒ/	top	/tɒp/	(cauliflower, what)

Diphthongs

/ɪə/	ear	/ɪə/	(beer, here, Italian, theatre)
/eɪ/	face	/feɪs/	(break, eight, fail, say, they)
/ʊə/	tour	/tʊə/	(plural, sure)
/ɔɪ/	boy	/bɔɪ/	(noise)
/əʊ/	nose	/nəʊz/	(aubergine, although, coat, know, shoulder)
/eə/	hair	/heə/	(careful, their, wear, where)
/aɪ/	white	/waɪt/	(buy, die, eye, height, high, my)
/aʊ/	mouth	/maʊθ/	(town)

Consonants

/p/	pen	/pen/	(happy)
/b/	bag	/bæg/	(rabbit)
/t/	tea	/tiː/	(ate, fatter, worked)
/d/	dog	/dɒg/	(address, played)
/tʃ/	chip	/tʃɪp/	(natural, watch)
/dʒ/	jazz	/dʒæz/	(age, bridge, generous)
/k/	cake	/keɪk/	(chemistry, kitchen, knock, toothache)
/g/	girl	/gɜːl/	(foggy)
/f/	film	/fɪlm/	(different, laugh, photograph)
/v/	very	/veri/	(of)
/θ/	thin	/θɪn/	—
/ð/	these	/ðiːz/	—
/s/	snake	/sneɪk/	(city, message, race)
/z/	zoo	/zuː/	(has)
/ʃ/	shop	/ʃɒp/	(description, machine, sugar)
/ʒ/	television	/ˈtelɪvɪʒən/	(garage, usual)
/m/	map	/mæp/	(summer)
/n/	name	/neɪm/	(sunny, knife)
/ŋ/	ring	/rɪŋ/	(thanks, tongue)
/h/	house	/haʊs/	(who)
/l/	leg	/leg/	(hill, possible)
/r/	road	/rəʊd/	(carry, write)
/w/	wine	/waɪn/	(one, why)
/j/	yes	/jes/	(used)

Stress

Word stress is shown by _underlining_ the stressed syllable: _water, amazing, Japanese_.

Letters of the alphabet

/eɪ/	/iː/	/e/	/aɪ/	/əʊ/	/uː/	/ɑː/
Aa	Bb	Ff	Ii	Oo	Qq	Rr
Hh	Cc	Ll	Yy		Uu	
Jj	Dd	Mm			Ww	
Kk	Ee	Nn				
	Gg	Ss				
	Pp	Xx				
	Tt	Zz				
	Vv					

Irregular verbs

Infinitive	Past simple	Past participle	Infinitive	Past simple	Past participle
be	was/were	been	let	let	let
beat	beat	beaten	lie	lay/lied	lied/lain
become	became	become	light	lit/lighted	lit/lighted
begin	began	begun	lose	lost	lost
bend	bent	bent	make	made	made
bet	bet	bet	mean	meant /ment/	meant /ment/
bite	bit	bitten	meet	met	met
blow	blew	blown	must	had to	(had to)
break	broke	broken	pay	paid	paid
bring	brought /brɔːt/	brought /brɔːt/	put	put	put
build /bɪld/	built /bɪlt/	built /bɪlt/	read	read /red/	read /red/
burn	burnt/burned	burnt/burned	ride	rode	ridden
burst	burst	burst	ring	rang	rung
buy /baɪ/	bought /bɔːt/	bought /bɔːt/	rise	rose	risen
can	could /kʊd/	(been able)	run	ran	run
catch	caught /kɔːt/	caught /kɔːt/	say	said /sed/	said /sed/
choose	chose	chosen	see	saw /sɔː/	seen
come	came	come	sell	sold	sold
cost	cost	cost	send	sent	sent
cut	cut	cut	set	set	set
deal /diːl/	dealt /delt/	dealt /delt/	shake	shook	shaken
dig	dug	dug	shine	shone	shone
do	did	done	shoot	shot	shot
draw	drew	drawn	show	showed	shown
dream	dreamt/dreamed	dreamt/dreamed	shrink	shrank	shrunk
drink	drank	drunk	shut	shut	shut
drive	drove	driven	sing	sang	sung
eat	ate	eaten	sink	sank	sunk
fall	fell	fallen	sit	sat	sat
feed	fed	fed	sleep	slept	slept
feel	felt	felt	slide	slid	slid
fight	fought /fɔːt/	fought /fɔːt/	smell	smelt/smelled	smelt/smelled
find	found	found	speak	spoke	spoken
fly	flew	flown	spell	spelt/spelled	spelt/spelled
forget	forgot	forgotten	spend	spent	spent
forgive	forgave	forgiven	spill	spilt/spilled	spilt/spilled
freeze	froze	frozen	split	split	split
get	got	got	spoil	spoilt/spoiled	spoilt/spoiled
give	gave	given	spread	spread	spread
go	went	gone/been	stand	stood	stood
grow	grew	grown	steal	stole	stolen
hang	hung/hanged	hung/hanged	stick	stuck	stuck
have	had	had	swear	swore	sworn
hear	heard /hɜːd/	heard /hɜːd/	swell	swelled	swollen/swelled
hide	hid	hidden	swim	swam	swum
hit	hit	hit	take	took /tʊk/	taken
hold	held	held	teach	taught /tɔːt/	taught /tɔːt/
hurt /hɜːt/	hurt /hɜːt/	hurt /hɜːt/	tear	tore	torn
keep	kept	kept	tell	told	told
kneel	knelt/kneeled	knelt/kneeled	think	thought /θɔːt/	thought /θɔːt/
know	knew /njuː/	known	throw	threw	thrown
lay	laid	laid	understand	understood	understood
lead	led	led	wake	woke	woken
learn	learnt	learnt	wear	wore /wɔː/	worn
leave	left	left	win	won /wʌn/	won /wʌn/
lend	lent	lent	write	wrote	written

Macmillan Education
Between Towns Road, Oxford OX4 3PP
A division of Macmillan Publishers Limited
Companies and representatives throughout the world

ISBN 978-1-4050-9960-8

Text © Sue Kay & Vaughan Jones 2008
Design and illustration © Macmillan Publishers Limited 2008

First published 2008

Review units by Peter Maggs and Catherine Smith

Project development by Desmond O'Sullivan, Quality Outcomes Limited

Designed by 320 Design Limited

Picture Research, Perseverance Works Limited, Sally Cole

Illustrated by Beach pp11, 19, 27, 47, 55, 67, 83, 95, 103, 108, 111; Gavin Reece p24; Ed McLachlan pp10, 21, 23, 25; 26, 28, 38, 46, 54, 56, 57, 66, 74, 82, 84, 85, 89, 94, 102, 110, 112, 113, 127, 129, 131, 133, 135, 137, 139, 141, 143, 145, 147; David Shephard p42; Adrian Valencia pp35, 119, 124; Kim Williams pp17, 18, 116, 121

Cover design by Andrew Oliver

Authors' acknowledgements
We would like to thank all our students and colleagues at the Oxford English Centre in Oxford as well as all our teaching colleagues around the world who are using Inside Out – your feedback has helped us identify what we should keep and what we could improve. Particular thanks go to the following people: Peter Tamkin, Phil Hopkins, Steve Jones (English Language Centre, Brighton); Howard Smith (Oxford House College, Oxford); Martin Barge, Debra Hills and Camille Steele (Bell School, London); Luca Copetti (Brussels); Sonja Yersenska (Czech Republic); Irene Kruglova (International Teaching Centre, Moscow); Inlingua schools (Thailand); Bangkok University; Sarah Shaw (British Council, Bangkok); Aleksandra Sauermann (Szczecin University, Poland); Antonella Vecchione (Liceo Scientifico, Varese, Italy); Ana Luisa Thode and Josefa Garbia (EOI, Malaga, Spain).

We are especially grateful to Peter Maggs and Catherine Smith for their excellent Student's Book review units, to Julie Moore (author) and Penny Analytis (editor) for the excellent CD ROM, to Philip Kerr for the wonderful New Inside Out Workbook, and to Helena Gomm, Caroline Brown, Peter Maggs and Chris Dawson for their important contributions to the New Inside Out Teacher's Book. We're also grateful to Scott Thornbury for allowing us to use extracts from his excellent book, An A–Z of ELT.

At Macmillan Education, we would like to thank Kate Melliss, Rafael Alarcon-Gaeta, Jemma Hillyer, Karen White, Balvir Koura, Deborah Hughes, Rowena Drewett and Stephanie Parker for all their hard work on our behalf. We are grateful to Jemma for her important work on the development of the digital components. Stephanie also deserves a special mention for the invaluable contribution she has made and continues to make to the management of this project. Finally, we would like to give a big thankyou to Rafael for his patience and support. We would also like to thank Sally Cole (freelance photo researcher), Alyson Maskell, Celia Bingham and Xanthe Sturt Taylor (freelance editors), as well as James Richardson (freelance audio producer).

Jackie Hill and Kim Williams – our wonderfully talented freelance designers – continue to work their magic. Inside Out would not be the stylish course it is without them, or without Andrew Oliver's fabulous cover design.

Many thanks also go to the Macmillan production and marketing teams around the world whose enthusiasm and encouragement have been such a support.

Our biggest thankyou goes to Des O'Sullivan (freelance project developer). Always thorough, always considerate and always there for us. We realize how lucky we are to be working with such a consummate professional.

Last but not least, we are so grateful to our families for their ongoing support and understanding.

David Riley 1955-2007

David was our first editor on Inside Out. His vision, wit, enthusiasm and unique publishing flair were instrumental in shaping the course. David always supported and defended the writers and the writing process. We will miss him for all sorts of reasons but it is his unswerving loyalty to us as authors and friends that we will miss most.

The authors and publishers are grateful for permission to reprint the following copyright material: Extract from '101 Ways to Slow Down', copyright © The Guardian 2000, first printed in The Guardian 09.09.00, reprinted by permission of the publisher; Extract '104 Things To Do With a Banana' by Wayne M. Hilburn from HYPERLINK "http://www.wmhilburn.com/bananas.htm" http://www.wmhilburn.com/bananas.htm reprinted by permission of the author.

These materials may contain links for third party websites. We have no control over, and are not responsible for, the contents of such third party websites. Please use care when accessing them.

Although we have tried to trace and contact copyright holders before publication, in some cases this has not been possible. If contacted we will be pleased to rectify any errors or omissions at the earliest opportunity.

The authors and publishers wish to thank the following for permission to reproduce their photographs: **Alamy**/Eye Ubiquitous p15(m), Alamy/Icelandic Photo Agency p15(b), Alamy/Garry Gay p36(b), Alamy/Axel Hess p45, Alamy/Ashley Cooper p60(r), Alamy/Ian Shaw p69(t), Alamy/Adrian Sherratt p71(a), Alamy/Paul Rapson p71(b), Alamy/Peter Titmuss p71(e), Alamy/Dominic Burke p71(f), Alamy/Vidura Luis Barrios p72, Alamy/Andrew Fox p75(1), Alamy/Photofusion Picture Library pp75(5), 75(6), Alamy/Roger Bamber p75(7), Alamy/Howard Barlow p75(4), Alamy/vario images GmbH & Co.KG p75(8), Alamy/FAN travelstock p79(b), Alamy/Dominic Burke p85, Alamy/Phil Rees p93(t), Alamy/Eureka p97(m), Alamy/Profimedia International s.r.o 97(ml), Alamy/Jon Arnold Images p107(b), Alamy/Tony Cordoza p109; **Aurora** p8; **Catwalking** pp36(tr), 36(tl); **Jenny Cockell** p149(t); **Corbis**/Stan Fellerman p5, Corbis/LWA-Dann Tardif p6(9), Corbis/Polypix/Eye Ubiquitous p12(m), Corbis/Klaus Hackenberg/Zefa p14, Corbis/Virgo Productions p20(m), Corbis/Christian Weigel/Solus-Veer p30(bl), Corbis/Louis Moses/zefa p31(ml), Corbis/Morgan David de Lossy p31(t), Corbis/Peter Dazeley p36(c), Corbis/Steve Prezant p41(t), Corbis/Schlegelmilch p42(b), Corbis/Darren Staples p42(c), Corbis/Frank May/epa p43(r), Corbis/Push Pictures p48(tl), Corbis/Tom Grill p48(bl), Corbis/Image 100 p48(m), Corbis/David Stoecklein p49(r), Corbis/C.Devan/ Zefa p53(bl), Corbis/Ashley Cooper p60(l), Corbis/Michael Prince p61(ml), Corbis/Richard Baker p71(c), Andrew Fox p75(3), Corbis/Dave & Les Jacobs/Blend Images p76, Corbis/Dallas and John Heaton/Free Agents Limited p79(t), Corbis/Ned Frisk p79(a), Corbis/Mike Theiss 86(mr), Corbis/Pat Doyle p97(t), Corbis/P. Deussen/A.B./zefa p105, Corbis/C. Lyttle p115(tl), Corbis/Bernd Vogel pp120, 125; **FPG** p70(all); **Greg Evans Picture Library** p92(b); **Eyewire** p52; **Gallo Images** p114(bl); **Getty Images**/Dave Nagel p4(l), Getty/Colin Hawkins p22(l), Getty/Tim McPherson p22(r), Getty/Matthew Peters p42(d), Getty/ Ezra Shaw p42(e), Getty/Dave Hogan p42(a), Getty/Michael Steele p42(f), Getty/Ariel Skelley p53(tr), Getty/Car Culture p81(b), Getty/Philip and Karen Smith p86(t), Getty/Paul Ellis/AFP p86(tr), Getty/Jed Jacobsohn p91(bl), Getty/Philip Lee Harvey p92(b), Getty/Alain Daussin p100(tr), Getty/Daisy Gilardini pp108, 114(mr), Getty/Paul Souders p114(tl), Getty/Art Wolfe p114(ml), Getty/Jamie Travis p114(t), Getty/Dea/E.Ganzerla p115(mr), Getty/Pankaj & Insy Shah p149(b); Getty pp 32, 50(tl), 77(all), 108(tr), (b), 100(tl), (bl), (mt), (mb), (br), (br); **Hulton Archive** pp20(l), 20(r); **Hola Images** pp61(l), 61(mr); **Matt Kay** p81(tl); **Dorling Kindersley** pp36(a), 36(d); **Lonely Planet** p63(b); **Macmillan Archive**/Bananastock pp6(3), 9,13(t), Creatas/Barnyard animals p97(tml), Digital Vision p114(mb) Digital Vision/Animal Faces pp96(m), 97(tmr), Dynamic Graphics/Living creatures pp96(b), 97(tl), 97(bl), 97(ml), 97(br), 97(bm), 98(b), Image Source p6(6), Brand X pp 8, 34, Photodisc p15(mt), Istock pp96(t), 97(bmr), 97(br), 97(m), 97(mr); **Magnum** p88; **Masterfile**/Brad Wrobleski p31(bl), Masterfile/Steve Prezant pp34(tl), 90(tl), Masterfile/Siephoto p48(r), Masterfile/Russell Monk p64(bl), Masterfile/Richard Smith p75(2), Masterfile/J. A. Kraulis p86(mr), Masterfile/Ron Fehling p92(tr); **Motoring Picture Library**/Neil Bruce pp92(t), (m); **NaturePl**/Dietmar Nill p97(t), NaturePl/Brandon Cole p97(tr); NaturePl/Jose Schell p97(bml), NaturePl/Rod Williams p97(mr), NaturePl/Doc White p99; **NHPA**/Daniel Zupanc p98(m); **Desmond O'Sullivan** p101(t); **Panos Pictures**/Liba Taylor p87(b); **Photodisc** pp7, 99(tl), (tr); **Photographers Choice** pp30(r), 37(t), (m), 59(t), 114(br); **Photolibrary** pp31(br), 31(mr), 61(r), 79(b), 79(c), 90(tl), 92(c), 93(b), 97(bl); **Photonica** pp6(5), 6(7), 41(b), 107(t); **Pictor International** p35(both); **Punchstock** p17(b); **Purestock** p68(l); **Reuters Archive** p64(tl); **Riser** pp59(b), 65(tl), 49 (background); **Louis Stettner** Promenade Brooklyn 1954 © ADAGP, Paris and DACS London 2002 courtesy of Gallery 292/Howard Greenberg Gallery p44; **Stockbyte** p4(r); **Stock4B** p41(m); **Stockfoods** p6(4); **Stone** pp6(1), 6(2), 12(t), 13(tm), 16, 17(t), 40, 51, 58(tr), 58(bl), 58(br), 69(b),73, 87(t), 115(tr); **Taxi** pp15(t), 30(tl), 58(tl), 63(t), 71(d); **The Image Bank** pp13(b), 68(r).

Photos of Ice hotel ® p106 / Tomas Utsi, Jan Jordan.

Photos on pages 64(tr) and 65(tr) & (br) kindly supplied by Original Volunteers.

Commissioned photography by Paul Bricknell p90, and John Cole p37.

Cartoons on p52 and p69 produced with permission from The Spectator.

Printed and bound in Thailand

2013 2012 2011 2010
12 11 10 9 8 7